For the Joy
Set Before Us

FOR THE *JOY* SET BEFORE US

Augustine and Self-Denying Love

GERALD W. SCHLABACH

University of Notre Dame Press
Notre Dame, Indiana

BV
4647
.S4
S35
2001

Copyright © 2001 by
University of Notre Dame
Notre Dame, Indiana 46556
All Rights Reserved
http://www.undpress.nd.edu

Manufactured in the United States of America

Designed by Wendy McMillen
Set in 11/13 Berkeley Book by Em Studio Inc.
Printed in the USA by Edwards Brothers, Inc.

Library of Congress Cataloging-in-Publication Data
Schlabach, Gerald.
For the joy set before us : Augustine and self-denying
love / Gerald W. Schlabach.
p. cm.
ISBN 0-268-02858-3
1. Augustine, Saint, Bishop of Hippo.
2. Self-denial. 3. Charity. I. Title.
BV4647.S4 S35 2000
241'.4—dc21   00-010689

∞ *This book is printed on acid-free paper.*

*To the many friends
who are less patient with St. Augustine than I,
but who have still been patient with me.*

Contents

Acknowledgments

Augustine's great capacity for self-examination reached its limits when he came, in *Confessions* 10.37.60, to his need for friendship and encouragement.

> For other types of temptation I have some kind of ability for self-examination, but for this scarcely any. . . . [For] to be without any praise whatsoever, and to test ourselves in this condition, how can we manage it? Must we not live an evil life, so abandoned and so inhuman a life that no one can know us without detesting us? What greater madness can be named or conceived than this? If praise usually is, and should be, companion to a good life and good deeds, we should no more abandon such accompaniment than the good life itself.

Centuries of hindsight allow boisterous young scholars to second-guess even the greatest of thinkers. I have tried to examine myself whenever that privilege has become something more like a temptation. But here, least of all, would I even be tempted to imagine that I might better Augustine, either at knowing how to manage without encouragement from others, or at finding words to confess my need for their company.

I owe a great debt, of course, to the committee that oversaw this project in its first phase, that of a doctoral dissertation. As adviser, Jean Porter was firm when necessary but always trusting and hopeful on my behalf. As friend in the years since then, her generosity continued into the very final stages of my revision process. John Cavadini will always remain my mentor, not only in reading Augustine, but in combining scholarship and Christian faith. The late John H. Yoder taught me years ago that one can hardly begin to love enemies without at least trying to understand disputants; he did not expect me to apply that axiom so enthusiastically to Augustine, but was patient nonetheless. I hope his perceptive questions have helped keep me from *mere* enthusiasm. Randall Zachman's advice and probing have sharpened my awareness of many critical issues.

To three other faculty members of Notre Dame's Department of Theology I am especially grateful: Todd Whitmore offered not just unfailing support but unflagging friendship. The influence of the late Catherine LaCugna was far greater than either of us would have expected amid the neophyte struggles of my first semester. Fr. David Burrell, c.s.c., modeled the possibility of combining deep rootedness in classical Western theology with receptivity to other cultures and canons. Thanks to the Internet and his own pioneering use of it, James J. O'Donnell of the University of Pennsylvania has been nearly as accessible as other professors; I wish to thank him for the way his electronic forum has allowed me to explore and gain confidence in Augustine studies, and for his personal encouragement. As I began to move my manuscript toward publication, Oliver O'Donovan offered a welcome mix of both encouragement and critique. So too did Allan Fitzgerald, o.s.a., when two reworked chapters needed a fresh set of eyes. None of these fine scholars shares responsibility for such mistakes and oversights as undoubtedly remain in my work, despite their best efforts. In fact, I may very well need this standard disclaimer even more than most scholars because I so often attempt the risky practice of addressing multiple audiences at once, yet alas, may not quite satisfy anyone.

No one promises that writing a doctoral dissertation will be a joyful experience—much less revising it precisely when fresher interests are developing. But sustaining me with a special, unexpected joy have been the friends and scholars in the Mennonite community who have heard me out when I have described my strange interest in Augustine. I think especially of Ted Koontz, John Richard Burkholder, Kristina Mast Burnett, Joseph Liechty, John and Tina Hartzler Ulrich, John D. Roth, Paul Keim, Shirley Showalter, Steve Nolt, Alan Kreider, and Willard Swartley. Since I came to Bluffton College, Rachel Reesor, Andrew Taylor, Gerald Biesecker-Mast, Loren Johns, Lisa Robeson, and John Kampen have joined this circle. As this project comes to a close and I continue to find myself exploring the resources of Roman Catholicism, I may not be offering my friends and colleagues much assurance about what may result from deep engagement with a figure such as St. Augustine, but I value their patience all the more. So to such friends I am dedicating this book.

Then there are the people whose one common characteristic is that I cannot imagine beginning or completing this project without their help. David Augsburger and Ingrid Schultz were instrumental in my decision to pursue a doctorate. Pete Blum has cheered, goaded, and served as confidant. The Kern Road Mennonite Church in South Bend is so full of supportive folk that I dare not begin listing them by name. To Bluffton College I am also grateful for the load reduction of a "mini-leave," which helped me complete my revisions. The good people of Nota Bene Associates provided the powerful and supple tools for research and writing that have been my constant companions for almost fifteen years; these tools also introduced me to the many remarkable and erudite friends I know mainly through the NOTABENE Internet forum.

First and last, there is family. My father Theron is my most important model of Christian scholarship, but above all, a close friend. My mother Sara has taught me a stubborn zeal for living life with warmth and simplicity, even amid hardship. My parents-in-law, Willard and Mary Handrich, have communicated unfailing trust that God would lead us, whether our adventures passed through a revolutionary country or a Roman Catholic university. My sons, Gabriel and Jacob, have been as patient as possible when the manuscript kept them from me (and from our family computer!). More importantly, they have kept me well-supplied with humor, hugs, chatty diversion, and much cheer. Finally, I struggle to thank my wife Joetta. More than I like to admit, she has held our household together when I have not lived up to our egalitarian ideals. And still she has offered love, friendship, and companionship in faith. For these dear ones, most of all, I am grateful to God.

> . . . in Deo amentur, quia et ipsae mutabiles sunt et illo fixae stabiliuntur: alioquin irent et perirent. In illo ergo amentur, et rape ad eum tecum quas potes, et dic eis: hunc amemus: ipse fecit haec et non est longe. Non enim fecit atque abiit, sed ex illo in illo sunt. . . .

Gerald W. Schlabach

Introduction

The making of moral judgments can be made *too* hard. Christian ethicist Stanley Hauerwas is right to chide his colleagues for long focusing on tough cases or moral quandaries while neglecting that character formation which makes us who we are. People in well-narrated traditions, after all, may look back on apparently tough decisions and say, "There really was nothing to decide; I couldn't do anything else."[1]

Obviously, however, making moral judgments can also be made too easy. Human beings have a boundless capacity for self-deception, rationalization, and moral short-cuts, all at the service of a lazy but trenchant longing for comfortable complacency. Hauerwas himself hopes Christian communities will cut through their own self-deception by training themselves to recognize that they are sinners and by allowing the story of Jesus to form them into disciples ready to carry his costly nonviolent cross.[2]

Even conscientious folk can make ethical judgment too easy for themselves. One way to do so with all the best of intentions is to attend to only one moral challenge at a time—without keeping an eye on other challenges in the knowledge that one's answer to the first might shape one's answer to the rest. The best reason for learning to think systematically about·theology and ethics is mutual accountability. We act well (or at least better) when we act expecting to explain our acts, first to those in our own most formative communities, but even to strangers whenever possible. One way a community (or a theologian in its service) exercises accountability is to show consistency and coherence of thought by taking the fragmentary insights that have emerged around diverse issues and integrating them into a single account. Even if we do not presume to construct from these fragments an encyclopedic *summa* of the whole of moral theology (as though we could anticipate every problem in advance), we should expect our insights to fit together solidly enough that we may trust the pattern of our accountability to hold, in spite of current gaps, as we seek to meet fresh challenges. We should probably never be altogether sure that the systems we construct constitute more than exercises in accountability. But we should surely expect to ask ourselves, *How will we answer many questions at once?*

I have found it difficult to do otherwise. The pages that follow represent my effort to identify for Christian ethics an integrated account of right self-love *and* proper self-denial. But this is only a rubric for anticipating many other questions.

Toward the end of chapter 1, I imagine a Christian woman who is confronting her need to practice greater self-concern, not because she has rejected her ethic of loving Christian service, but precisely because she has sought to practice it faithfully. Facing "burnout" from her deep involvement in a struggle for social justice, yet not wanting to settle into a comfortable middle-class lifestyle, she must be self-concerned precisely so that she does not become self-centered! What holds for this individual, I argue, also holds for entire Christian communities; to sustain an ethic of service and potentially costly witness in the world over time, even those who characterize Christian love as self-sacrificial must inevitably reintroduce considerations of self-love—not because they have been unfaithful to their ethic but precisely to the degree that they have been faithful.

Although I constructed the case of such a Christian woman, I hardly had to do so out of thin air. In many ways, she reflects the situation that my wife and I were in after five years of Christian service in Nicaragua and Honduras, in the mid-1980s, as representatives of the Mennonite Central Committee. For over eighty years that organization has been the arm of Mennonite churches in North America for relief, development, global education, and peacemaking. The Anabaptist-Mennonite tradition that has shaped these efforts has first of all shaped its members by arguing that the essence of Christianity is discipleship, that discipleship means following the way of the cross in all human relationships, and that to form a community that lives out this way is to align true social creativity with the very grain of the cosmos.[3] More than arguing, the tradition has done its shaping work by passing on stories of sixteenth-century martyrs who went to the stake rather than betray Jesus' love of enemies by taking up the sword, as well as stories of twentieth-century witnesses who had served distant neighbors around the world—sometimes in risky situations of war and social conflict—but who now may sit in a nearby pew.

In shaping, such a tradition also sends—it sends some of its most conscientious members out where they will face and pose new questions. The story of Mennonite Central Committee has been emblematic in this regard. A well-meaning desire to serve often exposes the limitations of *merely* serving those who need resources to develop their own communities for themselves. An effort to facilitate community development sometimes exposes structural injustices that have made development impossible and some kind of liberation urgent. And so, many of the Mennonites who have taken their church's witness of peace, service, and cross-bearing most seriously in recent generations have found themselves making a transition from serving, to advocating, to struggling for justice. While continuing to take discipleship seriously, they have ceased interpreting Jesus' Sermon on the Mount to teach long-suffering "nonresistance" and begun interpreting it to teach active "nonviolence." Whatever servanthood should mean, it dare not reinforce the servitude of the oppressed; whatever taking up the cross of suffering love for others should mean, it dare not rationalize the gratuitous victimization of others. As pacifists in revolutionary Nicaragua in the 1980s, my wife and I were hardly the first in the church to face these questions. But we knew its story well and we faced such questions in the faces of our Nicaraguan friends.[4]

Although self-denying love is key to the story of discipleship, then, that story may come to a chapter in which self-denial is also something of a problem. Liberation struggle in places like Latin America has had its counterpart in North American feminism. Mennonite feminists have converged with other feminists in questioning a tendency to identify Christ-like love too closely with a willingness to deny oneself for the sake of others. As Nadine Pence Frantz put it, "Women have borne the cost of discipleship, we have walked the second mile, we have given up our coat and our mittens as well. We have become acquainted with grief and sorrow. But we have not gained our life, we have found it squandered by those to whom we gave. And we have been told we are wrong to seek it." As a result, women in Mennonite and related "peace churches" ask: "How do I now live out of a sense of servanthood and service without losing myself, without sinning through the loss of myself?"[5] For some, traditional Christian language of self-denial and sacrifice has become altogether suspect.[6]

If we continue refusing to attend only to one problem at a time, however, we notice the intriguing case of *eco*feminism. Feminists who chart the common pattern by which patriarchy has rationalized both male domination of women and human domination of the natural world presumably share the feminist critique of degrading models of self-sacrifice, yet also critique the collective human egotism that environmentalists call "anthropocentrism." At a moment in history in which a human propensity to overstretch ourselves is reaching global proportions, it hardly seems the time to dismiss the imperatives of self-restraint and self-denial out of hand. Ecofeminism provides a particularly good reminder of the wisdom of juxtaposing various moral problems and holding ourselves accountable to all of them at once.

Actually, "juxtapose" may be too gentle a word. For to find a way through many moral problems at once is to grapple, to struggle, to live in tension, perhaps to grow tired, and perhaps to "burn out" in yet another way. This grappling alone involves a certain kind of suffering, all the more because the "problems" are not gentle abstractions but have faces. What then will sustain self-denial over time, through such struggle? Candidates are participation in a community of mutual love and aid, liturgical practices that lead to gratitude for God's love and responsive love of neighbor, and authentic spirituality that carries these connections between divine and human community into every corner of our lives. These and other resources for sustaining self-denial, however, are goods—desirable goods. But some would say that to seek any good self-consciously is to love ourselves in ways that bear the abiding imprint of a suspect egotism. Are they right?

Or, might we need some other kind of right self-love in order to sustain practices of self-denying love through time? My argument will begin with the suggestion that we are in the presence not of a contradiction but of a clue, and that it is a clue to more than one scholar's personal preoccupation, in more than one Christian tradition. In other words, my hope is that my own struggle has heightened my sensitivity to a larger historical and theoretical problem in Christian ethics. In writing on Christian service and social ethics elsewhere, I have stressed that what is most at stake is not the philanthropy or benevolence of individual Christians but God's salvific work to create whole communities of service within history. I have called this kind of community an "Abrahamic community," inasmuch as it is able both to celebrate God's blessing and to be a blessing to others, according to the call of Abraham.[7] Such a group must maintain a communal identity in which service to other communities is intrinsic, and thus negotiate a path of social engagement where the community neither dissolves *into* the larger culture nor excludes people and challenges *from* the larger culture. Having argued that living with some form of this tension is the key to Christian faithfulness, I have implicitly committed myself to exploring whether Christians and Christian communities can long sustain such a life of tension between their own community needs and the needs of other communities. The present project may not provide a full answer to that question, but does reflect it.

And so with many questions. This book does not offer a full treatise on discipleship, service, or pacifism, or on the challenges of social injustice, liberation struggle, or abuses closer to home. It does not explore as far as others might the pastoral practices we need to sustain committed Christians in times of burnout, or the communal practices of liturgy and mutual aid we need to sustain Abrahamic communities of service over time. Nor does it discuss ecofeminism thoroughly, but only as a warning against dismissing self-denial prematurely. Yet in some way this book *is* about all of these questions—their confluence, our accountability to all of them, and a corresponding need that the discipline of Christian ethics has for a coherent framework or doctrine of Christian love.

It is at this confluence of questions that I can best account for my encounter with St. Augustine. As Professor Van Harvey of Stanford University once asked me in a conversation at the American Academy of Religion, "Why would a nice Mennonite boy like you be studying Augustine at Notre Dame?" For me to answer that in the face of many questions I have found Augustine's brand of orthodox Christianity unexpectedly coherent and fruitful, is only to nuance the question. Why, indeed, Augustine?

———

Had I set out self-consciously to answer questions that my own life narrative has posed, it would never have occurred to me to study Augustine. I began my doctoral studies at the University of Notre Dame with all the usual prejudices against the late-fourth-century bishop; an initial survey course in the history of early Christianity let me read just enough of his writing to confirm those prejudices. "Bold rather than strong"[8] in my historical and theological assessment, I judged Augustine to have saddled Christianity with his sexual burdens, to have passed on a Platonic split between body and soul, to have cemented the church's alliance with the state, to have left Christian moral reflection more harsh and juridical than he found it, and so on. As a Mennonite whose Anabaptist ancestors once suffered persecution at the hands of established churches, I was particularly resentful of Augustine's rationalization for religious coercion. There matters would probably remain unexamined if I had not, in my boldness, let slip to my doctoral adviser Jean Porter that "I despise the man." Wisely she insisted that this was all the more reason to grapple with Augustine's theology. I could do so, after all, under the able tutelage of John Cavadini. And so, in the following months, Augustine began to intrigue me and even to convince me on a few issues. Whether or not I should now pray as Augustine once prayed to God, that "by inner goads you aroused me,"[9] Dr. Porter had goaded and Dr. Cavadini had aroused my interest in the study of Augustine. Quite to my surprise, I spent much of the next five years trying to argue through to a reasoned basis for some combination of resolute disagreement and intrigued agreement with Augustine.

Scholars have increasingly recognized, of course, that their own narratives do inevitably shape their inquiries. Even when they strive for the greatest possible objectivity, their traditions and social locations predispose them to ask (if nothing else) certain questions rather than others. The academy's most important checks against perverse interestedness continue to be care in the handling of evidence, respect for counter-interpretations, and all of the apparatus that allows scholarly mentors and peers to double-check one's research. In the body of the present work my foremost task is to be accountable in the standard academic way. Yet another kind of accountability has a complementary role to play. I am making my own interests transparent so that readers may judge for themselves whether those interests have skewed my reading of the historical texts, or whether they have played a more helpful role, by allowing me to read Augustine with fresh eyes.

Though I did not set out to study Augustine, a question I posed in only the second week of doctoral study anticipated why I would eventually study him so intensely. A seminar on the moral theory of Thomas Aquinas was exposing me for the first time to a Christian version of eudaemonism—a system of thought oriented around the question of how moral agents might realize their true happiness or good. Coming from a tradition that has emphasized Jesus' call to self-sacrificial love, I was amazed to read Aquinas's discussion of how even angels naturally love themselves by loving God as their highest good.[10] As the seminar went on to discuss Aquinas's treatise on happiness,[11] and his claim that no good short of a beatific vision of God could supply human happiness, I asked a clumsy question: "But what if, when we get to the beatific vision, what we see is a reality so self-giving that it turns the entire system on its head?"

My neophyte question was, in its clumsy way, essentially a version of the questions that so agitated the Swedish Lutheran theologian Anders Nygren some sixty years before: *Does not the love that God demonstrated through the ministry, teaching, and ultimately the cross of Jesus Christ so confront humanity that Christians must contrast the divine love at work in their lives with every form of natural human love? Does human love not inevitably assess the objects of its love according to rational standards of merit or justice that God in Christ has refused to make the basis of reconciled relationships with sinners, enemies—us? Does even the most noble human love not retain hints of nefarious self-interest or self-love?* The biblical exegesis and historical interpretation by which Nygren contrasted God's agape-love with human eros-love in the first fifteen centuries of Christian teaching has received ample assessment and rebuttal since Nygren published his massive study, *Agape and Eros,* in the 1930s.[12] Some people who are aware of this, and to whom I described my project as it was developing, have wondered why I continue to pay his position as much attention as I do. One answer must be that I started with assumptions much like Nygren's.

The less autobiographical version of that answer, however, and the one that appears in chapter 1, is that I am not alone: Nygren's thesis has been enormously influential and has framed debates in Christian ethics that continue well past the exegetical and historical objections. The reason for that, I suspect, is that within Christian ethics, Nygren plays something of the role that Immanuel Kant plays in philosophical ethics. Only a few philosophers in a given generation may become wholly convinced Kantians, yet every generation of philosophers must argue through to their acceptance or rejection of Kant's position, which now seems to be one necessary option in any typology of ethical systems. Likewise, whatever the exegete or historian has concluded about Nygren's work, Christian ethicists continue to come back to his thesis repeatedly; it is one of the major objections to which they must respond when they formulate any *other* conception of Christian love.[13]

For me, that "other" conception of Christian love eventually became an Augustinian one, not a Thomistic one. If I had carried out the overly ambitious project that I first envisioned—a comparative study of Augustine, Aquinas, and Martin Luther on self-love—perhaps I would understand more fully the reasons for that move. The rationale for the larger project I imagined, however, may offer an adequate explanation. While Aquinas and Luther both owed much to Augustine in their respective ways, part of the difference between them involves divergent assessments of self-love, both in the theological anthropologies that inform their accounts of salvation and in their ethics. What intrigued me about Augustine, in this regard, was that he could be read two different ways on self-love, and apparently *had* been read in two ways by these two major interpreters. Initially I intended to trace out the reasons for the apparent divergence. But what always interested me most was to discover how Augustine had held together what later traditions tended to split apart—self-love and that self-denial which plays a prominent part in the cruciform love of Jesus Christ.

However much I have come to disagree with Nygren, I cannot imagine an adequately Christian ethic that rationalizes away Jesus' call to follow him on a course that may sometimes lead to suffering— because Christ-like love always leads to the needy neighbor and enemy alike. To that extent I continue to accept Nygren's challenge and to worry with him about the tendency of medieval theology to make self-love (and thus self-defense, self-preservation, and the like) into an increasingly autonomous ethical principle. Augustine has intrigued me more than Aquinas for the very reason that Nygren ultimately found Augustine more threatening than Aquinas: Augustine's account of self-love seems more convincing precisely because it comes more closely integrated with an account of self-denying love. That account of self-denying love endeavors to sustain continuity with what I will call evangelical self-denial. With the term "evangelical self-denial" I refer in the first instance simply to that self-denial of which the Gospels speak, whatever this may turn out to be. In using this term, however, I also anticipate my thesis that Christian self-denial must in some way prove meaningful in light of Jesus' proclamation of the good news of God's Reign.[14]

While some have wondered why I bother with Nygren, others have wondered why I would either bother with Augustine or want to sustain a prominent place for self-denial in Christian ethics. Chapter 1 answers those questions at length. It argues that while the hard sayings and the cross of Jesus Christ give self-sacrifice a particularly prominent place in Christian ethics, every ethic in fact needs *some* account of self-denial, even eudaemonistic, feminist, or liberation ethics. At the same time, feminists have been right to resist the tendency in Christianity (of which Nygren is only the most extreme example) to make self-sacrifice the defining characteristic of Christian love, and to minimize duties of self-love and self-concern. If Christian ethics then needs a unified account of both self-love and self-denial, we find hints of how to proceed in Nygren's very sense that Augustine's "*caritas* synthesis" of agape and eros stood as his strongest rival. However unlikely a resource Augustine may seem for contemporary Christian ethics, his place at a watershed in the development of Christian teaching on love, together with the basic unity of his thought on self-love and self-denial, suggest that among classical theologians who have shaped the presuppositions behind Christian theology and ethics, Augustine's thought bears unrivaled importance.

In retrospect, my turn to Augustine does not seem quite so strange, nor he a total stranger. For if my own tradition has supplied some of the key problematics that I have taken to my reading of Augustine, it has also supplied insights that may have allowed me to discern dimensions of Augustine's thought that standard readings have sometimes underplayed. From Anabaptist critiques of any doctrine of justification that is purely forensic, I learned to notice ways in which Augustine—even the anti-Pelagian Augustine who had learned that human perfection must await eschatological completion—continued to insist that God's justifying work begin transforming or regenerating all of human life already in history. From Mennonite thinkers such as Guy F. Hershberger and John Howard Yoder I have become convinced that this transformation of human life takes on social and historical dimensions through the community of mutual love which is the church;

noticing how communal was Augustine's notion of the good that
Christians may rightly desire became the key to unlocking various in-
terpretive puzzles. From Yoder's *Christian Witness to the State*[15] and
other writings I have come to see history and society as a field of tension in which all human projects fall short of God's peaceable Reign
yet can still be called toward greater justice and more courageous
peacemaking; once Robert Markus taught me to recognize in Augustine's *City of God* a very similar view of history,[16] I was ready to recognize both the potential of Augustine's worldview and the tragedy of his
failure fully to sustain its eschatological tension. Meanwhile, I have
taken encouragement from peers in my own generation of Mennonite
scholars who have been recognizing anew that our tradition of discipleship, service, and peacemaking will only thrive if it remains rooted
in God's gracious love;[17] that encouragement has allowed me to apolo-
gize less and less often for what once seemed strange even to me—an
unwelcomed affinity with Augustine.

In his 1994 presidential address to the North American Patristics
Society, Frederick Norris argued that the discipline of early Christian
studies must certainly continue to do the work of establishing critical
editions, faithful translations, and careful interpretations. Nonetheless,
he continued, the demise of that historical objectivism under which
scholars once did such work, and a new sensitivity to the way communities of meaning receive, read, and transmit texts, should actually help the society do its work better. Norris thus welcomed new
readings of early Christian texts by theologians of Africa, Asia, and
Latin America. He welcomed readings from other disciplines too,
such as "religious studies, classics, history or literature," for, he said,
"I often find insights in such discussions which my community did
not see."[18]

I have made my forays into historical studies in the space that
Norris's welcome opened up. As an ethicist first of all, I have trusted
and assumed that the questions I bring not only from my community
but from the discipline of ethics would be welcomed as fruitful ones
from the other side of the interdisciplinary conversation. Yet for such
conversation to prove fruitful in fact, the ethicist must also continue
welcoming the interrogation of historians. I have come to think of this

book as situated, therefore, in a field of tension defined by two sets of polarities.

The first is a set of two questions: What might Augustine have to offer? But how are we to appropriate Augustinian thought without appropriating too much? I argue that contemporary Christian ethics should consider reappropriating at least the overarching structure of Augustine's doctrine of Christian love because it integrates both right self-love and proper self-denial. Yet we should be ready to ask whether we might be appropriating too much, for Augustine integrated all aspects, of all loves, through a vision of the good of mutual love that *also* tempted him to paternalistic coercion carried out with the backing of imperial violence and presumption.

Now, the term "reappropriation" has started to become a commonplace in the field of historical theology, along with the term "retrieval." But if we do not sense a second set of tensions here, we should. The prospect of reappropriating "too much" from Augustine carries a normative tone, a hint of ethical judgment. The second field of tension, then, is between the methodologies of ethical argument and historical investigation. Historians, despite the demise of objectivism, and despite the welcome that I heard in Norris's speech, remain properly nervous about imposing normative problems upon the historical record. "Reappropriation" dare not mean that we strip-mine a tradition for pretty gems we happen to like, only to render the landscape unrecognizable for students who come after us.

I have tried to negotiate this field of tension by requiring myself to appropriate or reject Augustine's ethical judgments and ecclesial policies only on the basis of a principle of selection that he himself might be able to recognize, on his own terms. To arrive at such a principle of selection has, I hope, required me to be responsible with the historical record and accountable to the canons of historical research.

In the end, however, I make no claim that this is strictly a historical study. Rather, it is a species of conceptual analysis, in conversation with historical texts. The hope is that we can make clearer distinctions in and among concepts we have inherited, by examining them at or near their sources. The goal is to enliven our imaginations so that we may think about a set of contemporary ethical issues in ways that have been refreshed. The possibility that nonetheless remains is this: So long as we stay clear that the questions we are taking to ancient texts are not exactly the questions that the ancients were asking, then the lens of our own fresh questions might yet allow us to see things in the historical record that we would otherwise have missed.

––––––––

We will be reading the historical texts because normative questions have urged us to do so. I am committed on grounds other than Augustinian texts to an interpretation of Christianity that gives central place to nonviolence. With that presupposition in place, I am engaging Augustine as a conversation partner from whom we might learn and retrieve as much as possible. In making a retrieval, I am not in the first or last instance claiming to offer a definitive interpretation. Admittedly, I approach Augustine looking for fault lines in this thought—openings through which I and other like-minded Christians may enter into his views without necessarily accepting them wholly. Even so, I must also admit to a certain hope that once inside the ongoing debate that *is* Augustinianism, Christians who, like myself, are committed both to a critique *and* to a retrieval of St. Augustine's thought may persuade others to join in his fresh interpretation.

Whatever St. Augustine has to offer us he offers not because he stands as an unquestioned *auctoritas* in the canon of Christian theologians, but because the overall structure of his thought proves to be cogent in the face of a potent mix of theoretical and pastoral challenges. Those challenges may demand that we reject some of Augustine's specific ethical judgments and ecclesial policies. Only what coheres after and in spite of critical appraisal will bear normative import. And even then, the ultimate test of cogency will not be the intellectual satisfaction of a good, broadly explanatory theory. Rather, that ultimate test of cogency will be the service that theology renders—and the grace toward which it points—for Christians who would live their lives in fitting response to the narrative of God's saving faithfulness in Jesus Christ, through the power of the Holy Spirit. That is a test that has only barely begun at the point where any theological project ends.

For the Joy
Set Before Us

CHAPTER ONE

The Problem of Self-Denial

I have never found any tension between the pastoral office and the scientific task of scholarship. It is not a matter of mutual tolerance, but of a fruitful interrelationship.

Anders Nygren, "Intellectual Biography"

Theological ethics in the Christian tradition cannot do without an account of proper self-denial; neither can it do without an account of right self-love. The hard sayings and the cross of Jesus Christ present permanently discomforting challenges to every Christian life and require the church to grapple with their meaning in every age. Those challenges and that grappling have so shaped the ongoing life-reflection we call Christian ethics that one must wonder how this ethic could be Christian at all if it did not call and predispose its practitioners to respond to the needs of others even at cost to themselves. Still, when Christian ethicists have spoken of self-sacrifice as though it were the most telling trait in love that is truly Christian, they have opened Christian theology to serious critique from those who have suffered oppression and who object that they cannot freely or lovingly sacrifice what they have already been denied. Dismissals of either Christ-like self-denial *or* Christian self-love thus seem premature.

In seeking to hold together proper self-denial and right self-love, we will speak intermittently of "evangelical self-denial." In the first instance this term simply refers to that self-denial of which the Gospels speak. Whether or not we understand Jesus' challenge, and however we grapple with its meaning, we cannot excise Jesus' call to deny ourselves from the Gospels. Without claiming that either we or a Christian thinker of another age has fully understood and heeded Jesus' call, we leave a marker for that call and initially

1

ask only how a given theologian has endeavored to sustain its claim. Yet sooner or later we will have to say more. Sooner or later that part of the Church's grappling which we call theology will have to explain *how* self-denial can be part of "the gospel"—good news, the *euangelion* of God's Reign—that the Gospels record Jesus proclaiming and realizing in his person. Can self-denial really be gospel? By whatever account Christian self-denial is good, even for those who are denying themselves, it will be "evangelical self-denial" in a second sense that is richer, fuller, more theological, but also subject to ongoing revision. By implication, such an account may carry with it an account of right self-love, for in seeking to participate in the good, moral agents are loving themselves. My argument, at least, will be that only such self-denial as is meaningful in light of God's intended good for human beings is proper—and properly evangelical. But to move from the first to the second meaning of "evangelical self-denial" will, in a way, be the task of this book.

In the thought of St. Augustine the Christian church once had a unified account of self-love and self-denial. The fourth-century convert, philosopher, theologian, and bishop, whom most major branches of Western Christianity have claimed as an authority, spent a lifetime debating with himself and with others about exactly how love of God and neighbor unify the whole Christian life—and thus order love for self and for temporal goods as well. To be sure, the complexity of Augustine's conversation with himself makes appropriation of his thought hazardous; later Christians have not always learned the best lessons from him. Amid Augustine's long and sometimes shifting debate, in fact, he himself alternately obscured, failed to note, or even fractured crucial links that unified his thought. Yet insofar as the overarching structure of Augustine's doctrine of Christian love remains coherent and sound, it offers a model for reunifying our account of Christian love.

It will repay us, then, to rediscover the links that unified self-love and self-denial in Augustine's thought, and thus to suggest how contemporary Christian ethics might continue to do so. To do this we will engage in a critical reflection on some of the most important texts that Augustine left to posterity, thus "conversing" with Augustine's thought. As in any respectful conversation, we must do everything possible to allow our partner to speak in his own "voice." As with any figurative conversation partner who is in fact long dead, that means holding ourselves accountable to the historical record and the canons of historical inquiry. Yet in the end, our hope will be that the conversation prove fruitful—in this case by allowing us to draw an ethical argument from the historical texts.

At first glance the criticism Augustine receives from a wide range of contemporary positions may seem to render him an unlikely source of unity. Augustine has critics who fault him for foisting too much self-denying, anti-body austerity on later Christians—but also has critics who fault him for allowing too much self-love into Christian thought. This very spread of criticism is intriguing. Perhaps Augustine understood something about the unity of self-love and self-denying love of others that neither set of critics has recognized. Second thought therefore suggests that reading Augustine more closely may prove fruitful in surprising ways. For if we find that we cannot do without accounts of either right self-love or proper self-denial, what first appears to be a dilemma may in fact turn out to be a clue. Though the problem of unifying these accounts would remain with us, we may then see it as a fruitful problem.

In any case, we should recognize contemporary debates over the nature of Christian love as an Augustinian problem. By Augustine's telling, human beings are prone to fracture their love into scattered loves.[1] Those who have presented and those who have contested self-sacrifice as the most telling trait in truly Christian love have all represented fragments of Augustine's thought: Reinhold Niebuhr recovered Augustine's doctrine of sin but made little of Augustine's faith that the Holy Spirit was at work transforming Christian lives in time through mutual love in the church. Anders Nygren arrayed Lutheran arguments against Augustine, but the Luther he cited still owed a great debt to the ancient bishop. Feminist critics of Niebuhr, Nygren, and their students have rarely appealed to Augustine, and then with reservations. Yet when some feminists have sought to recover a place for self-love and for delight, or when others have wondered if trinitarian theology might offer the ultimate ground for selfhood and mutuality, they have begun to restore elements of Augustine's legacy that Christian ethics had risked neglecting. So whether contemporary debaters have blamed Augustine or invoked him, then, and whether they have named Augustine or ignored him, their entire debate has been Augustinian—at least insofar as all have wrestled with his legacy. That pattern deserves greater attention.

A Premature Agreement

Though many Christians associate self-sacrifice with authentic love, two Protestant thinkers who gained prominence in the 1930s not only articulated that view, but set the very terms for twentieth-century debates over the nature of Christian love.[2] They are the Swedish theologian, church historian, and Lutheran bishop Anders Nygren; and Reinhold Niebuhr, who became a formidable American spokesman for a movement known as Neoorthodoxy.

Anders Nygren

Anders Nygren's study of agape and eros actually began, he has said, when as a boy he overheard his schoolteacher father discussing theology with an acquaintance. "A great deal went over my head, but I caught something here and there, and in particular a sentence of my father's, 'But Christian agape means something quite different.'"[3] That the meaning of agape and eros are "quite different" turned out, for Nygren, to be something of an understatement. Surveying fifteen centuries of Christian reflection and teaching on love, Nygren's presupposition eventually became his conclusion, that agape and eros are not only quite different but entirely different, "opposed," perhaps even engaged in a "life-and-death struggle."[4]

However we evaluate Nygren's thesis, it has been enormously influential. As Thor Hall, one of his North American interpreters, summed up that influence in 1978, "No churchman who has been anywhere near awake during sermons for the last forty years or so can have missed hearing—at least once from every preacher—an exposition of the difference between *eros, philia,* and *agape,* the three Greek terms for love. . . . Most of us nowadays consider the point made. That was not so forty to fifty years ago."[5] Among ethicists, especially Protestant ones, Nygren's project helped found a school of thought that sometimes bears the name of Agapeism. "Agapeists" do not necessarily accept all of Nygren's conclusions or draw distinctions as sharply as he did. Yet they continue to hold that agape is what structures Christian ethics, even as they debate over just how it does so.[6]

For Nygren, agape was the uniquely Christian love, seen most fully in the cross, where God in Christ descended, humbled, and sacrificed himself for sinners. It did not seek its own immortal good, but dared to lose its life. In fact, argued Nygren, agape is Christianity's defining characteristic, its *Grundmotiv* or fundamental motif. In turn, it gives Christian ethics a radical distinctiveness. Fellowship with the God who has come to humanity out of sheer, self-giving love is what "wholly determine[s]" the content of Christian ethics. "Agape is creative," it is "a value-creating principle," Nygren wrote repeatedly. It does not discover but rather creates value in its objects without presupposing any good there of their own; it is spontaneous and unmotivated. In other words, it is not attracted to the value, the beauty, or the good it discovers in its objects, but rather it creates value in them *ex nihilo*.[7]

Though determinative for Christian ethics, agape is preeminently God's love for sinners who have no grounds of their own for hope, according to Nygren. His strongest case for the centrality of the agape motif to Christianity was his argument that it characterized and linked the religion of both Jesus and Paul. That case was especially arresting because it ran directly counter to the dominant theological thought of Nygren's day. Nygren received his first theological degree in 1912, and as Hall has noted, it was not an auspicious time to be launching a theological career. Adolf Harnack's *What Is Christianity?* and Albert Schweitzer's *Quest of the Historical Jesus* were only the latest and most prominent works shaking the theological confidence of many by driving a wedge precisely at this point, a wedge between Jesus and Paul. Harnack especially had popularized the thesis that the simple ideas of Jesus of Nazareth, rather than the complex notions of Paul, express the essence of Christianity. Nygren found "the seeds of Paul's theology deep in the message of Jesus," as Hall put it.[8] The experiential source of Paul's "ceaseless wonder" at God's gratuitous love, according to Nygren, was that he *"the persecutor became a disciple and apostle. . . .* Were it a matter of worthiness, he would least of all have deserved to become an apostle of Christ." This showed Paul "the absolutely unmotivated character of God's love" and placed the cross of Jesus Christ at the center of both his preaching and theology. Christ's cross, his death for sinners, commends God's own agape toward human beings.[9]

All this is familiar, but key to Nygren's argument was the precedent he found for Paul's theology not only in the raw event of crucifixion but in the very teachings of Jesus of Nazareth.[10] Nygren argued that "the Agape motif forms the principal theme of a whole series of Parables." Thus, the gratuity of God's unmerited, "groundless" agape, which would later form the core of Paul's theology, itself formed the very fabric of Jesus' teaching. Certain parables demonstrated Jesus' understanding of God's love with particular poignancy.[11] Nygren lingered longest over the Parable of the Laborers in the Vineyard. The action of the vineyard's householder in paying a day's wages to those who only worked an hour, just as he did those who worked an entire day, was "directed against the thought of worthiness and merit, against every attempt to regulate fellowship with God by the principle of justice." This was the picture of God's "spontaneous, 'unmotivated' love."[12]

As taught by Jesus, demonstrated on the cross, and discerned by Paul, the pattern of God's agape contrasted entirely with the eros motif in Hellenistic theories of salvation, Nygren argued. Eros was the Platonic conception of love, especially. Even in its noblest religious form, which had nothing to do with "erotic" sensuality, it was acquisitive, egocentric, and desirous, for the object of its desire was the beauty of the divine, with which its subject desired union. Though eros begins in human need and longing, what evokes it is the value already present in the object of longing. Thus, it is precisely what agape is not. It is acquisitive, not self-giving; it moves upward toward, not downward from, the divine; it is not spontaneous but motivated. Eros recognizes rather than creates value; it is the draw of that value, the evocative power of that good, the attraction of that beauty, which gives eros its quality.[13]

Eros, according to Nygren, is profoundly egocentric. Religious eros for union with the divine may, in its nobility, obscure the self-centered character of eros in a way that crassly sensual eros does not. Yet once we notice that selfish character, believed Nygren, we can trace the egocentrism of eros down deep, all the way to its core. "Eros is essentially and in principle self-love. . . . It is not too much to say that self-love is the basic form of all love that bears the stamp of Eros. Love for God and love for one's neighbor (or for any other object than God) can alike be reduced to self-love."[14] If scholarly debate on Nygren has attended overwhelmingly to the issue of self-love, here is the reason. Should Nygren's position hold up, self-love is the telltale sign in any Christian doctrine of love that is ultimately destined to undermine New Testament agape.

The greatest threat to the purity of the agape motif as Nygren understood it was not, after all, a frontal assault from the eros motif itself. Rather, that threat disguised itself with a name other than eros and undermined agape from within Christian theology. Nygren's own greatest rival was the very possibility of a synthesis between agape and eros. The strongest objection to Nygren's position would be the coherence of this reconciling rival. Like an unwelcomed peace activist or principled double agent in times of Cold War, such a reconciler would supply perspectives to the worlds of agape and eros that might allow them to recognize themselves as part of a single world, and thus make peace in spite of their differences. And the argument for synthesis would cohere particularly well if the position of agape within that rival position remained intact, sustainable, perhaps even stronger. In that case, the "threat" of betrayal would not be a threat at all, except to those with some stake in a stand-off.

Augustine had made the most formidable attempt at such synthesis; the name by which Augustine allowed eros to infiltrate Christian love, according to Nygren, was *caritas*. Given the critical role that Augustine had played in the history of Christian teaching on love, plus the importance of Augustine's synthesis as the best objection to Nygren's own argument, it is hardly surprising that Nygren dedicated more pages to Augustine than to any other single figure. Augustine stood at the frontier between the eros and agape motifs, wrote Nygren. He represented both motifs in his very person; in his thought, neither motif defeated the other. Yet by bringing eros and agape together Augustine created a third motif. *Caritas* is both, yet neither, of the two. Augustine, in short, was the main developer of the Christian doctrine of love as it came down to us through the centuries. Thus he became more influential even than the New Testament.[15]

Augustine held eros and agape together, in Nygren's telling, by finding complementary roles for the two formative influences upon his thought—Neoplatonism and the New Testament proclamation of God's love. Neoplatonism made a place for the eros motif by showing the true object of human longing. But Neoplatonism cannot attain that object. Only Christianity shows us how to attain and cling to God. Still, eros remains the *way* to God. Agape fits *into* the eros framework. Agape merely corrects the chief fault of eros, its subtle yet haughty pride or *superbia*. Augustine, Nygren alleged, failed to see the "great and fatal contradiction" in using that same Neoplatonic ascent to recount his own religious experience, to frame his doctrine of Christian love, and thus "to maintain both Eros and Agape at once." Yet even as he leveled his critique, Nygren implicitly underscored the continuing importance of Augustine's conception of Christian love for theological and ethical reflection.[16]

Nygren believed he discerned the center of Augustine's thought in this formula: God commands, then gives what God commands.[17] Appropriate to its synthetic quality, to be sure, *caritas* was a complex of themes and thoughts. The closest thing to a simple definition derives from what Augustine found so engaging in the phrase from Psalm 73(72):28 that he often quoted: "*Mihi adhaerere Deo bonum est.*" *Caritas* is clinging to God as one's highest and only good, in the abandon of an undivided heart. As Nygren read Augustine, then, *caritas* is primarily a love *for* or *to* God, rather than God's love for us. Augustine was convinced that the love "poured into our hearts through the Holy Spirit that has been given to us" (Romans 5:5) is a love we then have for God. Though such love may be God's gift, it is then our love for God, and Nygren believed that such an interpretation obscured the priority of God's love for us.[18]

Above all, Augustinian *caritas* betrays authentic Christian love, according to Nygren, because it always retains egocentric, acquisitive self-love at its core. The Neoplatonic framework ensured that *caritas*-love remained fundamentally acquisitive. This in turn betrayed its eudaemonism, its ethical orientation toward the human's own desire for well-being. To Nygren, "there cannot be the slightest doubt that [Augustine's] doctrine of love, so far at least as our analysis has yet dealt with it, rests substantially on the foundation of Eros and has very little in common with Agape-love." Nygren insisted that for Augustine, even God's own love aims at evoking love back *to* God; Christ comes and God reveals God's love so that we might in turn learn to love God rightly. Thus, argued a mystified Nygren, even *God's* love appears in Augustine's construct to be self-seeking. More obvious still, Augustine's *caritas* synthesis also undermined authentic love of neighbor, according to Nygren. Constrained by the prominence of neighbor-love in the New Testament witness, Augustine endeavored to patch love of neighbor into his system. But since God and self were the two poles that oriented that system, Augustinian love of neighbor at best was *only* a patch. Augustine would have us refer all love of neighbor back to our love for God, but Augustinian love for God always began in the self-love that perceives God as one's good.[19]

For Nygren, then, Augustine's synthesis of self-referential love or eros and self-denying love or agape was as calamitous as it was subtle and original; synthesis itself was suspect to Nygren, since he believed that any attempt to combine eros and agape must necessarily betray the latter. Though Nygren's work has fallen into disrepute both for exegetical and historical reasons, his thesis continues to require examination. If nothing else, Nygren exercised vast influence by framing what have proven to be fundamental questions for both Christian ethics and for Augustine studies.[20] More than that, the philosophical and theological problem that drove Nygren's exegetical and historical investigation persists, whatever the flaws in his investigation. For quite apart from the merits of his historical reading, Nygren's *Agape and Eros* stands as an important exposition of one conception of Christian love and ethics (though at one extreme even among those who share that conception). And if Nygren's instincts were right, Augustine's were wrong—in which case any effort to unify self-denial and self-love must prove as misguided as Augustine's effort to synthesize agape and eros allegedly was.

Terms of Debate: Mutual Love and Acquisition of the Good

We can begin to see the sense in which contemporary debates over the nature of Christian love constitute an Augustinian problem, as well as some preliminary reasons to consider reappropriating Augustine's thought for Christian ethics. So far it has been enough to see in Augustine one alternative to the understanding of Christian love that Nygren represents.[21] To Nygren, Augustine's was surely the *most* persuasive alternative, and the overarching thesis of the present project is that Augustine's approach is a cogent one. This certainly does not mean that Christian ethics can appropriate Augustine's thought uncritically or in all its details. Nor does it mean that Augustine's approach is the only alternative to Nygren's. Yet those elements of Augustine's "*caritas* synthesis" that most bothered Nygren should at least pique the interest of skeptical critics.

The place Augustine made for self-love is obviously one element that may pique such interest. Augustine's defenders have shown that Nygren's worries ran deeper, however, and in the process they also have shown why Augustine offers Christian ethics more than just an account of self-love. Augustinian *caritas* was so problematic for Nygren because it was central to Augustine's "immanent teleology," that is, the system by which he understood salvation to involve a movement not only from the Creator but back toward a goal or *telos* in union with the Creator.[22] In Augustine's teleology that goal was a universal order of mutual love; by evoking, righting, and guiding human desire this *telos* was to motivate active love for God and all creatures. Mutual love and right desire were both fundamental here. Two dimensions of Christian love that feminists have sought to recover for Christian ethics,[23] therefore, were already present in Augustine's doctrine of love.

Typically, teleological systems analyze and orient human action and human life itself through at least three main stages: In the distance they define some good as the object or purpose of action; close at hand they motivate the subject of the action accordingly; and in between they narrate an account of acting, questing, or growing toward fulfillment of the good. Nygren objected to teleology at every one of these stages. Motivating action according to the good seemed on one side to arouse egocentric self-interest, and on the other side to rule out love for sinners, enemies, and all who do not conform to the agent's order of value and goodness. Further, to grow and move toward the good through human agency seemed to require an acquisitive quest that looked to the Lutheran theologian suspiciously like justification by works.

I will argue in chapter 3 that Augustine's way of acquiring the good was not in fact "acquisitive" in Nygren's sense of the term, for it required trusting faith in God alone, through a continence that receives the good as God's gift rather than human achievement. Seeking to acquire comes in the middle stage of a teleology. Various interpreters of Augustine have already made clear that at the other two stages of teleologically guided human action, neither the end of mutual love nor the motivating desire for that love needs be egocentric, as Nygren thought. John Burnaby and Oliver O'Donovan have demonstrated that for Augustine even self-love could instead be theocentric.[24] Burnaby was one of the first to reply to Nygren, with a 1938 book that has since become a classic in Augustine studies, *Amor Dei: A Study of the Religion of St. Augustine.* O'Donovan's *The Problem of Self-Love in St. Augustine* represents his own wide reading within the Augustine corpus, and his judicious use of the secondary literature that intervened between

Nygren's book and O'Donovan's; on most points it approximates the consensus that two generations of discussions with Nygren have produced.

Burnaby believed he knew how Augustine could have met Nygren's core concern about the inevitable egocentricity of any love of God that we can speak of as true love of self. Whether such love is egocentric or theocentric "must depend, he would say, on your conception of the Supreme Good. If the *Summum Bonum* is by its very nature the *bonum commune,* a good which can be possessed only by being shared, then the desire and pursuit of it can never be the desire and pursuit of a *bonum privatum.*"[25] Burnaby argued that Nygren's neglect of mutual love or *philia* indicated "a serious, perhaps a fatal defect in [Nygren's] whole construction."[26] Nygren had misunderstood Augustine because he was unable to recognize communal notions of either love or good as authentically Christian.[27]

Augustine's notion of the common good, argued Burnaby, is key to understanding how he could approve of a certain kind of self-love while condemning others. "It is Augustine's constant doctrine, from the *De Moribus Ecclesiae* onwards, that the only love of self which deserves to be so called is the love of God as Supreme Good."[28] Perverse self-love is really love of one's own power and preeminence, Burnaby insisted; this "*amor suae potestatis* [is] the craving for independence, the soul's attempt to escape from the rule of God and to be its own master."[29] Such is the self-love that Augustine condemned in the *City of God—amor sui usque ad contemptum Dei.*[30] This "love of self that runs to the contempt of God," wrote Burnaby pointedly, "is neither egoism nor egocentrism, but 'egotheism'—not selfishness but blasphemous rebellion."[31]

O'Donovan has made this even clearer: The love of self that wishes good for itself only by loving God above all else can hardly be egocentric. It only loves itself by way of refraction, loving the self that God wills it to be and that God alone gives. Its good, its *telos,* is not of its own choosing, creation, or formation.[32] Self-love is egocentric only, then, if one looks to the self rather than God to discern one's purposes and goals. O'Donovan made his case by analyzing four different aspects to any love, as Augustine spoke of it.[33] Of these, the most satisfactory was "benevolent love," which rationally recognizes an objective order of created good and, in addition, freely affirms this order and seeks to help realize it. To love any creature, including oneself, is to seek the good of that creature not according to a teleological order that one imposes but according to God's will for it within the teleologically ordered good of the whole.[34] Not even Augustinian self-love is egocentric, therefore. Rather, it is theocentric. To love ourselves rightly by loving ourselves in God is to love ourselves with benevolent love, *amor benevolentiae*. This is a love that we must learn, preeminently from scripture.[35] In fact, only as we learn to love ourselves rightly would Augustine trust us to love our neighbor properly; otherwise we might lead our neighbor toward some false good.[36]

In seeing how two outstanding interpreters of Augustine have met Nygren's charges, we gain a fuller sense of what Augustine might have to offer contemporary Christian ethics. Burnaby and O'Donovan have taken Nygren's influential way of framing contemporary debates over Christian love and turned that framework on its head. If Augustinian love is not egocentric or "acquisitive" in Nygren's sense of the word, it is because Augustine offered us a theocentric vision of Christian love in which the good is neither private nor imposed by the human agent who is drawn toward it. God's own will to create an ordered ecology of mutual love, and God's own noncoercive way of seeking that good, thus define the terms for debates in Christian ethics over the nature, content, and criteria of love and loving action.

Interpreters like Burnaby and O'Donovan have not, however, pointed Christian ethics toward an Augustinian account of proper self-denial that might stand in the place of Nygren's. Nor have they explained how Augustine would have us seek the good in a way that is not egocentric and "acquisitive."

Reinhold Niebuhr

Critics of Nygren have suggested that recovering Augustine's thought might provide one alternative to the tendency within twentieth-century Christian ethics to associate Christian love closely with self-sacrifice. There are different ways to appropriate Augustine's legacy, however. Reinhold Niebuhr laid claim to it mainly by recovering what he took to be Augustine's doctrine of sin, in which pride, egotism, and self-assertion were fundamental.[37] Feminists seeking to counter strongly self-sacrificial notions of Christian love have thus devoted at least as much space to Niebuhr as to Nygren. Reviewing Niebuhr's notions of

sin, salvation, and Christian love will underscore the dangers that
ensue when Christian ethics loses its accounts not only of self-love but
also of mutual love—and loses a teleological framework for both. If
Niebuhr's theology lacks these elements, one reason may be that his
appropriation of Augustine was too selective.

Niebuhr's emergence as one of the most formidable thinkers in
twentieth-century American Protestantism coincided with his reflections on the requirements and limitations of Christ-like love.[38] Originally he shared the pacifist tendencies of liberal Protestantism and the
Social Gospel movement in particular, but by the early 1930s he had
become liberal pacifism's most trenchant critic. Niebuhr argued that
Jesus' ethic involved a self-giving altruism so thorough-going that it
offered little direct guidance for the political tasks of Christians who
might take responsibility for building and sustaining a relatively just
social order. Niebuhr called his position "Christian Realism," and its
framework was a theological anthropology that he presented as nothing
less than a recovery of the orthodox, "Augustinian" doctrine of sin.[39]

A polarity between human limitation and human transcendence
defines the human condition at its most fundamental level, according
to Niebuhr.[40] Precisely because human beings are capable of transcending their creaturely limitations, they are capable of overestimat-
ing themselves, while underestimating their weakness and dependency
on God and others. Fundamentally, then, sin is for Niebuhr pride and
self-love. Pride may express itself through the exercise of power, knowledge tainted with ideology, self-righteousness, or self-deification. By
projecting the interests of one's own person or group over against the
claims of others, pride is always a manifestation of self-love as well.[41]

Niebuhr structured his treatment of redemption around a double
paradox in the Pauline text, "I am crucified with Christ, nevertheless I
live; yet not I but Christ liveth in me . . ." (Galatians 2:20, KJV). The
first paradox: God has created the self in such a way that "it cannot realize itself within itself. It can only realize itself in loving relation to its
fellows." Thus, "The self in this state of preoccupation with itself must
be 'broken' and 'shattered' or, in the Pauline phrase, 'crucified.'" The
second paradox is that the Christian does then experience a new selfhood. "The new self is more truly a real self because the vicious circle
of self-centredness has been broken. The self lives in and for others,
in the general orientation of loyalty to, and love of, God." The Pauline
"nevertheless," wrote Niebuhr, opposes not only the self-destructive

egotism of the sinful self, but "Christian conceptions of fulfillment and mystic doctrines of salvation in which the final goal is the destruction of self." The double paradox, therefore, is that redemption is "the negation of a negation": The life of the redeemed self is the life wherein "not I but Christ liveth in me," a "self only by grace," wherein divine mercy causes Christ's perfection to stand in for human achievements that the self can at best intend. Since even sanctifying, empowering grace becomes available by way of a "double negation," the stress in Niebuhr's thought is always on the grace of forgiveness.[42]

At the heart of Niebuhr's theological anthropology is another paradox: Guiding all human relations according to the "law of love" is an ideal that lies outside the possibilities open to human beings within time and history; yet the "law of love" remains the law of life even within the natural, historical life of human beings. His central plank was that "Christ as the norm of human nature defines the final perfection of man in history." That perfection was not so much the fullness of human virtue or pristine sinlessness but "the perfection of sacrificial love." Even as the cross shows that divine perfection involves itself in the suffering and tragedy of human history, it "also indicates that the perfection of man is not attainable in history." The key to comprehending this paradox is the contrast Niebuhr drew between sacrificial love and mutual love, at least mutual love as he understood it.[43]

Jesus' ethical ideal was for Niebuhr one of "pure disinterestedness" or "sacrificial *agape*."[44] It transcends, yet enlivens, the ordinary moral problems of politics, economics, or a single human life. After all, ordinary morality always works toward some kind of prudent "armistice" between contending claims and interests, rather than the relinquishing of such claims and interests. "The absolutism and perfectionism of Jesus' love ethic sets itself uncompromisingly not only against the natural self-regarding impulses, but against the necessary prudent defenses of the self, required because of the egoism of others."[45] A life dedicated to living out such an ideal must necessarily lead to the self-sacrifice of the cross:

> The final majesty, the ultimate freedom, and the perfect disinterestedness of divine love can have a counterpart in history only in a life which ends tragically, because it refuses to participate in the claims and counterclaims of historical existence. It portrays a love

"which seeketh not its own." But a love which seeketh not its own is not able to maintain itself in historical society.[46]

Thus, the highest moral possibility that human beings can sustain over time through their institutions and cultures is not *sacrificial* but rather *mutual* love—which to Niebuhr meant *reciprocal* love. The self-sacrificial love of Jesus Christ may provide the ultimate standard of human nature, and individuals or small groups may even witness briefly to that standard through authentic altruism. But within the on-going course of history, mutual love provides the only achievable and sustainable ethical norm. Sacrificial love "cannot justify itself in history. From the standpoint of history mutual love is the highest good." The purposes and obligations of human society can only find their fulfillment in mutual love, through which all conflicting claims and interests are "proportionately satisfied and related to each other harmoniously." For that very reason, sacrificial love may even conflict with the norm of mutual love in history, for sacrificial love is an affront to the norms of justice.[47]

The norm of mutual love, wrote Niebuhr, is knowable through historical experience and attainable within history; reason and natural religion do not need the life and death of Jesus to ascertain "that life ought not to be lived at cross purposes, that conflict within the self, and between the self and others, is an evil." Harmony can be in the interest of any enlightened ego; in fact the noblest of such "mutual love" retains the taint of egoism and expresses eros insofar as human agents desire a more harmonious social order out of self-interest. Still, the sacrificial love of the cross clarifies what is only partially knowable otherwise, that mutual love cannot sustain itself without transcending itself, "for the self cannot achieve relations of mutual and reciprocal affection with others if its actions are dominated by the fear that they may not be reciprocated. Mutuality is not a possible achievement if it is made the intention and goal of any action. Sacrificial love is thus paradoxically related to mutual love. . . ."[48]

Niebuhr's penchant for paradox may of course reflect the very paradox of the Gospels, where Jesus promised his followers that "Whoever seeks to gain his life will lose it, but whoever loses his life will preserve it" (Luke 17:33). Niebuhr often reiterated what he once called *the* paradox of the moral life:

[T]he highest mutuality is achieved where mutual advantages are not consciously sought as the fruit of love. For love is purest where it desires no returns for itself; and it is most potent where it is purest. Complete mutuality, with its advantages to each party to the relationship, is therefore most perfectly realised where it is not intended, but love is poured out without seeking returns.[49]

If Jesus promised rewards to followers who took the way of self-sacrifice, that paradox "merely" showed that "egoism is self-defeating, while self-sacrfice actually leads to a higher form of self-realization. Thus self-love is never justified, but self-realization is allowed as the unintended but inevitable consequence of unselfish action."[50] Perfect mutual love is attained when no one seeks it for oneself, but only seeks the good of others through sacrificial love.[51]

Niebuhr's formulation is certainly a compelling one. Appropriate to its paradoxical and critical mode, it should long continue to play a cautionary role even for Christian ethicists who do not finally find it satisfactory. Without denying its analytic power, then, one may note that it encounters at least three problems:

First, even on Niebuhr's own account there must be some non-paradoxical continuity between the limited mutual love that is possible within history and the perfect mutual love of eternity. For, in yet another Niebuhrian paradox, the human perfection that is only possible outside of history does not entirely consume, devalue, or negate the "natural and historical vitalities" of our present human life.[52] How can this be, if the mutual love which results from sacrificial agape is possible only insofar as human beings abandon any desire or eros for the mutually beneficial relationships of history in which each has a stake? Are we consciously to desire mutual love in history or not? Or rather, will our love always be less than Christian when we inevitably do? Somehow Niebuhr would allow us to envision a transcendent order of mutual love among all creatures and God, yet hold suspect any desire to participate in a reflection of that order already in this life. According to his account, any paradoxical achievement of authentically mutual love within the limitations of historical existence depends on not intending to achieve it for ourselves. Thus, Niebuhr's treatment of mutual love finally begs for a response analogous to Augustine's remark that if one can say that God is ineffable, God is *not* ineffable.[53] If

Niebuhr can explain the paradox of the moral order, it may not be quite so paradoxical after all. It must thus be possible to love and act in truly Christ-like self-denial while knowing and desiring that one's sacrifices may contribute causally to an order of mutual love whose realization one recognizes to be a good for oneself. It cannot be impossible, much less wrong, to motivate and sustain the possibility of self-denying love by presenting mutual love as its end or purpose—its *telos*.[54]

The second problem in Niebuhr's formulation is that throughout all his discussions of mutual love he tended to conflate it with mere reciprocity. Niebuhr and other Agapeists have surely been right to note that even publicans are capable of a love that salutes their own and is only ready to do good to others on the condition that they will return such love (Matthew 5:46–47). Yet they have not taken adequate account of the possibility that there is a kind of mutual love so authentically Christian that it marks those who practice it as Jesus' disciples (John 13:34–35). While Agapeists have consistently defined Christian love as a love that "seeketh not its own" (1 Corinthinas 13:5), they have seldom noticed that in a trio of other New Testament texts the renunciation of self-interest finds its meaning, motive, and reason in a still larger purpose—the cause of Christ with which the faithful have come to identify their own good.[55] Self-denial is not a good in itself and self-sacrifice is not a freestanding duty. If Christ himself endured the cross for "the joy that was set before him,"[56] then even his own supremely sacrificial act looked with longing toward the *telos* of mutual love he had proclaimed as God's Reign. What makes joy in the mutual love that is "set before us" something more than mere reciprocity is what Jesus Christ shows us about the way God creates and restores relations of mutual love: God has taken the first step, has loved and suffered first. Thus, all who seek mutual love in Christ-like ways will likewise be prepared to risk and to act first—not without hope nor altogether without thought of receiving love in return (as Niebuhr and Nygren believed), but without any *guarantee* of receiving love in return.

Third, as feminists have pointed out, stressing the self-sacrificial trait in authentically Christian love seems to offer little good news to those upon whom society is already too quick to impose sacrifices or whose sense of selfhood is already shattered.

A Premature Dismissal

Feminists and others have poignantly shown the pastoral and conceptual problems that ensue precisely when Christians accept New Testament agape as normative for their lives in such a way that they seek to place others' needs invariably above their own. We cannot begin to survey all relevant feminist literature. However, one group of feminist authors has directly engaged Nygren's and Niebuhr's conceptions of self-sacrificial Christian love. Because of his prominent place in twentieth-century Christian ethics, especially in North America, Niebuhr in particular has drawn their attention. Surveying these critiques will certainly underscore the danger of premature agreement upon a definition of Christian love that tends to equate such love with self-sacrifice. Yet to dismiss self-denial from Christian ethics (or any ethic) would also be premature. It is not clear that Christian feminists are attempting to do without an account of self-denial altogether. What should become clearer, however, is that they cannot.

Feminist Critics

Feminists have found various reasons to debate whether it is possible to be both a feminist and a Christian, but the apparent centrality of self-sacrifice in the Christian tradition is especially problematic. While the cross has long been central to the faith of all Christians, men and women, much of the tradition has insisted that women especially take on the role of suffering servant. An overarching question for debate is whether this double standard is merely an abuse of Christian insights, or whether it is instead a damningly logical outgrowth of fundamental Christian claims.[57] In framing that question, a series of feminists have challenged the presuppositions about Christian love and self-denial that Niebuhr shared with Anders Nygren and others.

Valerie Saiving.   In a ground-breaking essay of 1960, Valerie Saiving found in Nygren and Niebuhr clear examples of a "widespread tendency in contemporary theology"—the tendency to describe the human condition in a way that mainly reflects the male condition, not a universal human situation that females share to the same extent. The result is that theology's description of God's redemptive response to the human condition does not respond to the experiences and needs of women. Because contemporary theology tends to focus on "man's predicament as rising from his separateness and the anxiety occasioned by it," argued Saiving, it also tends "to identify sin with self-assertion and love with selflessness." A more adequate account of the female human condition must recognize that "the temptations of woman *as woman* are not the same as the temptations of man *as man,* and the specifically feminine forms of sin . . . have a quality which can never be encompassed by such terms as 'pride' and 'will-to-power.'" Rather, at the root of characteristically female sins, argued Saiving, is "under-development or negation of self."[58]

Judith Plaskow.   Though Niebuhr had claimed that sin is fundamentally the pride and self-love whereby humans seek to deny their creaturely limitations, he had actually recognized in passing that sin could also express itself as sensuality—the attempt to hide one's freedom and to lose oneself in the vitalities of creaturely life.[59] As Judith Plaskow first observed, Niebuhr had "made things too easy for himself" by identifying sensuality mainly with sexual impulses and neglecting to explore other ways that people deny their own freedom by losing themselves in these vitalities.[60] A broader understanding of sensuality, taking into account women's experience, must recognize it in the attempt to pay attention to everyone's needs except their own. In this broader sense, Plaskow argued, sensuality *is* "women's sin."[61]

Not only was Niebuhr's definition of sin "one-sided," however, so was his definition of grace, insisted Plaskow. "Here again, . . . the human experience Niebuhr addresses is not women's experience. His view of grace, like his doctrine of sin, partly neglects the needs of women and partly reinforces a traditional understanding of women's role." If anything, his treatment of grace compounded the problems in his treatment of sin. Only because he emphasized the sin of pride without adequately exploring the sin of sensuality, wrote Plaskow, could Niebuhr claim that "the primary fruit of grace [is] sacrificial love." Even when Niebuhr moved on to the redeemed self that affirms "Nevertheless I live," noted Plaskow, he explained this critical phrase "almost entirely in terms of what it does not mean." Throughout his discussion of grace, Niebuhr's focus was on judgment, the "shattering" of the old self-centered self, and forgiving grace.[62]

Insofar as Niebuhr attended to sanctification at all, noted Plaskow, he identified sacrificial love as the primary fruit of empowering grace.

The problems in Niebuhr's doctrine of sin could thus undermine the sanctified life itself: "The shattering of the self from beyond is received as grace only where the self's sin is pride and self-absorption. Where sin is not 'too much' self but lack of self, such shattering is at least irrelevant and possibly destructive rather than healing." Where a woman is committing what Plaskow called the sin of self-lack—drifting, being passive, not taking responsibility for herself and her own needs—holding up sacrificial love as the norm for the redeemed life will only reinforce this sin. A person caught in the sin of self-lack requires "a different sort of grace from the shattering of the self," for she has no self to be shattered and may already be other-directed to a fault; grace must elicit "self-reconstitution along principles very different from those Niebuhr envisages."[63]

Susan Nelson Dunfee.   What Plaskow had called the sin of self-lack, Susan Nelson Dunfee later called "the sin of hiding."[64] "Hiding" was for her the fundamental sin of escaping from freedom, which Niebuhr had initially identified with sensuality and which Plaskow had called the primary form of sin for women. The problem in Niebuhr's thought, Dunfee argued, went deeper than simple neglect of the phenomenon of sensuality or the sin of hiding. In Niebuhr's thought the sin of hiding had actually ceased to be a real possibility. Humanity's true fulfillment, according to Niebuhr, is in the law of self-transcendence, expressed in total self-giving. "The sin of hiding has become a nonpossibility, and the sin of pride has become *the* sin; and true humanity, as seen in the one true man Jesus Christ, is known through total self-sacrifice. Self-sacrificial love, then, becomes the goal, the supreme human virtue, for all humanity."[65]

Niebuhr's thought faces severe difficulties, Dunfee argues. If humanity, even in its highest form, remains both finite and free, as Niebuhr claimed, the very ideal of one person sacrificing herself totally for another in perfect self-transcendence may in fact express "the very desire to deny one's finitude totally, and thereby transcend one's finitude—which is the sin of pride." Further, Niebuhr's own insights into the sin of hiding, however undeveloped, show that self-sacrifice cannot be the goal of human life. Niebuhr had "made humanity's highest virtue identical with the sin of hiding"! Not only did this involve Niebuhr in the logical contradiction of making a sin into a virtue, it also meant that he implicitly encouraged those committing the sin of hiding to continue doing so. "One then becomes glorified for never truly seeking to become fully human"; and because there is no judgment on the sin of hiding, there is no call to forgiveness and release.[66]

A theology such as Niebuhr's, therefore, perpetuates "woman's bondage to her hiddenness." It equates any desire to be a self with self-assertion and riddles that desire with guilt and anxiety. "As long as the sin of pride remains *the* sin and as long as the sin of hiding remains an unnamed sin, woman is caught in a double bondage to her guilt." This is a guilt that total self-sacrifice can never assuage, since it only goads her to a deeper sense of guilt, "the guilt of not being a self, the guilt of denying her full humanity and hiding in a deformed existence." Women must "repent of their real sin, the sin of having no self to sacrifice"; until they can do so, "they will know no end to the cycle of guilt and violence turned inward."[67]

The Need for Some Account of Self-Denial

Not all Christian feminists are ready to jettison their tradition's conceptions of sin and salvation, of course. While seconding the feminist critique of Niebuhr's definition of sin, Wanda Berry, for example, has warned that feminist as well as other liberation theologians may have become too preoccupied with Niebuhr's kind of analysis. Feminism, she argued, needs either to recover the sacrificial and juridical metaphors that predominate in Western liturgical and theological traditions, or to find new images that express recognition of responsibility for one's own life in the way that orthodox doctrines of sin and forgiveness long have done. Feminism cannot afford to blame social structures for all evil and oppression without acknowledging personal dimensions of responsibility.[68]

The same holds true for self-denial. Feminism itself will probably need either to recover or to find new ways to speak of right self-denial. After all, there is reason to doubt that any ethic can do without some such account—least of all a Christian ethic, even of the liberating sort.

First of all, if a Christian theology does not finally grapple with the New Testament's own hard sayings—its call to take up the cross, and to place other's interests ahead of one's own—then some will ask whether that theology can still claim to be Christian, and others will ask why it should bother.[69] For all that feminist critiques of Niebuhr help us to sharpen the problem of self-denial, they may have missed one critical point. Niebuhr's theological anthropology represented a synthesis from various sources, yet we should not underestimate the role that biblical interpretation played in his theology from beginning to end. As Dennis McCann has noted in a comparative study of Niebuhrian thought and liberation theology, Niebuhr's abiding conviction was that Jesus' ethic was uncompromising in its demand for a nonresistant love that preferred even the good of the evil enemy to one's own good.[70] Whatever problems in Niebuhr's work, he at least struggled to come to terms with Jesus' "love ethic."

Second, liberation struggle itself surely requires self-sacrifice. To imagine a liberation theology without any self-sacrifice may be a luxury that only North Americans and Europeans can afford. When liberation struggle is more than a "culture war"[71]—when the stakes in fact are life and death—any participant must contemplate costly self-denial. The Guatemalan poet Julia Esquivel has insisted that "The option the Christian woman takes in the struggle for a new society rules out egocentrism. This option is a continuous voluntary, joyful offering of her own life for the common good." No woman, particularly from a middle-class background, can understand the injustice that her economically impoverished sisters suffer or identify with them in solidarity without "acquiring the ability to give up a personal life project for a communitarian one." In undergoing what Esquivel calls a "'conversion' to the poor and to the project of their liberation," she "can no longer make choices which are isolated from the society in which she and they live. Her life project can no longer be purely individual, isolated from her people. Her entire life is involved with the pain, struggles, risks and goals of her people."[72]

Further, *any* ethic needs to identify the places in its system where self-denial is necessary. This is so even with eudaemonistic ethics, which begin with questions of how human beings might gain the good, happy, fortunate, or blessed life. To have normative "bite," any ethic must identify points at which an agent will refrain from acting in a way that presents itself as advantageous. Anyone willing to take the so-called "moral point of view" (which steps back from one's own pursuit of the good life to examine as objectively and self-critically as possible whether one's actions are also compatible with the good for others) must certainly contemplate moments of self-denial. Thus, Judith Plaskow's feminist critique of Niebuhr included an argument that one of Niebuhr's key concepts "includes no criteria in terms of which a particular exploitive act can be ruled illegitimate";[73] to provide such criteria would in fact mean identifying points at which self-denial becomes a duty.

As feminism moves beyond critique to the reconstruction of a fuller ethic that systematically confronts a variety of problems, we can expect it to need some account of self-denial. While feminists have been criticizing Christianity for equating self-love with sin and self-sacrifice with sanctity, for example, environmentalists have blamed Christianity for devaluing the natural world and legitimating human exploitation of so-called lower creatures.[74] If we add an ecological critique to a feminist critique, what emerges is the intriguing case of "ecofeminism." Ecofeminists point out that the ideologies and worldviews which legitimate dominance over both women and nature have not only coincided historically but also undergirded each other.[75] They argue that society will break with neither pattern of exploitation unless it breaks with both. In the context of our current inquiry, however, this must suggest that if we attend to both feminism and ecofeminism, we will need to avoid degrading both ourselves *and* the earth. In other words, human beings will need to conceive of ways to love themselves rightly yet without the domineering collective self-interest that environmentalists refer to as "anthropocentrism."

Can Self-Denial Be Sustained?

It seems that we cannot do without an account of Christian love in which self-denial always remains a real possibility, but neither can we accept a notion of Christian love that expresses itself most characteristically in self-abnegation. What then? We should come to see the problem of self-denial not only as a dilemma but as a clue. We should come to see it as a fruitful problem.

A Heuristic Problem

Let us imagine a Christian who is committed to practicing an ethic of love whose ultimate standard is the sacrificial love of Jesus Christ. This person could be a man or a woman, but since we have attended to feminist critiques, we will continue to speak of a woman. She has generously devoted her energies not simply to family or church but to grassroots political activities in the name of social justice. Amid a particularly grueling time, she starts to ask herself how long she can continue at such a pace. She worries that she will "burn out" and settle for a temptingly comfortable middle-class lifestyle that she considers self-centered. Yet she begins to recognize that she must be honest. She must replenish her resources and care for herself. She must be self-concerned precisely so that she does not become self-centered.[76]

This is not the challenge of self-denial as it poignantly presents itself in extreme situations of martyrdom on one hand, or abuse on the other. It is the problem of self-denial in "ordinary time." Yet it ought to be of at least as much interest to Christian ethicists. If nothing else, the problem has great heuristic value as well as pastoral importance. This is the problem of self-denial as it presents itself not so much when Christians abuse their ethic of service and self-denying love, but precisely insofar as they seek to practice it faithfully.

The need to balance care for oneself and for others is hardly unique to Christians, of course. According to Carol Gilligan, author of *In a Different Voice: Psychological Theory and Women's Development,* honesty about one's own needs presents a critical transitional issue for anyone moving toward moral maturity along a track in which caring and responsibility are the primary ethical concerns.[77] Moral maturity, she has argued, involves the ability to look at a moral dilemma in a way that integrates perspectives from both abstract principles of fairness and concrete caring for the needs of all the parties involved. The transition to moral maturity begins "with reconsideration of the relationship between self and other, as the woman starts to scrutinize the logic of self-sacrifice in the service of a morality of care"; a woman who does so "begins to ask whether it is selfish or responsible, moral or immoral, to include her own needs within the compass of her care and concern."[78]

Although Gilligan's work focuses on the moral development of individual women, it highlights a logic intrinsic to any ethic that makes self-sacrificial love a virtue, and thus poses a problem for any woman or man. At the same time, her work promises that this problem may be a fruitful one to have. For an individual, at least, it is the key to making a transition into moral maturity.

Self-Denial: The Shape of the Problem

For Christian communities as well as for individual Christians, for men as well as for women, the problem of self-denial is Gilligan's question writ large. This is the question of what might sustain a community of service over the long haul—what might sustain a community that institutionalizes mutual love, yet does so knowing that the larger purpose of its life together is potentially costly witness on Christ's behalf and service on others' behalf. The communal version of the problem of self-denial is intimately related to the problem as it confronts an individual Christian such as a Susan Nelson Dunfee or a conscientious objector to military service or a member of a Catholic Worker house serving the inner-city homeless. Since participation must in some way be voluntary in any Christian community that encourages and witnesses to the kind of Christ-like love that may require self-sacrifice, it can hardly sustain its communal witness and service if its members cannot sustain their own.

The church's pastoral problem must be its ethicists' question. This is the question of whether a love ethic that may demand right self-denial does not also require right self-love as a condition for the very possibility of right self-denial, not just as a concession to finitude or fallenness. Self-denial is not love itself; yet the willingness to suffer or refrain from advantage is a precondition for acting on behalf of others. The critical role of such a willing predisposition has led some ethicists to identify self-denial as the most telling mark of authentically Christian love. The current project focuses attention on self-denial not because it is the whole of love, but precisely because it is not. To avoid confusing self-denial with love itself, we must inquire into the preconditions and the sustainability of self-denial too. We must tell its story. Will and willingness do not form from nowhere.[79]

Can self-denial be sustained? For theological ethics, the question is double-edged. If Christian ethics cannot place self-denial in a larger framework that identifies what sustains it personally and pastorally, then theology may not be able to answer critics who are troubled that Christianity puts the cross of self-sacrifice somewhere very near its center. Accounting for how self-denial can be "evangelical" in our second and more theological sense—the sense in which it is only meaningful and proper in light of the good that God intended and Christ proclaimed for human beings—may actually be necessary simply to sustain receptivity to continually hear the Gospels' call to deny ourselves.

The "problem of self-denial," then, is the question of how to sustain, personally and in community, a demanding ethic of love and servanthood. To give and sacrifice for years and generations without replenishing personal and community resources seems a psychological, spiritual, and economic impossibility. Thus, if a church can offer no serious theological basis for personal self-development and communal flourishing, then contemporary psychology alone (whether "pop" or "pastoral") will supply rationales for self-concern to individuals, while communal self-preservation will revert to a kind of tribalism. And none of these is likely to discriminate well among the considerations of self-interest that it allows, or provide clear criteria for when self-denial becomes obligatory.

CHAPTER TWO

The Structure of Augustinian *Caritas*

Whoever has charity sees the whole at once
with the understanding's grasp

Augustine, *Homilies on 1 John*

"There can be no separation of love," Augustine once re-marked. He was standing in the cathedral of Hippo in 416 preach-ing on 1 John; he was now a seasoned bishop, biblical expositor, and theologian. For some thirty years he had been reflecting deeply on how the human person may relate rightly to all objects of human love—temporal goods, oneself, one's neighbor, and God.[1] By now he stood assured: the path of every authentic love led to God; and then, in God, one rediscovered the love of every creature, secure. Thus, he could tell those assembled, "you may choose for yourself what you love, and all the rest will follow."[2]

Augustine had not always enjoyed such assuredness. In 388, scarcely two years after what has become one of the most renowned conversions of Christian history, he had already come to see love of God, and with it love of neighbor as self, as the central prin-ciples that unify Christian theology, Christian life, and the Christian scriptures. How to coordinate the two loves was not quite so clear at first, however. Writing against the Manichaeans to whom he had once belonged, the promising young lay apologist had argued in *The Morals of the Catholic Church* that human beings could have no greater good than the unchanging, invulnerable, and loving en-joyment of God.[3] A resurgent Platonism of recent centuries, which we now refer to as Neoplatonism, had come to dominate Roman intellectual circles and to predispose many to embrace Christi-anity. It offered Augustine a language in which to say, with the Psalmist, that in contrast to *"omnes qui fornicantur abs te,"* all those who fornicate against God, "*mihi autem adhaerere Deo bonum est*"—for me to cling to God is the good.[4] Yet scripture added a second love at the center of Christianity, saying that while the greatest command was to love God with one's all, love of neighbor was very much like the first love.[5] Augustine had no doubt that love for God and love for neighbor must ultimately stand or fall together, and that "no one should think that while he despises his neighbor he will come to happiness and to the God whom he loves." But how this might be—whether both loves develop in tandem, or whether one leads to the other—a younger Augustine could only speculate.[6]

If the older Augustine was right, an interpreter should be able to begin with any of Augustine's four main loves and still find that all receive their orientation rightly in the love of God. Yet Augustine's doctrine of love did not spring into his mind like a forgotten Platonic memory, in full and timeless form, even when his mind bent most toward things Neoplatonic. From his earliest days as a Christian his abiding intuition was that only by loving and clinging to God can a person love God's creatures rightly. Even that intuition had a history, however, whose unstable beginning he marked at his adolescent discovery of Cicero's *Hortensius,* exhorting him to love wisdom above all earthly things.[7] Though all paths of Augustinian love lead to and from the love of God, his own path led through a recurring set of preoccupations and puzzles as surely as it led toward its abiding goal. The interpreter may best retrace his path by noting at once the goal that gave it meaning, and then working back toward this unifying love of God "from below," by attending to evidence from his own struggle to love rightly.

After all, even as the bishop stood more confidently in the pulpit, expounding on the great themes of Christian love from 1 John, uncertainties remained. The bishop theologian was not altogether different from the newly converted apologist. Though he had long since worked out the basic structure of Christian love, initial conceptual puzzles had given way to nagging practical problems in the application of this doctrine. The occasion for some of his most eloquent preaching on Christian love was in fact an ugly schism. Augustine's mutable recommendations about how to restore Christian unity sometimes belied his eloquent words and coexisted uneasily with the steady convictions that underlay and unified Augustine's thought.

This combination of difficulties and stable intuition has been Augustine's legacy to the centuries. Just as he came quickly to many of the abiding convictions around which his thought cohered, yet puzzled long over how they cohered and how to apply them in practice, the interpreter soon finds that it is easier to identify underlying themes than it is to recognize every variation on these themes as convincing or even consistent.[8] For those who would move from description to normative appropriation of his thought, the task is even more complex. While many of Augustine's specific moral judgments have earned trenchant criticism, the underlying structure of his reflections on Christian love has nonetheless had enormous influence on Christian theology and ethics in the West, often quite independently of those judgments. Whenever Christian thinkers highlight Jesus' two great commands to love God and to love neighbor as self, and then use them to structure and summarize the whole of Christian ethics, they are following Augustine's lead.[9] Such would hardly be the case if it were not possible to differ with him on particular ethical judgments, yet affirm the underlying structure of his thought. What then is that structure?

The Four Loves

Love for God

Augustine's understanding of Christian love or charity, with love of God at its center, seems straightforward enough:

> I call "charity" the motion of the soul toward the enjoyment of God for His own sake, and the enjoyment of one's self and of one's neighbor for the sake of God; but "cupidity" is a motion of the soul toward the enjoyment of one's self, one's neighbor, or any corporal thing for the sake of something other than God.[10]

Writing *On Christian Doctrine* in the late 390s at about the same time that he penned his *Confessions,* Augustine built up this definition of *caritas* both from a carefully reasoned philosophical argument and from the authoritative teaching of scripture. The central thesis of *On Christian Doctrine* was that the twofold love of God and neighbor is key to interpreting all scripture.[11] Scripture made this claim for itself, he believed.[12] But when reason and scripture supported each other the claims of each were stronger.[13] To make the biblical claim intelligible, rather than mere assertion, Augustine began with basic (*a priori*) categories that he believed common to all people's experience. Some things we enjoy; other things we use; still other things (human beings themselves) we both enjoy and use.[14] If we confuse these categories by enjoying that which we ought rather to use, we are as foolish as travelers who become infatuated with the vehicles and delights of their journey, only to forget the homeland which is their journey's end and instead wander aimlessly in a "perverse sweetness."[15] Equal companions on such a journey might present a special case of utmost importance, for they both aid us on the journey (thus proving useful in a way, even as they too use our aid) and share in the joy of restful arrival at home. But only that which makes us blessed (*beatos*) is enjoyable without qualification. This must be a life that is one of immutable truth— stable, secure, invulnerable to loss, and trustworthy. Nothing mortal qualifies. Thus, "The things which are to be enjoyed are the Father, the Son, and the Holy Spirit, a single Trinity, a certain supreme thing common to all who enjoy it, if, indeed, it is a thing and not rather the cause of all things, or both a thing and a cause."[16]

Thus any love must, according to Augustine, ultimately refer in some way back to love of God if it is to be right love; this teleological orientation was stable from the beginning to the end of Augustine's theological career. In his early *Morals of the Catholic Church* he began by arguing that no one can possess the blessed or happy life except by enjoying a supreme, perfect, and invulnerable good, which must be God, for any other object of love could disappoint.[17] An early argument such as this was certainly quite Platonic. Some thirty years later, Augustine could write a trenchant critique of the Platonists in book ten of the *City of God*. Yet even there he continued to affirm that the two great love commands of scripture pointed toward the Final Good of human beings of which philosophers debate; that good was to cling to God. "We are commanded to love this Good with all our heart, with all our soul, with all our strength: and to this Good we must be led by those who love us, and to it we must lead those whom we love."[18]

Still, Augustine's very definition of Christian charity in *On Christian Doctrine* hints that love for God itself might not be quite so straightforward in its meaning. For one thing, Augustine was quite content to let the ambiguity of the Latin genitive stand; *amor Dei* or *caritas Dei* could refer either to human love *for* God, or *God's* love for humans, or *both at once*.[19] Though that is a complexity that confronts readers in his writings generally, it is not the problem here. As Augustine defined Christian love in *On Christian Doctrine* 3.10.16, the first great love command warranted his focus on the human side of *caritas Dei*.

The problem in Augustine's definition is that the center which holds it together itself seems more elusive than stable. Love for God is clearly the basis for all other loves, in his definition, such that even love of neighbor is for the sake of God. Yet to define love for God itself, Augustine had to do so in relation to other loves, including the false loves that it was not: Charity was not cupidity; charity was not an ultimately unstable, mutable, mortal love for those things which one could not finally "enjoy," because they were themselves unstable, mutable, and mortal.

The difficulty in the definition is a difficulty in the doctrine. Augustine's reasoned arguments for the supremacy of the love for God almost always seem to proceed by way of negation. Love for God was the love that remained when all others failed, whether existentially or logically. What, therefore, did love for God really mean for Augustine? The question may seem odd, for few things are clearer in Augustine's writings than the centrality of this love. Yet finding a positive definition of its content proves a surprisingly elusive task. Scripture may fill in some content, but often by way of divine commands. A skeptic asking for the reasons behind these commands might conclude that Augustinian love for God is finally a vacuous concept. Existentially it may be an empty, needy longing, while logically it may be purely formal.

The question would have jarred Augustine less than we might expect, however. The very premise of his *Confessions* was the problem of how human beings can call upon God when they do not even know God. The believer might confess what scripture testifies, that "You are great, O Lord, and greatly to be praised: great is your power and to your wisdom there is no limit." Yet God is so great that after considering further the biblical confession that Augustine has mouthed, God may seem too immense, too inscrutable, and too unlike us in the way that God loves, for us to love God in return. Or—as Augustine sometimes put the problem when working in a more practical and pastoral mode—we simply cannot see God. That in fact is why, according to 1 John 4:20, we must learn to see God with the heart, through a love of neighbor that bears fruit in the mutual love of Christians.[20]

Augustine himself has forced his readers to proceed with him "from below." In order to understand what love for God meant for him, we must proceed with him through that process of elimination by which he not only found sinful human loves to be unsatisfactory, but also found right human loves to be unstable apart from a stable love for God. Even *that* love for God, however, would itself be nothing but one more unstable human love unless God's own love established and animated it—as he so often repeated—through the love of God that is "poured into our hearts through the Holy Spirit that has been given to us" (Romans 5:5).

On the surface it might seem that to accept this procedure requires us to accept the claim that Augustine's pilgrimage as he narrated it in his *Confessions* is a "singularly clear example" of the Platonic way of salvation through ascent, or what Plato called "the right way of Eros." Augustine did in fact recount various "Platonic ascents"—introspective philosophical exercises wherein the seeker looks within for the *logos* and (so the seeker hopes) finds it through successively higher and more universal insights into the form of that *logos* which shapes all that is. But the lesson of these ascents, and the larger question of Augustine's debt or allegiance to Neoplatonism, is trickier than it first appears.[21]

Augustine's Platonic ascents always failed, except perhaps for one. The most successful ascent, which he shared with his mother in Ostia, was a gift not of their own devising; its lesson was that no creature could claim to have made itself, but that everything from initial creation through final invitation to "enter into the joy of your Lord" was God's gift and God's doing. Even the Ostia vision indirectly indicted Platonic seekers for their pride, therefore. Other ascents, which failed outright, consistently confronted seekers with the humility rather than the grandeur of the divine, and thus, the sinful failure of Platonism in its proud refusal to accept Christ's incarnation. All that might ultimately remain of Augustine's Platonism was a language for making sense not of the prospects for human beings to attain the divine, but rather of the failure of every attempt to grasp God.[22]

Human love for God therefore had ultimate value only insofar as it showed itself impossible, thus giving way to the mystery of God's grace, God's unwarranted love, God's initiative in Jesus Christ.[23] In so doing it also gave way to the testimony and guidance of scripture, which in fact increasingly displaced philosophy as the basis for Augustine's doctrine of love. The humility of the canonical text as Augustine first encountered it, after all, bore an intimate relationship with the humility of God in Jesus Christ, which was the foundation upon which charity built.[24] "Obedience" to the "commands" of love would finally prove to be not fearful compliance but responsive *love of what God loves,* according to the record of God's own loving action.

Love of Temporal Goods

To "love the world or the things in the world" (1 John 2:15) was, for Augustine, not only a sinful affront to the love of God, but futile and foolish. The sin in such love was nothing short of adultery against God; James 4:4 told him that those who fornicate against God rather than cling to God were those who loved the world.[25] The complications of life in time, however, reminded him that to love those things that time snatches or bears away may be pointless besides. Moth, rust, and finally death would thwart every effort to lay up treasures on earth for oneself, or even for one's children.[26] Thus, although God made all things in the world, we face a choice. That choice is "either to love things temporal and pass away with time's passing, or not to love the world, and to live forever with God. The river of time sweeps us on; but there, like a tree growing by the river, is our Lord Jesus Christ." In taking human flesh, dying, and ascending to the stable eternity of heaven, Christ had entered time that he might "plant himself as it were beside the river of things temporal. If you are drifting down to the rapids, lay hold of the tree: if you are caught up in the world's love, lay hold of Christ."[27]

The lesson had at first been a bitter one.

To relinquish ambition, upward mobility, and wealth did not initially seem to be so difficult or bitter for Augustine. As a talented young man, Augustine had risen rapidly from his status as a provincial professor of rhetoric into the emperor's court in Milan. Yet to hear him tell it, philosophical wisdom was so much the higher good that his career began to nauseate him; he was so ready to abandon it before his conversion that he could renounce it with little trauma soon afterward. When Augustine wrote of his ongoing temptations as a Christian bishop, the "desire of the eyes" that might lead others to covet wealth and luxury goods had diminished to nagging curiosity.[28]

To relinquish the "desire of the flesh" was more difficult for Augustine, of course, but was finally manageable. To dismiss first the woman to whom he had long been faithful, and then to abandon sexual activity altogether, involved bitter pains that exercised a formative influence on his later theological reflection. Even so, a decision for the celibate life allowed him to draw a clear line; sexual desire might never cease to "assail" him, yet he could know for certain whether the gift of celibacy had "been fulfilled" in him. He might never will perfectly in this area, but he could at least will to will, thus withholding consent from contrary desires. Sensual desires for food, drink, even music, thus became his ongoing struggles in this regard.[29]

Ambition was a subtle temptation, however, for he did not actually have to aspire to public recognition *in saeculo,* so long as a few friends offered their praise. Of the three categories of temptations that Augustine found in 1 John 2:16—*concupiscentia carnis, concupiscentia oculorum,* and *ambitio saecul*[30]—the last one gave him the most long-standing trouble, according to his own confession. For while the external perquisites to be gained through successful worldly ambition never returned to tempt him seriously,[31] their demise actually left an unalloyed desire to be influential and respected among the friends and colleagues he valued most.[32] Whether the exchange expressed mutual love and respect or reciprocal pride and conceit was almost impossible to sort out, Augustine found. Everyone seems to need some of the former, so desperately that they easily grasp at the latter. Of the false joy that human relationships might proffer, Augustine prayed: "I ask you, has this third kind of temptation ceased for me, or can it cease throughout all my life, this wish to be feared and to be loved by men?" Any line here was an uncertain line in the sand, even (or especially) among his closest friends. The difference between the true joy he found in edifying a friend with a word of counsel or edifying an assembly with a sermon, and the false joy he found in the praise they then returned to him, was almost impossible to discern. Thus, "For other types of temptation I have some kind of ability for self-examination, but for this scarcely any. . . . [T]o be without any praise whatsoever, and to test ourselves in this condition, how can we manage it?"[33]

Friendship that fell short of true love of neighbor was itself a temporal good. Here Augustine recorded his bitterest lesson in the futility of all attempts to cling to temporal goods. Here too, Augustine did not hesitate to speak of wrongful, unfounded love of friends as fornication against God, and as a competitor against rightful clinging to God.[34]

Just as Augustine was embarking on his career, a friend died. This friend, whom Augustine declined to name, was a childhood playmate whose companionship Augustine had only recently rediscovered. Looking back, however, Augustine concluded that theirs had never been a true friendship, even at its best, for they had fused it together themselves out of a community of shared interests, such that the "sweetness" they shared came from "ardor in like pursuits" rather than concern for one another, much less enjoyment of God. Augustine was certain of this, after all, for he had first led his friend into Manichaeism, and then, after a deathbed baptism, had sought to dissuade him from true faith. Theirs could not have been a true friendship, he insisted, "for friendship could not be true unless you [God] solder it together among those who cleave to one another by the charity 'poured forth in our hearts by the Holy Spirit, who is given to us.'"[35]

Augustine grieved deeply and wept bitterly, to be sure. "Sorrow entirely clouded over my heart; death appeared wherever I looked." Every sight in his hometown of Thagaste tormented him, every activity he had shared with his friend was a "cruel torture." His friend had been "half of his soul," as though their two bodies had shared one single soul; suddenly Augustine's own death loomed as a threat to annihilate all that remained of the life they had shared.[36]

Augustine's grief suggested to him a dispiriting lesson about his love itself, however. Finding a certain solace in the experience of grief, bitter though it was, Augustine noticed that even before his friend's death, the experience of friendship had been what he loved, more than the friend itself. "So wretched was I that I held that life of wretchedness to be more dear to me than my friend himself. For although I wished to change it, yet I was more unwilling to lose it than I was to lose my friend." As friends, they had used each other to create, in a pact of reciprocal instrumentality, the experiences that they had valued above one another.[37]

Tragically, however, Augustine knew nowhere else to turn for comfort except similar friendships. In a strictly mortal world, friendship that had no basis except delight in earthly things was as indispensable as it was doomed to sweep on in the river of time. Without some solace, "Wretched was I, and wretched is every soul that is bound fast by friendship to mortal things, that is torn asunder when it loses them, and then first feels the misery by which it is wretched even before it loses those things." To look honestly at the vulnerability of mortal things, including friendship itself, was to see a raw and brutal truth that none can long bear. Thus he needed new friends desperately, and he moved from Thagaste to Carthage to start anew. Yet he concluded that to find one's only available comfort in other mortals was to begin another loop around a cycle of futility. The more one enjoyed them, the more vulnerable one was to new losses. The soothing effect of time, which none can refuse, might not bring new sorrows immediately, yet still brought "causes of new sorrows." All that replaced despair in the interim was illusion, "a huge fable and a long-drawn-out lie" that corrupted the collective soul of friends with "its adulterous fondling." For even with the greatest collegiality, all manipulated all in a thousand "friendly" and "pleasing gestures" that fueled what was only an illusion of unity.[38]

So operate *superbia* and *ambitio saeculi*—the pride and ambition that characterize our present age.[39] God alone, the only true "Lord," is able to "dominate over others without pride."[40] For dominate and manipulate each other we must, when friendship is for us a strictly temporal good. If we are to make of any friendship what we hope and desperately need it to be, after all, we must treat one another as temporal goods. Still, what "madness," what foolishness, what futility, that we do "not know how to love human beings in a fittingly human way [*humaniter*]!"[41]

Love of Neighbor

Amid sin and futility, how then can creatures such as we learn to love rightly? Augustine's answer at first may seem merely pious. Alternately, it may seem callous and inhumane, rather than *humaniter.* Amid the grief that had sharply focused for him the problem of human friendship, "To you, O Lord, ought [my soul] have been lifted up, to be eased by you."[42]

Augustine had not loved a human being rightly, he insisted, because he had not loved God in trust.

But blessed is anyone who loves you, and a friend in you, and an enemy for your sake. For he alone loses no dear one to whom all are dear in him who is not lost. But who is this unless our God, the God who made heaven and earth and fills all things because by filling them he made them. No man loses you except one who forsakes you. . . .[43]

To love other creatures rightly, a human being must relativize that love—devaluing its object in one way, yet rediscovering its true and stable value in another way. When we love friends or neighbors rightly, the value they lose is their value as a tool of our own egocentric self-interest; the value we then recognize in them is their value insofar as God, the source of all things, creates and secures them. To love one's neighbor rightly, in other words, Augustine's abiding conviction was that we must not first love the creature but must first love God.

Still, what "first" means here was difficult even for Augustine to say, since humans cannot actually see God. Clearly love of God was *ontologically* prior—first in ultimate importance according to both logic and God's creative intention. It was also *authoritatively* prior, according to Jesus' statement of the greatest commandments. Yet in what sense should it come first *chronologically* as a person grows in love? This was the puzzle. For if we must suspend our love for human beings until we enjoy an entirely stable and perfect love for God, then existentially, love of neighbor might actually prove less rather than more stable, as it awaits insecurely the completion of this elusive goal.

Whenever Augustine attempted to work out the relation between love for God and love for neighbor according to some lexical priority—whether motivational, epistemological, or developmental—he failed to construct satisfactory explanations. Not surprisingly, these tend to be the passages that have troubled and repelled critics such as Nygren. Such critics, however, may not have paid adequate attention to clear indications that Augustine himself never seemed satisfied with his own explanations. In Augustine's first attempt to explain the relationship between the two great loves, in chapter 26 of *The Morals of the Catholic Church,* he could think of "no surer step [*gradus*] toward the love of God than" the love of one human being for another. Alternately, he continued, perhaps love of neighbor was "a sort of cradle [*quasi cunabula*] of our love of God." Somehow love of neighbor might lead to or nurture love of God, but how really to explain this? In one sense, he mused, the two loves rose together; in another sense, "while the love of God is first in beginning, the love of our neighbor is first in coming to perfection," for "perhaps divine love takes hold on us more rapidly at the outset, but we reach perfection more easily in lower things."[44]

Critics of Augustine have found the instrumental connotations inherent in images such as "step" and "cradle" more troubling than Augustine's own stated perplexity here.[45] Yet elsewhere, in book one of *On Christian Doctrine,* Augustine systematically explored the categories of enjoyment (*frui*) and use (*uti*) that might make sense of such metaphors, and he himself refused to settle upon an instrumental formula. Oliver O'Donovan has probably overstressed the tentative tone of Augustine's attempt to explain Jesus' second great love command as a love that *uses* the neighbor in order to *enjoy* God.[46] But O'Donovan has rightly pointed out that for all the times throughout Augustine's career that he described the proper human relationship to nonhuman temporal goods as one of use, only in this first book of *On Christian Doctrine* did he suggest that love of neighbor might involve a kind of use. In any case, already by the end of book one, Augustine seems to have moved on to other formulae that had fewer instrumental overtones. In the end, we are to enjoy God and enjoy one another in God. Or, we are to enjoy our neighbor for God's sake.[47]

Augustine's reflections on the relationship between love for God and for neighbor consistently stabilized around this love for friends or neighbors *in God* and *for God's sake.* The phrase "in God" especially allowed him to suspend the perplexing search for a lexical priority, and instead to orient all loves according to a single gestalt, a single theocentric vision of love-as-a-whole-in-coordination-with-its-parts. Thus, when Augustine contrasted true godly love with the wrongful and futile way in which he had once loved his friends, no phrase in his word of beatitude was happenstance: "But blessed is anyone who *loves you,* and a friend *in you,* and an enemy *for your sake.*"[48]

How then are human beings to love other human beings "in a fittingly human way?" In recounting his wrenching reaction to the death of his friend in the *Confessions* 4, Augustine had left the reader hanging for a few pages. Still delaying to explain fully, he paused once again before showing what it means to love other human creatures "in God." To understand, the reader apparently must first catch a glimpse of how, in a world of flux, parts relate to the whole and our loves long to rest in both.[49]

"'Convert us and show us your face,'" Augustine began; unless through faith we see the face of a personal God, in and beyond all else that we perceive, our attempts to comprehend both the beauteous parts and the wondrous whole of reality will fail. When the human soul is fixated (*figitur*) on things of beauty apart from God, all that finally stays attached (*figitur* again) to the soul is sorrow. This, of course, is what Augustine portrayed the death of his friend as having taught him; *all* things in fact rise, strive to be, hasten all the more quickly to their death for their striving, yet by passing in succession contribute to the whole as surely as do the individual words in a sentence. Since our fleshly senses are naturally slow and must operate within the limitations of time, we keep wanting to stop—as it were—in mid-sentence. All things are no less objectively good or beautiful because our subjective perception of them apart from the whole brings us sorrow; indeed, "for all these things" our soul ought in fact to "praise you, O God, creator of all things." But when we love creatures only according to the perceptions that our bodily senses afford, that love catches us tight. After all, "in such things there is no place where [the soul] may find rest, for they do not endure. They flee away, and who can follow them by fleshly sense? Or who can grasp them [*quis ea comprehendit*], even when they are close at hand?"[50]

Now, "if fleshly sense had been capable of comprehending the whole," it would find greater delight in this whole than it does in single parts—but it cannot. Hence we must pray to see God's face, and until we do so see, we must trust in this personal God, "our God," who not only made all things but is better than all things together. Amid the tumult of perception, Jesus Christ speaks to us: "Hear you: the Word himself cries out for you to return, and with him there is a place of quiet that can never be disturbed, where your love cannot be forsaken." The Word of God does not depart as do the myriad of parts dwelling in time; thus we ought to establish our dwelling place in this Word. Herein lies the hope rather than the annihilation of temporal goods, including human creatures insofar as they exist in time. "Entrust to the truth whatever you have gained from the truth, and you will suffer no loss." In case such counsel sounded too Platonic, Augustine quickly added the biblical promise: "All in you that has rotted away will flourish again; all your diseases will be healed." Temporal goods would not then drag one down into an abyss, "but they will stand fast with you and will abide before the God who stands fast and abides forever."[51]

Against this vision of parts abiding in a whole, which itself finds its life in the personal God whom Jesus Christ makes known to us, what it means to love our friend or neighbor or enemy or in fact any creature whatsoever *in God* begins to come clear:

> If you find pleasure in bodily things, praise God for them, and direct your love to their maker, lest because of things that please you, you may displease him. If you find pleasure in souls, let them be loved in God. In themselves they are but shifting things; in him they stand firm; else they would pass and perish. In him, therefore, let them be loved, and with you carry up as many as you can.

Though the notion of carrying up others to God—actually, *seizing* and carrying to God—would later help Augustine rationalize coercion in the name of love for neighbor, the method he recommended at this point was purely persuasive. One was to say to one's neighbor what one now knew to be true for oneself: "Let us love him, for he has made all things, and he is not far from us. He did not make all things and then leave them, but they are from him and in him. Behold where he is: it is wherever truth is known."[52]

The message was not just for virtuous friends whom one might love because goodness was already obvious in them, but rather for sinners, enemies, and "transgressors," whom one must urge to return repentantly and cling to the God who made them. For Augustine, the "enemy" was not a separate category from the "neighbor," although enemy love does play a privileged role within neighbor love. All people are to be loved equally, wrote Augustine in *On Christian Doctrine*. If some are nearest to us according to "place, time, or opportunity," and are thus our neighbors naturally, that merely happens "as if by chance" and inherently constitutes no greater moral obligation than the casting of a lot. "Among those who are to enjoy God with us [i.e., neighbors], we love some whom we help, [and] some by whom we are helped. . . . Be that as it may, we should desire that all enjoy God with us and that all the assistance we give them or get from them should be directed toward this end." Not only does this "pattern of behavior befit" those Christians who are united in love for God, but "[t]hus it is that we also love our enemies."[53]

Repeatedly, in sermons and letters as well as treatises, Augustine insisted that love of neighbor must extend to the enemy.[54] The ultimate grounding for such love was God's character as one who rains good things even on the unjust; we see God's character in Jesus Christ, who came into the world as a lover of enemies when all of us were in fact his enemies.[55] Love of enemy, Augustine also said often, is the greatest test of neighbor love and highest perfection of the Christian.[56] After all,

> . . . it is a comparatively small thing to wish well to, or even to do good to, a man who has done no evil to you. It is a much higher thing, and is the result of the most exalted goodness, to love your enemy, and always to wish well to, and when you have the opportunity, to do good to, the man who wishes you ill, and when he can, does you harm. . . . But . . . this is a frame of mind only reached by the perfect sons of God. . . .[57]

Early in his career especially, Augustine tended to speak of the enemy as a particularly good lesson in the patience, perseverance, and dispassionate inner freedom one needed for moral perfection.[58] By itself, that rationale for enemy love showed little concern for enemies themselves, and supplied no content to the good that love for them should seek. But as Augustine gained clarity on what it means to love a friend or neighbor "in God," the good of the enemy also became more prominent in his reflections.

The only real difference between loving a friend "in God" and loving an enemy "for the sake of [*propter*] God" was temporal, or perhaps eschatological. The prepositions *in* and *propter* from the formula of *Confessions* 4.9.14 reflect larger patterns in Augustine's thought quite deliberately. To love one's neighbors *in* God was to wish that they be in right relationship with God and with God's intended ecology for all creatures "in God," who is their Supreme Good. It was actively to seek for them the good of that relationship, and to respect their place in God's order by declining to treat them as mere instruments for some private good of one's own devising. None of this was any less true of the enemy, who is also a neighbor. Yet for the enemy its fulfillment is not yet a matter of sight but purely one of faith and hope. Only faith can see, and love can hope, that God is somehow incorporating the enemy into the web of right relationships "in God."[59] To begin loving the enemy even now, was to love the enemy *propter Deum,* for the sake of God.

In this life, conflict and enmity may be inevitable, and certainly Augustine himself had many opponents and enemies—heretics, schismatics, and cultured despisers of Christianity—whom we might now describe as his "others." But to analyze their status under such a category alone would have meant, for Augustine, to abandon hope and settle complacently for their perdition. God has loved us as sinners, argued Augustine, in much the same way that a good carpenter looks lovingly upon an unhewn trunk; the carpenter's love "is set upon what he will make of it, not upon its present state. Even so has God loved us sinners. . . . [S]urely his love for us sinners is not to the end that we remain in our sin. . . . You [also] love in [your enemy, therefore], not what he is but what you would have him be; and thus when you love your enemy, you love a brother." The positive content in love of enemies could only begin to become clear, in fact, when one *stopped* seeing them *as* enemies.[60]

In order to love friend or enemy alike, according to *Confessions* 4.12, one's highest obligation was to urge them to repent and cling to the God who made them. To do this they must recognize that they had no good as an independent possession, and that instead the very goodness of their life was God's gift, which they could only rightly return: "The good you love is from him, but only in so far as it is used for him is it good and sweet." God had given that gift in creating us, but newly restored life came only through Christ's descent, incarnation, teaching, deeds, death, resurrection, and ascent. All love for God, and all ensuing love of neighbor, finally rested on and responded to the prior loving descent of God in Jesus Christ.[61]

If the language of descent and ascent in 4.12 of the *Confessions* resonated with Platonic quests for unity with the divine, it also resonated with the Christological hymn of Philippians 2. But more than that, the agapeic *kenosis,* wherein Christ Jesus "did not regard equality with God as something to be exploited, but emptied himself, taking the form of a slave, . . . humbled himself and become obedient to the point of death—even death on a cross," had permanently upended Platonism and implicated its pride. To neighbors who thought themselves on a quest but were in fact erring in the very way they quested, Augustine's final word of admonition reversed the terms of ascent and descent entirely: "Even now, after the descent of life to you, do you not wish to ascend and to live? But how can you ascend when you have set yourselves up high and have placed your mouth against heaven?

Descend, so that you may ascend, so that you may ascend to God. For you have fallen by ascending against God."[62]

Any response to such an admonition involved both self-denial and self-love. That would be true for one's neighbors, whose good one must above all seek by helping bring them into right relationship with the God who was their Supreme Good, yet whose face was personal. And that had always been true for oneself.

Love of Self

Once one sees Augustine's doctrine of love in a single gestalt—once one sees with him a single theocentric vision of love-as-a-whole-in-coordination-with-its-parts—there can be no question about the proper place of right self-love in the moral order of the universe, at least as he envisioned it. Critics of Augustine such as Nygren have misconstrued Augustine's notion of right self-love as egocentric because their analysis has itself been, technically speaking, ego-centric.[63] For the self Augustine would have us love is never the self *in itself,* but always the self *in God.* Even if the analyst attends to the self's inner workings of motivation and will, the self that would love itself rightly would turn its own attention *not* to itself but to God, according to Augustine. It would will what God wills. It would love what God loves. It would love itself but indirectly, only by way of refraction through its love for God. It would discover its good nowhere except "in God." And in God, as a gift of God's love, it would will to "find itself in the place just right."[64]

For I myself am a creature too. In the gestalt unity of love as a whole, insofar as I participate in it, I cannot help but desire for myself exactly what I desire for my neighbor and for every creature, namely, that each one together fulfill its part within the whole common good of the universe, of which the Supreme Good or *Summum Bonum* is none other than God. "There can be no separation of love: you may choose for yourself what you love, and all the rest will follow"—including right self-love.[65]

This is why Augustine never wavered in his conviction that "it is impossible for one who loves God not to love himself."[66] That conviction, which Augustine early stated in his *Morals of the Catholic Church,* continued even through later works such as *City of God.* To be sure, the massive social critique in *City of God* rested on a thesis about the perverse self-love at the heart of human society: "We see then that the two cities were created by two kinds of love: the earthly city was created by self-love reaching the point of contempt for God, the Heavenly City by the love of God carried as far as contempt of self."[67] Increasing recognition of how fundamental was the sin of perverse and prideful self-love might lead the mature Augustine to speak of right self-love more circumspectly: "Now God, our master, teaches two chief precepts, love of God and love of neighbour; and in them man finds three objects for his love: God himself, and his neighbour: *and a man who loves God is not wrong in loving himself.*"[68] Yet if anything, this circumspect double-negative way of vindicating right self-love highlights the logic of Augustine's position: One loves oneself rightly by loving oneself only indirectly, by refraction through the love of God, by loving the self that lives or should live "in God."[69] Late in his career Augustine could still insist that "we love ourselves all the more, the more we love God."[70] Once we recognize that this love of self "in God" is what Augustine meant by right self-love, we must also recognize that the perverse self-love upon which the earthly city rests is something else altogether. It is not really love at all, but a false love.[71]

Echoing Jesus' dictum that those who seek to gain their lives would lose them, while those who lose their lives would gain them (Luke 17:33), Augustine might, to be sure, present right self-love as a paradox:

> Let us, then, love not ourselves, but Him; and in feeding His sheep, let us be seeking the things which are His, not the things which are our own. *For in some inexplicable way, I know not what, every one who loves himself, and not God, loves not himself; and whoever loves God, and not himself, he it is that loves himself.*[72]

Yet the paradox of self-love was not quite so paradoxical as it seems.[73] Inadvertently, Augustine *did* explain, even here, that which he claimed was "inexplicable." For even as one "seeks the things that are God's" to the abandonment of one's claim upon "the things which are one's own," one seeks one's truest good within the common good of all, *as one among God's own.*

The very perversity of perverse self-love actually confirms how it is that right self-love can be right. By the mid-390s Augustine had begun to recognize a fundamental root of all sin in the love of one's own power.[74] Soon he was taking care to distinguish such self-love from right self-love. In book one of *On Christian Doctrine,* for example, he noted that whenever the human spirit moved beyond a proper rule over its own body and sought to rule over other human beings who were its peers, such a spirit had turned vicious. "When it endeavors to dominate those who are naturally its peers, other men, its pride is altogether intolerable."[75] Its apparent self-love was actually hatred—in fact, self-hatred. So by the time he wrote the latter chapters of *On the Trinity* in the late 410s, Augustine was able to describe with great precision and poignancy how human beings fall when they overreach themselves as though they could dominate the whole universe to their own ends.

In book twelve of Augustine's complex treatise *On the Trinity* he offered a kind of narrative psychology of the fall, not as it first occurred in Adam and Eve, but as each human soul recapitulates the fall in its historical existence:

> What happens is that the soul, loving its own power, slides away from the whole which is common to all [*a communi universo*] into the part which is its own private property [*ad privatam partem*]. By following God's directions and being perfectly governed by his laws it could enjoy the whole universe of creation [*universitate creaturae*]; but by the apostasy of pride [*superbia*] which is called the beginning of sin it strives to grab something more than the whole [*plus aliquid universo appetens*] and to govern it by its own laws; and because there is nothing more than the whole it is thrust back into anxiety over a part [*in curam partilem truditur*]. . . .[76]

Human beings, in other words, already possess all things through joint participation with all other created things in the common whole of the universe.[77] God has given the whole creation to each part, and especially to humanity, as a gift. Yet in their pride, human beings want something more; in love with their own power, they want to grasp, control, and dominate the whole for their own private good, as though the universe itself were their own private possession. Obviously this is impossible, because there is nothing more than the whole [*amplius universi-tate*] . . . , and so by being greedy [*concupiscendo*] for more it gets less. That is why greed [*avaritia*] is called the root of all evils.[78]

Besides God, after all, nothing is larger than the whole. By seeking more than God has already given them as a gift, human beings inevitably end up with less and demean themselves. Since they, mere parts of the whole, have sought joy in domination, their reward is their desire; fittingly, God allows them to care for a measly part [*partilem*].

All other sins follow from this basic sin, in Augustine's psychology. To care for a small part of the universe in humility and gratitude might yet be an act of praise and trust in God. But human beings continue to enjoy the illusion of power over the whole even though they do not have it, and manipulate other "bodily shapes and movements" near but external to them according to self-interests and fantasies that further alienate them against the whole. Thus each one refers

all its business to one or other of the following ends: curiosity, searching for bodily and temporal experience through the senses; swollen conceit, affecting to be above other souls which are given over to their sense; or carnal pleasure, plunging itself in this muddy whirlpool.[79]

What begins "from a distorted appetite for being like God" through human attempts to dominate the whole, instead makes human beings "end up by becoming like beasts."[80]

Right self-love which proceeds indirectly through love of God thus follows a course entirely opposite that of perverse self-love:

For man's true honor is God's image and likeness in him, but it can only be preserved when facing him from whom its impression is received. And so the less love he has for what is his very own the more closely can he cling to God. But out of greed to experience his own power he trembled down at a nod from himself into himself as though down to the middle level. And then, while he wants to be like God under nobody, he is thrust down as a punishment from his own half-way level to the bottom. . . . And how could he travel this long way from the heights to the depths except through the half-way level of self?[81]

Where perverse self-love alienates human beings by setting them over against the whole, right self-love discovers its true creaturely purpose in relationship with the personal God who is the Supreme Good of the whole. Where perverse self-love grasps tightly to its own goods, right self-love clings to God. Where perverse self-love must prove its own power by determining its own good, right self-love receives its good in and from God. Where perverse self-love would make itself the center of the universe, right self-love recognizes God as the center. Where perverse self-love, for all its grasping and manipulation, still fails to maintain its handhold at the center of its universe, right self-love, which clings to God, finds itself in the place just right, where it can reflect God's image and thus receive "true honor." Where perverse self-love fails in spite of itself, therefore, right self-love succeeds in spite of itself. For by loving less "what is [one's] own," a person receives, in relationship with God, the life that God in fact willed and created for that person.

The One Love: Triune, Incarnate, Eschatological

> So with one and the same charity we love God and neighbor; but God on God's account, ourselves and neighbor also on God's account.[82]

If all creatures have their being, goodness, and very life from God, then the love of God must ultimately unite all authentic loves in God.[83] This was the inexorable conviction toward which all of Augustine's reflections on Christian love led—a conviction at once as complex and simple as the gestalt vision that it sought to articulate. If a reader or parishioner did not immediately catch Augustine's vision of love as a whole, this was no cause for concern, and no excuse not to begin loving the brother or sister one *could* see. "Let no one say: 'I don't know what to love.' Let him love his brother, and love that [same] love." Anyone who did so in truth would become intimately acquainted with God's love even while learning how to respond to the neighbor's specific needs. "[A]fter all, he knows the love he loves with better than the brother he loves. There now, he can already have God better known to him than his brother, certainly better known because more present, better known because more inward to him, better known because more sure. . . ." Ultimately, all love is "one and the same love" in God, who "is love," according to 1 John 4:16. God's very life as a Trinity of persons is irreducibly relational, after all: "Embrace love which is God, and embrace God with love. This is the love which unites all the good angels and all the servants of God in a bond of holiness, conjoins us and them together, and subjoins us to itself. . . . [So in fact] you do see a trinity [or *the* Trinity] if you see charity."[84]

The love of God that drew all things into itself, therefore, was both elusive *and* concrete, as transcendent and incarnate as the God who is its source and object. Its requirements must ever be open-ended; one could never reduce them to precepts one might manage legalistically apart from relationship to the living God. Yet a relationship to this mysterious, transcendent God could never be other-worldly in any facile sense; one could never love the God of Jesus Christ without loving all that God loves, in the irrevocably vulnerable and earthy way that Jesus Christ reveals God to love. Finally, human participation in God's own love must be through the continuing gift of God's own self in the Spirit of Jesus Christ; one could never recognize, assent, and be vulnerable to the mystery of God's presence in concrete others without "the love of God poured into our hearts by the Holy Spirit which is given to us"—through the third person of the Trinity, whom Augustine believed is charity itself, which binds persons together in true unity:

> Wherefore, whoever names the Father and the Son ought thereby to understand the mutual love of the Father and Son, which is the Holy Spirit. And perhaps the scriptures on being examined . . . do show us that the Holy Spirit is charity.[85]

Oliver O'Donovan has pointed out that a single paragraph in Augustine's treatise *On the Trinity* (6.5.7) "contains everything central to Augustine's doctrine of love"; the paragraph is on the Holy Spirit, who "subsists"[86] with the first two persons of the Trinity in the same "unity and equality of substance."[87] The Holy Spirit, wrote Augustine, "is that by which the two [Father and Son] are joined each to the other, by which the begotten is loved by the one who begets him and in turn loves the begetter. Thus *They keep unity of the Spirit in the bond of peace* (Eph. 4:3)" through their mutual self-giving. It is this unity which through grace commands Christians to live in unity; it is this love that finds expression through the two great love commands upon which depend the Law and the Prophets. It is this triune communal life of the "one, only, great, wise, holy, and blessed God" which effects and animates mutual love of neighbor through God's own self-giving. For as God blesses us by, in, and through the gift of God's own life, "we are one with each other," living in one spirit with God as we cling to God. The human life of the Christian community participates in God's own life, for the Holy Spirit is the very bond of all true community:

> So the Holy Spirit is something common to Father and Son, whatever it is, or is their very commonness or communion, consubstantial and coeternal. Call this friendship, if it helps, but a better word for it is charity. And this too is substance because God is substance, and *God is charity* (1 Jn. 4:8, 16).[88]

O'Donovan has concluded that the "self-love or mutual love of the Godhead is the link through which the self-love of the universe, the love of [human for human] and for God, is derived from the divine being."[89] For any one creature, right self-love is *only* right insofar as it participates in the cohesive love of the whole for the whole, as made possible through participation in God's own trinitarian life.[90] Neither the self-love of the whole universe for the whole, nor the unity of humankind, was, in Augustine's mature thought, "an immanent fact about the cosmos," as it would have been in both Stoic and Neoplatonic thought. Rather, it is "an eschatological achievement, the accomplished work of the Holy Spirit in the church of Christ." Or, in the meantime, it is an "evangelical proclamation," a forward-looking "summons" rather than "nostalgia for lost unity." The "teleological thrust of love" in Augustine's thought "was always toward exact mutuality of subject and object, a state that must obtain when 'God shall be all in all.'"[91]

One sign of how thoroughgoing was Augustine's vision of love's embrace is the way it eventually drew in what love for God had first seemed to rule out—a careful love of temporal goods. The "things of the world" that Augustine had first taught Christians to "despise" or at most "use,"[92] and that 1 John itself presented as a competitor to love for God, recovered a certain dignity once Christians rediscovered their place in God, in relation to God, according to God's will. Only in one sense were love for God and love for the world mutually exclusive, as

1 John 2:15 insisted.[93] Genesis 1 taught, and Augustine's listeners had reason to object, that all God had made was good. John himself spoke of God's love for the world.[94] Without backing away from his warning against loves that would carry his listeners away in the river of time, Augustine the pastor offered a positive suggestion and a complementary metaphor. One might acknowledge with God's Spirit the goodness of all creation, yet not love creatures to the abandonment of their Creator, if one treated them as a fiancée should treat an engagement ring. A woman would be guilty of infidelity if she loved the ring in place of her betrothed, yet certainly she could love his gift rightly if she saw in it a sign and pledge of his love. "Even so, God has given you all these things: therefore, love him who made them. There is more that he would give you, even himself, their Maker."[95]

The reason that Augustinian love for God first looked so elusive— or even formal and empty of material content—is that a relationship with the transcendent God must always have an open-ended quality, in anticipation of ever-new content, instruction, and unifying charity, opening out to new relationships to all things "in God."

Still and all, the actual historical content of this love *would* in fact be empty, or at most merely speculative, had this transcendent God not filled up its content in the incarnation of Jesus Christ. Precisely because *caritas Dei* is mutual love, any love for God and for creatures "in God" must be a grateful and fitting response to God's prior self-giving in Jesus Christ,[96] which God's gift of self now made possible through "the love of God poured into our hearts by the Holy Spirit which is given to us." As Augustine said again and again (often at some critical juncture in his critiques of Platonism), we need a mediator, a true mediator who has taken up our clay and taken on the form of a servant in humility.[97] Through Jesus Christ, prayed Augustine in book eleven of the *Confessions,* "you [God] have sought us when we did not seek you, and sought us so that we might seek you, your Word, through whom you have made all things, among them myself also, through whom you have called to adoption a people of believers, among them me also."[98] The content of right love, which places a believer in right relationship to God and to "all things," came through God's initiative in Jesus Christ, who first begins to reknit human relationship to "all things" by incorporating the believer into "a people of believers," whose mutual love anticipates God's ultimate purpose for all creatures in the cosmos.

This incarnational and eschatological movement from and to God is more basic and indigenous to Augustine's thought than modern analytic categories of deontology and teleology. The scriptures, which Augustine spent his mature years expositing, revealed God's will and filled out the material content of love; even love of God and neighbor were hermeneutical keys to interpreting scripture, not independent principles that might replace the narrative of scripture.[99] But even scripture revealed Jesus Christ above all, and he it was who both summarized the meaning of God's commands and focused the direction of God's purposes.

> "Convert us and show us your face," O God of hosts, "and we shall be saved."[100]

For those who see in Jesus Christ the face of the very God who created the hosts of heaven and earth, the will of this God can never be an arbitrary command, and the good of human beings can never fully be known apart from Jesus Christ. By showing us what God loves and how God loves, Jesus Christ is the one who must fill up the content of love for God and all other loves "in God." For the will of God is that we love what God loves; we cannot love God if we despise God's commandment. While we ourselves cannot possibly see God's will for all creatures as one coordinated whole, we can glimpse the character of that will in the canonical narrative of God's saving actions in history, and preeminently in the person of Jesus Christ. The preeminent revelation of that commandment is Christ's own fulfillment of the law through Christ's own love.[101]

Specification of the content of love for God, then, begins where the first fruits of a new creation begin to appear in the community of mutual love. Here too we are to see what God loves. For if believers are members of the body of Christ, and even enemies of Christ are brothers and sisters yet to be incorporated into the body of Christ, then it would be impossible *not* to love Christ when we love the brother or sister, suffering and rejoicing together as each member suffers or rejoices. "Loving the members of Christ, you are loving Christ; loving Christ, you are loving the Son of God; loving the Son of God, you are loving the Father. There can be no separation of love: you may choose for yourself what you love, and all the rest will follow." In turn, love for God necessarily includes love for others. "None may make one love an excuse from another. Christian love is altogether of one piece, and as itself is compacted into a unity, so it makes into one all that are linked to it, like a flame fusing them together." The people of believers living as a community of mutual love is itself the eschatological appearing of God's own mutual, trinitarian love in history. For "thus the end will be one Christ, loving himself; for the love of the members for one another is the love of the Body for itself."[102]

Longing surely remains. Yet even the longing of right self-love, the longing for personal reintegration in God, directs itself toward that city where God, whose very life is communal, will be all in all. So, prayed Augustine,

> I will enter into my chamber and there I will sing songs of love to you, groaning with unspeakable groanings on my pilgrimage, and remembering Jerusalem, with heart lifted up toward it, Jerusalem my country, Jerusalem my mother, and you who over her are ruler, enlightener, father, guardian, spouse, pure and strong delight, solid joy, all good things ineffable, all possessed at once, because you are the one and the true good. I will not be turned away until out of this scattered and disordered state you gather all that I am into the peace of her, the mother most dear, where are the first fruits of my spirit, whence these things are certain to me, and you conform and confirm me into eternity my God, my mercy.[103]

"Uncertainty Everywhere"

The promise in Augustine's thought does not come without problems. The overarching structure of Augustine's doctrine of thought certainly looks promising insofar as it offers an integrated account of what he considered to be the four possible categories of human love—for God, neighbor, self, and temporal goods. In potentially helpful ways, that integration retains a key and arguably biblical place for mutual love. Even so, we must face the danger that mutuality might actually lock out one other emininently biblical love—the love for enemies. Augustine has subsumed enemy love within neighbor love. If some of the ways that Augustine sought to practice "love" for his ecclesial enemies were problematic, the critic may understandably conclude that either his emphasis on mutual love or his apparent de-emphasis of enemy love is the source of these problems.[104]

The overarching structure of Augustine's conception of Christian love or *caritas* has seemed promising as we have charted it "from below," by moving with him through what he considered to be the four possible categories of human love. Though his early and abiding intuition was that one may only love creatures rightly by loving and clinging to God as one's highest good, his own experience and explanation for what this means began in the futility of love for temporal goods, proceeded through the limits and possibilities of loving friend or neighbor and self rightly, and finally found the unity of all right human loves in a gestalt vision of love-as-a-whole-in-coordination-with-its-parts. One could love a creature rightly only by refraction, as one loved God and thus loved "in God" what God loves—that is, by loving the creature for and as what God lovingly created it to be within the rightly ordered ecology of the whole universe. This included oneself and, circumspectly, even reincorporated temporal goods.

Still, the structure of Augustinian *caritas* would be purely formal and open-ended except for the incarnational revelation of Jesus Christ. For in Christ we may see what and how God loves, and thus see the character or "face" of the God who is the Supreme Good of the whole universe. The content of love for God and all creatures in God finds further specification in mutual love among Christians, as the redemptive work of Christ bears its first fruits in the Christian community. That mutual love is, for Augustine, nothing less than the eschatological appearing within time and history of the promised fullness when "God will be all in all."

Mutual love in history admits to certain ambiguities, however, and so we must anticipate a series of problems. As Reinhold Niebuhr would remind us, mutual love in history may not be uniquely Christian at all, and—more fatefully still—it always has the potential for excluding strangers and enemies from its circle. Augustine was not unaware of the danger of group egotism. He did not fail to notice that for all that "John the apostle" spoke of "brotherly love," Jesus himself said in Matthew 5:46 that "it is not enough for us to love our brothers," for if we only love our own and love does not "stretch so far as to reach our enemies," then we are no different from the "publicans." Even without this text before him, Augustine sometimes derived an exhortation to authentically Christian love from the more general observation that co-conspirators in sin (like "publicans") seem to enjoy a kind of charity among themselves. Finally, one limitation of the earthly peace which Augustine analyzed in book nineteen of the *City of God* was that all people wish peace for their own kind but correspondingly wish to impose their wills on other people. Yet to be aware of a danger is not the same as to avoid its trap. The border at the edge of the community of mutual love came to coincide with the most contested border between Augustine's theory of love and his practice of love.[105]

Insofar as Augustine kept clear that the church is a still-unfinished eschatological community, his conception of the community of mutual love did not necessarily exclude any enemies. As an eschatological community longing for that fulfillment of creation when God will be all in all, the church as Augustine understood it is still drawing in its enemies.[106] Christians should see in their enemies the brothers and sisters that God might yet make them.[107] In fact, even the earthly city as Augustine understood it encompassed the entire human community—a single family whose solidarity even in sin resulted from a still more basic bond of created human solidarity.[108] In this earthly city, whose peace Christians are to seek,[109] justifiable warfare is for Augustine always more of a police action—aimed at restraining and perhaps correcting errant *members* of the human community—than a self-defense of one's own community against outsiders.[110] Augustine may have been blind to the degree to which he derived his vision of a single human community from the imperial worldview by which Rome pretended to rule the whole world. But however questionable was the mix of reasons for which Augustine modified Jesus' commands of nonresistant enemy love, he only justified exceptions for the sake of what he judged to be charity on behalf of others, not oneself. As Paul Ramsey argued, in Augustine's just war theory collective self-defense could only appeal to the protection of innocents, on the principle of neighbor love, not to some autonomous principle of self-defense.[111] Strictly personal self-defense had no place in Augustine's ethic at all.[112]

In practice too, Augustine's understanding of enemy love did at least some work restraining the collective egotism of those groups with which he himself identified, while defending the dignity of their enemies. In 412, for example, Augustine wrote to the Roman proconsul

Apringius, an older and less devout brother to Marcellinus, who was likewise a proconsul and a close friend of Augustine. A group of Circumcillions—the armed resistance movement associated with the rival Donatist church of North Africa—had been indicted for capturing a group of Catholics that included Augustine's fellow priests, for killing at least one, and for torturing and mutilating others. Marcellinus had extracted confessions from the Circumcillions without resorting to torture, and this Augustine commended. But now Augustine must appeal also to Apringius, "begging and praying you by the mercy of Christ," not to return evil for evil by sentencing the criminals to new tortures or capital punishment. Even before a non-Christian judge, Augustine claimed, he would "insist that the sufferings of the servants of God, which ought to serve as a pattern of patience, should not be sullied with the blood of their enemies." If no lenient punishment were available short of returning upon them a torture and execution such as they had inflicted, claimed Augustine, "we should prefer to let them go free, rather than avenge the martyrdom of our brothers by shedding their blood." Perhaps his motive included an element of self-interest, for making martyrs of Donatists could be a public relations disaster for the Catholics. "Strive to outdo the wicked in goodness," he urged therefore, since Catholics and Donatists were competing for the laurel of continuity with North Africa's martyr tradition. Nonetheless, if Apringius heeded Augustine's plea, true benefit would in fact accrue to these "enemies of the Church": "They cut short the life-span of a minister of the Church by killing him; you must lengthen the span of years for the living enemies of the Church that they may repent."[113]

Still, restraint was far easier for Augustine to argue once "enemies of the Church" were already in custody, under the power of his Roman friends. Here, as we say, lies the contested borderline at the outer edge of Augustine's community and practice of mutual love. Augustine's motives were mixed, his practice inconsistent. Objectively, his appeal for clemency already took for granted that it was appropriate for nominally Christian imperial officials to be imposing sanctions upon the rival Donatist church. Civil authorities of course had their own purely civil reasons to punish *any* crimes of the sort that the Circumcillions had committed, but Augustine's very plea for mildness was blurring the domains of church and state: "For when you act," he told Apringius, "the Church acts, for whose sake and as whose son you act."[114]

Thus, we cannot reconstruct an Augustinian doctrine of love in isolation from his policy toward the rival Donatists. His very passion to restore an order of mutual love in North Africa inspired much of his most eloquent teaching on all dimensions of Christian love. Chapter 5 will argue that Augustine's Donatist policy in fact struck a fissure in his doctrine of love, so that to appropriate his thought at all we must do so selectively, reading Augustine against himself. For such a reading to be something other than gratuitous, however, we must have a principled basis of selection. Chapter 3 will provide a principle of selection that Augustine would recognize: *The good that all right love seeks must be had through the continence that clings to God in trust, rather than through manipulative and coercive grasping.*

We will not do justice either to Augustine or to our own contemporary problematic if we see the ambiguities in Augustine's account of Christian love solely as historical problems, which the inadequacies of his own theological construct bequeathed to later centuries of Christians. We have already noted and will note yet again that according to Augustine's gestalt vision of Christian love, one would not be loving any friend, neighbor, or enemy truly if one did not somehow "seize and carry them up to God." Such a formula is fraught with risks, for it easily rationalizes violent measures in the overconfident assurance that one knows what is really best for the erring. Yet anyone who has honestly wondered how to respond to the simple moral dilemma of a panhandler shares a problem that Augustine did not so much construct as discover: Love argues *both* for intervention on behalf of what we judge to be others' true good, *and* for respect of their dignity as creatures of God who must appropriate that good for themselves. Shall I buy the panhandler a hamburger because I smell alcohol on his breath, or shall I respect his right to make his own mistakes? If measured coercion is creating Catholics who are now grateful that imperial sanctions have freed them from the "schismatic" Donatist church, should I change my mind and approve of coercion as an act of love?

Risks are inherent in any conception of love, not just in Augustine's doctrine—at least if love is to have some content. The dignity of the other, and the corresponding duty of nonmaleficent respect, constitute only one half of love. Misguided benevolence may risk coercive paternalism; but solitary nonmaleficence risks complacent detachment. Augustine did not invent the tension inherent in all love, or at least in all Christian love. Anyone who follows Jesus' command in

Matthew 5:44 to love one's enemies and pray for one's persecutors must at some point ask *what* to pray for. Anyone who heeds Paul's reminder in Romans 12:14 to bless one's persecutors must at some point ask *how* to do them good. To be sure, Proverbs 25:21–22 had reminded Paul of the priority of supplying basic human needs such as food and water, and he had listed them in Romans 12:20; but anyone who truly cares about the good of one's enemy (and not just an alternative non-lethal form of vengeance that shames like "coals of fire") must eventually ask what else besides these most basic of human goods will truly be good for the enemy. Whether or not Augustine solved this problem, he certainly saw it clearly. As he preached on 1 John, his congregation might wonder at Augustine's claim that even when one loves an enemy,

> it is always the brother that you love. How so? you ask. I ask in turn, Why do you love your enemy? Because you wish him to have good health in this life? but suppose that is not in his interest? Because you wish him to be rich? but if riches themselves should rob him of his sight? To marry a wife? but if that should bring him a life of bitterness? To have children? but suppose they turn out badly? Thus there is uncertainty in all the things you seem to desire for your enemy, because you love him: *uncertainty everywhere.* Let your desire for him be that together with you he may have eternal life: let your desire for him be that he may be your brother.

Communion "in God" was ultimately the only certain good for which love might aim. Love could not settle for respect alone, but must aim for the good of sharing the Supreme Good. Anything less would mean abandoning sinners in their sin, which "surely" God in God's "love for us sinners" had not done. Thus, when Christ bid us love our enemies, his intent cannot have been "that they should always remain such: that would be an instruction to hate, not to love."[115]

Yet as soon as one insists that love requires positive content, one must also pause before the dangers of imposing overconfidently one's conception of the good upon others. And so one must say yet again the inverse, that love cannot claim to be seeking the other's good if it has in any way begun to lose respect for the other. Or better, one must find a way to speak both sides of love at once, compromising neither one's respect for the dignity even of enemies, nor one's longing for the good of others—a good that ultimately draws even enemies into communion as brothers and sisters.

In the deep grammar of Augustinian continence we will find at least one way to speak both sides of love at once. Just as evangelical self-denial is not by itself positive love of enemy, although a predisposition to make sacrifices is a condition for love of enemy, so too, Augustinian continence is not the whole of Augustinian *caritas*. Continence, however, is critical for speaking both sides of love. For on one side, continence requires that we seek the good only in trustful and nonmanipulative ways. Higher goods do not justify greater moral compromises as means to their acquisition; quite the contrary. In the grammar of Augustinian continence, higher goods can *only* be had respectfully and continently, as gifts of God that are not of one's own creating. On the other side, then, continence does not merely do the negative work of self-restraint. For if some goods—but especially *the* good of communion with God and "in God" through mutual love—can only be had continently, then from the human side, continence is precisely what makes the fullness of *caritas* effective. Continence is the operative mode of Augustinian *caritas*.

CHAPTER THREE

The Grammar of Augustinian Continence

For where not I, there more happily I.

Augustine, *On Continence*

Augustine's theocentric doctrine of love envisioned a love for God that responds in gratitude to God's love, and longs to love rightly all things "in God"—as God loves them and seeks their good in ordered relation to the good of the whole creation. It is a doctrine both coherent and tantalizing. Once students of Augustine catch a glimpse of his gestalt vision of love-as-a-whole-in-coordination-with-its-parts, it may captivate their imaginations in much the same way that Cicero's *Hortentius* first captivated Augustine's—stirring and enkindling him "to love, and pursue, and attain and catch hold of, and strongly embrace . . . wisdom itself, whatsoever it might be."[1]

Yet as Augustine himself soon learned, human beings can imagine such a love yet find themselves congenitally unable to practice it. Even after Augustine's vague longing for wisdom recognized the God of Jesus Christ as its proper object, still, he confessed, "I was not steadfast in enjoyment of my God." Once converted to a more stable love for God, his heartfelt cry implied that at last he had learned to love rightly: "Too late have I loved you, O Beauty so ancient and so new, too late have I loved you!" Yet a page later he tacitly recognized that even then, after years as a Christian and ordination as bishop, he still did not cling to God "with all [his] being," as the first great love command requires. Thus, he must continue to pray: "All my hope is found solely in your exceeding great mercy. . . . O Love, who are forever aflame and are never extinguished, O Charity, my God, set me aflame!"[2] Perhaps the problem was that Augustine had wrongly begun his quest to love God and never abandoned the illusion that Cicero's *Hortentius* once evoked in him—that love for God was something *he* might "pursue," *he* might "attain," *he* might "catch hold of," and *he* might "strongly embrace." Anders Nygren's thesis was that Augustine made and retained exactly this fundamental, and fundamentally self-seeking, mistake. John Burnaby and Oliver O'Donovan have argued against Nygren that Augustinian *caritas* is theocentric rather than egocentric; chapter 2 sought to illustrate and reinforce their arguments by supplying what Nygren baldly neglected, an exposition of Augustine's notion of love for oneself and all creatures "in God."[3] Yet all of these points may still fall flat if Nygren was right to insist that Augustinian *caritas* was, from its core, acquisitive. In the sense that Nygren understood acquisitiveness, even an Augustinian love set in theocentric order might seek the objects of its longing through egocentric eros, which Nygren described as "a form of self-assertion of the highest, noblest, sublimest kind," one that is self-seeking in its effort to gain divine life, and that operates through "the will to get and possess."[4]

Augustine left us a reply, but it is so obvious that it is easy to overlook. Continence, he believed, is the way that human beings reintegrate all loves through one love, the love of God. God commands continence, and God must give what God commands.

> All my hope is found solely in your exceeding great mercy. Give what you command, and command what you will. You enjoin continence. "And as I knew," says a certain man, "that no one could be continent except God gave it, and this also was a point of wisdom to know whose gift it was" [Wisdom 8:21]. By continence we are gathered together and brought back to the One, from whom we have dissipated our being into many things. So much the less does he love you who loves anything else, even together with you, which he does not love for your sake. O Love, who are forever aflame and are never extinguished, O Charity, my God, set me aflame! You enjoin continence: give what you command, and command what you will.[5]

We should take Augustine at his word long enough to test the intelligibility of his claim. For as we will see, one can only acquire Augustinian continence in a way that is *not* acquisitive in Nygren's willful sense; the very logic of continence requires that one receive it as a gift, not seize it as a prize. In fact, one can only become continent *in a continent way*—by relinquishing control, by respecting, by asking for help, by receiving as a gift.

Fittingly then, and tellingly, Augustine portrayed the interior movement of his conversion itself as a chaste embrace with a "virtuously alluring" woman whose very name was Continence. To "have" a dignified, serene, and joyous woman named Continence in the "embrace" of a right relationship required that he *not* "have" her in a domineering, disrespectful way, for to violate her would be to destroy the very beauty that he longed to enjoy, and that gave her her name. Continence, it seems, is a way of *having* by *not having*.[6]

Higher Continence

If continence is Augustine's reply both to the student's question about how to love God, and to the skeptic's allegation that none can acquire such love without taint of self-assertion, then no wonder it has been easy to overlook. When Augustine spoke of continence he often seemed to have had narrowly sexual continence in mind; even when he spoke of continent love for God in a broader, more general sense, he often employed sexual metaphors.[7] Certainly his own conviction that to become a Christian would require him to become celibate has left readers with an example of Augustinian continence that readily eclipses all others. Further, if biographer Peter Brown has read Augustine fairly, the bishop himself contributed to later preoccupation with sexual continence when he used the problematics of sexuality to appeal to the jury of popular Christian opinion against Pelagian optimism about human willpower and self-control.[8] Whether Augustine was actually the controversialist most obsessed with sexuality amid the Pelagian debates, or whether that dubious honor belongs to his tenacious opponent Julian of Eclanum,[9] the controversy over sexuality increasingly dominated Augustine's attention. It should hardly surprise us if many issues with some tangential relevance to Augustinian continence readily distract readers from noticing the pervasive role that continence plays in the Augustinian theory and practice of Christian love.[10]

Augustinian continence is a more general phenomenon of self-control and self-denial; positively, in fact, it involves right acquisition through respectful relationship. Of course, even when we attempt to trace out the larger role of continence in Augustine's thought, we can hardly afford to ignore evidence from his own life narrative, including his experiences with sexuality. But in Augustine's thought and experience, each informs the other.

In recent years scholars have begun to recognize that Augustine's belabored attention to "concupiscence" grew not from a crude preoccupation with sexuality but from a complex analysis of the sources of human behavior—of social as well as sexual behavior, of lust for power as well as pleasure. Gerald I. Bonner's 1962 article "*Libido* and *Concupiscentia* in St. Augustine" was pivotal in this regard. Bonner noted that many before him had tended "to study Augustine's teaching on sexual concupiscence in isolation from his doctrine of the lust for power." In contrast, Bonner's reading of Augustine generally, and of the *City of God* especially, made it apparent that

> Augustine did not envisage any division such as developed in later Christian thought, where preoccupation with sexual concupiscence assumed preponderant, and at times deplorable proportions, and where the will to power and domination has been, if not exactly baptised, at least treated with the same sort of respectful consideration which is accorded in modern society to usury and financial speculation.

Bonner reminded scholars, for example, that in *City of God* 14.15 Augustine had listed lust for vengeance, for possession of money, for victory at any price, for boasting, and above all for domination as drives that express human disobedience and multiply human evils. More recently, Peter Brown has offered a general definition of Augustinian concupiscence. He called it a shadowy "drive to control, to appropriate, and to turn to one's private ends, all the good things that had been created by God to be accepted with gratitude and shared with others"; for Augustine, concupiscence "lay at the root of the inescapable misery that afflicted mankind."[11]

It is time to extend to continence the same pattern of analysis that recognizes concupiscence as a general phenomenon capable of twisting *all* human relationships. In other words, it is time to pursue Augustine's suggestion that continence is crucial not just for dealing with errant sexuality, but for the righting of all human relationships. Augustine did not always make this explicit, and so a central task of the current chapter will be to discern how the grammar of continence shaped his teachings on love even when he did not explicate that grammar. If the grammar of Augustinian continence has gone unnoticed, then here is another reason: grammars *usually* go unnoticed, for their purpose is not to call attention to themselves but rather to enable people to speak of many *other* things in intricately consistent ways. What Augustine took for granted can sometimes be more important than what he made explicit. The notion of a grammar helps us identify his background assumptions and organizing categories of thought, which may well have been more stable than were any of the explicit theological formulae that he continued revising throughout his career, precisely because they were less self-conscious.[12] Whether or not this is so, we have a solid base of textual evidence from which to begin and to contend that in Augustine's thought, continence has a purview that extends far beyond sexuality.

"In truth, you command me to be continent with regard to 'the concupiscence of the flesh, and the concupiscence of the eyes, and the ambition of the world,'"[13] wrote Augustine at a critical juncture in book ten of the *Confessions*. Robert A. Markus has suggested that the center of Augustine's *Confessions* is in fact "that most astonishing tenth Book."[14] What makes it "astonishing" is the depth of Augustine's self-examination and his recognition that even now as a bishop, the sins that had (mis)shaped him and that remained present in his memory also continued to tempt and trip him amid his present struggle. Augustine had narrated in the first nine books how he had "dissipated [his] being into many things" through wrongful, scattered, and concupiscent loves, and how "by continence" he had begun to be "gathered together."[15] James O'Donnell has suggested in his commentary on the *Confessions* that Augustine had followed the threefold desires of 1 John 2:16—lust of the flesh, lust of the eyes, and worldly ambition— as he structured the narrative of his moral dissolution and reconstitution in those first nine books.[16] Now, at this critical junction in book ten, as Augustine turned to examine his current moral state, he organized his accounting of all possible sins around these same three categories of concupiscence.[17] If his love was to remain single—unified in one love for the One God—he must be continent with regard to all possible sins and temptations.

As we have recognized, some of the rhetorical moves that Augustine made within the Pelagian controversy encouraged later readers to focus exclusively on the sexual dimension of both concupiscence and continence. Yet the Pelagians also forced Augustine to clarify what had long been implicit in his thought—that sexual continence is only one instantiation of a "higher continence" of the heart. Sometime between 417 and 421, Augustine wrote a treatise *On Continence,* as well as a parallel treatise *On Patience.*[18] Though scholars have not given major attention to these two works, they are among Augustine's clearest and most succinct statements of his case against Pelagian confidence in human ability to become righteous.[19] While acknowledging that sexual continence is the kind "most chiefly and properly to be called continence," Augustine sought to shift the focus of his debate with the Pelagians to "the higher continence, concerning which we have been some time speaking, [and that is] preserved in the heart."[20] From this "higher continence" of the heart, argued Augustine, proceeds *every* right thought and deed according to a desire for the good that is strong enough to refuse consent to evil desires.[21]

Notice Augustine's passing claim that he had actually been speaking of this higher continence "for some time." Perhaps the phrase only refers to the previous paragraphs, where Augustine had (in another translation) been speaking "at length" about continence in its broadest sense.[22] The term *"superior continentia"* appears nowhere else in the Augustinian corpus, after all. Yet if Augustine was claiming unselfconsciously that the notion was really nothing new because he had been discussing it on many earlier occasions, his very lack of self-consciousness would be quite fitting. For even when Augustine did not name continence at all, much less "higher continence," the logic of continence was shaping his doctrine of Christian love. Continence as a general phenomenon was present as a grammar even when it did not appear in the vocabulary of a given treatise. As with any grammar, the speaker was employing it to speak of many *other* things, and only occasionally did he make it explicit. The key to demonstrating this will be the pattern by which Augustine employed another set of terms— verbs for having and for possessing, for grasping and for clinging, for acquiring and relating to all the goods that may be the objects of human love.

In the deep and formative grammar through which Augustine articulated his doctrine of love, trustful clinging to the God who is one's highest good consistently contrasted with every kind of manipulative grasping after other goods.[23] In the Augustinian phenomenology of love, cupidity acts with concupiscence and attempts to grasp at the objects of its wrongful love, while *caritas* acts with continence and clings to God as the source of all good gifts one might rightfully love. We may chart the pattern this way:

| *cupiditas* | grasps | through concupiscence |
| *caritas* | clings | through continence |

As with any heuristic device, this chart is useful because it is something of a simplification.[24] Still, the links or contrasts here between *caritas-continentia, continentia/concupiscentia,* and *caritas/cupiditas* all have strong textual basis, and this suggests that the pairing of *cupiditas-concupiscentia* should be consistent with the pattern. We have already seen (1) Augustine's statement in the *Confessions* that by continence we reorder our loves in the love of God (*caritas-continentia*), and (2) that *continentia* is what we need to counter every form of *concupiscentia.*[25] (3) In *On Christian Doctrine* 3.10.16, Augustine not only juxtaposed definitions of *caritas* and *cupiditas* in a way that implied they are opposites, but went on to confirm this by presenting the reigns of charity and cupidity as a zero-sum equation.[26] This leaves (4) the relationship between *cupiditas* and *concupiscentia.* Admittedly, the difference between these two terms was slight enough that Augustine sometimes used them interchangeably.[27] But while *cupiditas* is the simple desire in "wrongful desire," *concupiscentia* seems to be *cupiditas* that has begun to move into action with the interior intention of grasping its object for its own purposes.[28] If nothing else, *concupiscentia* indicates a more agitated state of *cupiditas,* as initial capitulation to desire gives way to lustful habit.[29]

In any case, what is clear is that the operations of charity and continence are entirely coordinate, while the two larger movements of cupidity and charity are mutually exclusive. And what is clear will become clearer still as we trace the pattern by which Augustine employed terms for grasping and clinging. Tracing this pattern of word usage will show us why and how continence is basic to the operation of all right love, inasmuch as it controls the self rather than others and trusts God to give the good that it needs and longs for—even the good of one's own self-control. That pattern obtains even when Augustine did not directly employ the word "continence." For as he once remarked, love is "the hand of the soul":

The accomplishment of righteousness in that we live here in labour, in toil, in self-restraint, in fastings, in watchings, in tribulations; this is the exercise of righteousness, to bear this present time, and to fast as it were from this world. . . . He then fulfills the law who abstains from this world. For he cannot love that which is eternal, unless he shall cease to love that which is temporal. *Consider a man's love: think of it as, so to say, the hand of the soul.*[30] If it is holding anything, it cannot hold anything else. But that it may be able to hold what it is given to it, it must leave go what it holds already. This I say, see how expressly I say it; "Whoever loves the world cannot love God; he has his hand engaged." God says to him, "Hold what I give." He will not leave go what he was holding; he cannot receive what is offered.[31]

Least of all might one grasp God, seize salvation, or devise the restoration of one's self. These, the greatest of goods, were also the greatest of gifts. While readers such as Nygren have portrayed the overarching structure of Augustine's *Confessions* as a Platonic ascent by which the seeker attempts to find unity with the divine,[32] and others have pointed to specific exercises of ascent within the *Confessions* as evidence of Augustine's Neoplatonism,[33] all of these ascents in some way failed.[34] The one ascent that most nearly succeeded (at Ostia, *Conf.* 9.10.23–26) did so not through Augustine's grasping but as a gift.[35] The lesson of these failures, and the lesson implicit in Augustine's overall failure to ascend through his own will and devising to a stable love of God, is that one must in a way be continent even toward God. Though clinging to God with a stable love is salvation itself, such love is a gift of God's love alone, which humans cannot grasp for themselves. They must receive it in continence and, to *be* continent, receive continence itself as a gift.[36] To show this will go a long way toward meeting the deepest concern that drove Nygren's critique of Augustine—his properly Lutheran anxiety that Augustine's *caritas* synthesis must inevitably subvert the sovereignty of God's love, which no human love can spark, much less earn.

More central to the present inquiry, however, an examination of Augustinian continence will also show how love for the good provides a motive that sustains rather than subverts the possibility of loving self-denial. *A fortiori*, it will show how Augustine integrated self-love and self-denial in a single account.

Grasping and Clinging

Love is "the hand of the soul," for "[i]f it is holding anything, it cannot hold anything else."[37] Augustine only used this image in a single sermon.[38] Yet the notion behind it figures in a text no less important for the study of Augustine's doctrine of love than his *Homilies on First John*. There Augustine noted that one must resist all three categories of temptation—the desire of the flesh, the desire of the eyes, and the pride of life—in order to make room for charity.[39] Such resistance, of course, is continence.[40] Continence is not love itself, to be sure, yet I will argue that for Augustine right love always moves in coordination with the movement of continence. As Augustine noted in the *Confessions*, "You [God] have commanded upon us not only continence, that is, to withhold [*cohibeamus*] our love from certain things, but also justice, that is, whereon we are to bestow [*conferamus*] our love."[41]

The hand that opens in order to cling to God, after all, must be a hand that continently refrains from grasping all those smaller goods it might close in upon and manipulate. According to Augustine, nothing is more like yet more unlike the movement of charity than the movement of cupidity—"*quid similius et quid dissimilius?*"[42] Charity and cupidity aim in utterly opposite directions, yet they operate in similar ways. The phenomenology by which human beings grasp hold of goods in a way that may ultimately destroy both the objects of their desire and themselves, therefore, reveals much about the phenomenology by which human beings cease to grasp, clinging instead to the God who is too great for them to manipulate, and begin to respect all that they receive from and in God, as gifts they cannot fully control.

Such assumptions formed the deep grammar of Augustine's writings; only rarely did he state their logic deliberately, yet he employed their logic constantly in much of what he said about love and desire. Augustine might describe the human condition in terms of rising and falling, for example; if a prideful rising led to a degrading fall according to the macro-movement of Augustine's cosmology, then in the micro-movement of every human heart the fall recurs precisely when human beings overstretch their *reach* in a vain attempt to control their own destinies.[43] Or Augustine might note that while God intended all people to be equals, covetousness is the desire at work when they pridefully dominate and seek higher positions.[44] Or he might describe love for God as a chaste embrace, in obvious contrast with every other way of holding tight and being held tight by temporal goods. Or he might speak, again and again, of clinging to God, and simply let all the overtones in Psalm 73(72):27–28 reverberate.[45]

Or, when speaking of ways that human beings acquire and possess, Augustine might simply choose some verbs over others. Augustine inherited patterns of word usage from the Latin language generally, and from available biblical translations especially, but his own preferences emerge strikingly enough to suggest that the phenomenology of grasping and clinging formed part of the deep grammar of Augustine's thought. Grasping was concupiscent; clinging was continent.[46]

The Grammar of Grasping

Whenever there is some inquiry into a wicked deed [*facinore*] and what caused it, we usually believe that it would not have been done except when it appears that there could have been desire [*appetitus*] to acquire [*adipiscendi*] some of what we have called lower goods, or from fear of losing [*metus amittendi*] them.[47]

Apparently, the desire to acquire and to keep—which together constitute the single act of grasping—is basic to all wickedness.[48] Still, the desire to acquire and keep is likely to motivate many more deeds than those that are wicked. The mere fact that one acquires or has some object is hardly enough to vitiate an action; the propriety of the object is certainly relevant too, if not decisive.[49] Acquiring, having, and grasping, after all, are basic to every human existence. To reach out, seize, acquire, contain, hold, and possess—*appetere, rapere, adipisci, capere, adprehendere,* and *possidere*—these are the actions by which human beings manage their physical existence and eat every bite they need to survive.[50] Just as important to Augustine, and in a sense that was probably not even metaphorical to him, these are the mental actions by which human beings take in images of all they perceive and then hold those images within their memories—seeking to grasp (*adprehendere*), understand (*capere*), comprehend (*comprehendere*), and acquire (*adipisci*) wisdom.[51]

However, Augustine displayed a certain reticence when he spoke of the proper ways for human beings to relate to the objects they desire, love, and in some way acquire. The more important (or "higher") an object, the more problematic human endeavors to grasp it were likely to be. This is the pattern that emerges when we examine Augustine's use of verbs for having and grasping:

Temporal goods.   Everyone must necessarily grasp and possess at least some nonhuman temporal goods, but even so, Augustine insisted, a person ought not grasp them so tightly that they actually ensnared the person in their grasp instead. Obviously one might need to snatch up objects such as books, and Christians also should seize (*rapere*) any good they could from pagan arts, if what they gathered (*capienda*) could serve spiritual ends.[52] This was the proper Christian approach to temporal goods generally; those on pilgrimage amid the earthly city must use temporal goods without being held tight (*capitur*) by them.[53] But clearly one should not acquire (*adipisci*) worldly goods, bodies, honors, power, and revenge if doing so required departing from God or God's law.[54] Something in the sinful human heart willingly desired to be captivated, whether by adolescent love, or by God's own beauty.[55] As Augustine surveyed his life according to the three concupiscences of 1 John 2:16, he used verbs of grasping to note that one was therefore vulnerable to ensnarement even when one reached out to grasp necessities like food and drink, knowledge, or affirmation from others.[56] That is why, as the Psalmist had said, God must pluck people out of their snares before that happened.[57]

In any case, the attempt to grasp at temporal goods could be both sinful and in vain. When dishonest and unjust people cheat others, they grasp and embrace in wrongful, concupiscent ways—"they fornicate against you out of love for passing, temporary trifles and filthy lucre, which defiles the hand that seizes it [*quod cum apprehenditur manum inquinat*], and by embracing a fleeting world [*et amplectendo mundum fugientem*]. . . ." So, too, for the ambitious who sought to rise socially through the lies of rhetoric. Augustine himself had been such a young man, and the flight of what the fleeting world offered could be quick indeed: "If any good fortune smiled upon me, it was too much trouble to grasp after it, because almost before I could take hold, it had flown away."[58]

Thus, it is really one's own illusions of permanent, private possession that present the most serious temptation, since external goods themselves only provide occasions for temptation. According to *On the*

Trinity 12.10.15, temptations from the external physical objects one needs to manipulate in order to survive are relatively minor.[59] The real and serious danger when one "does something to obtain the things that are sensed by the body" is the danger that one will mix perceived need with illusions of permanent possession and private control. This is the action of "the soul, loving its own power," as it seeks to possess things privately rather than in common with others; its embrace is not chaste but adulterous. What it actually snatches at are "deceptive semblances of bodily things inside," which it combines with the vain thought that they have divine attributes, namely, permanence and the ability to serve as one's true end and good.[60]

Neighbors.   That the attempt to control permanently is the critical moral variable in human grasping emerges even more clearly from the way Augustine used his grammar of grasping when human beings are the object.

Augustine's general reflections on the death of his friend in book four of the *Confessions* show that wrongly grasping is both sinful and ultimately in vain, but his specific choice of words underscores the point. Upon first recounting the death of his friend, Augustine insisted that theirs had not been a true friendship because God must glue (*tu agglutinas*) together such friendship among those who cling to God (*haerentes tibi*) through the *caritas* of the Holy Spirit. By contrast, the "love that comes from the body's senses" could also apply a glue (*glutine*) to the soul, but one that worked through fixation (*infigatur*) with passing goods. The soul might seek to rest in its attachment to the human friendship which is among the greatest of the many beautiful but temporal goods that God had created; yet because such goods flee on in time, desiring them apart from God ends up tearing away part of the soul. Thus, even before they flee and while they are still close at hand (*cum praesto sunt*), "who can grasp them?"—"*quis ea comprehendit*"?[61]

On the other hand, the way to love a neighbor, friend, or enemy rightly was, for Augustine, to "carry up to him with you as many as you can." At first the notion may in every case seem to suggest violent forms of grasping. Even if modern English speakers filter out the over-powering connotations of the imperative "*rape ad eum tecum quas potes*," the Latin verb *rapere* still carries troublesome associations of its own. In Latin itself, *rapere* could serve as the word for sexual rape, though it had a wider range of meaning. A *raptor* was a thief who seizes things belonging to others. Augustine might characterize Christians as dovelike creatures who lacked a grasping, rapacious nature. What Christ had *not* done was seize the equality with God that was in fact his own; but what the serpent of Eden had done, and tempted Adam and Eve to do, was seize what was not their own.[62]

If, in spite of all such overtones, Augustine nonetheless insisted that one might somehow *rapere* other human beings who are one's equals and carry them up to God, the reason was that this implied a relinquishing of control—at least eventually, at least in theory. This was the subtle difference between *rapere* and *-prehendo* verbs; there were ways in which it was possible to *rapere* others in order to release and free them, but the attempt to *comprehendere* or *adprehendere* another person (in any noncognitive sense) was inherently selfish and domineering. The logic of *rapere* might be paternalistic, insofar as one intervened for other people's good even when they did not yet recognize the goal of the intervention as for their good. And although Augustine did not initially intend the paternalism of *rapere ad Deum* to encourage violence, its connotations probably prepared him to rationalize coercive policies toward "schismatic" Christians. Yet for all that, the image itself is at least not egocentric: the power that one exercises in carrying others up to God is not a dominance that one loves for its own sake; rather, the good is the neighbor's and the possession is God's. Augustine's use of the term *rapere* was a seamless part of his theocentric vision of Christian love, wherein a person "refers" every love "to that love of God which suffers no stream to be led away from it by which it might be diminished."

> For when [Jesus] said, "With your whole heart, and with your whole soul, and with your whole mind," He did not leave any part of life which should be free and find itself room to desire the enjoyment of something else. But whatever else appeals to the mind as being lovable should be directed [*rapiatur*] into that channel into which the whole current of love flows.

If seizing and carrying other humans up to God is always potentially ambiguous and subject to misuse, that ambiguity does at least cut two ways, and one of those ways might be altogether nonviolent. Thus, when the Roman orator Victorinus publicly embraced the Christian faith, the jubilant Christian community was ready to seize (*rapere*) the new convert into its heart; its members clutched him (*rapiebant*) with the two grasping hands (*rapientium manus*) of love and joy.[63]

Truth, wisdom, happiness, eternal life.   In some sense, people should of course seek to learn, apprehend, comprehend, and otherwise grasp the truth. Yet Augustine exhibited a certain reticence even here; he seems to have used *comprehendo* and *adprehendo* most freely in their apparently neutral, cognitive meanings when their subjects were not in fact grasping the truth. In books five and six of the *Confessions* Augustine criticized philosophical Skeptics who did not believe that human beings could comprehend (*comprendere*) any truth with certainty. He was not arguing for a more optimistic intellectualism here, as though human beings *could* comprehend or grasp the truth on their own; rather, his argument was that only through the authoritative instruction of scripture and the Church could they comprehend the truth. Later, when Augustine's parishioners recognized that their earthly city's rejoicing would one day cease, just as the grass withers and the flower fades, they did right to ask, "How can I apprehend the Word of God" that abides forever? But the scripture before him provided an answer that stressed God's initiative before their own: "The Word was made flesh, and dwelt among us."[64]

As Augustine well knew, the nature of the goods that humans should in fact reach out toward with desire (*appetere*) and the problem of how to acquire (*adipisci*) the Supreme Good were central questions for ancient philosophy.[65] Oliver O'Donovan has observed that Augustine most consistently appealed to natural human self-love and the universal desire for happiness when the apologetic task required him to take up the language of this philosophical tradition and urge his listeners to have mercy on themselves by recognizing the truth of Christianity and loving God.[66] O'Donovan's observation extends to Augustine's use of terms that seem to imply that humans might be the agents who acquire truth, wisdom, happiness, and eternal life; outside of the apologetic and homiletic context, such terms become more rare. And even when he appealed to the desire of readers and listeners to acquire such goods for themselves, he eventually went on to insist that they could only "acquire" such goods as gifts, which were not therefore their own making.

Though human beings may not agree on what will make them happy and blessed, they do seem to have a universal will to grasp and retain blessedness.[67] God has given bodily and temporal goods so that we might grasp (*capiamus*) spiritual and eternal things.[68] Augustine might also speak of acquiring wisdom, the truth, the Supreme Good, and, along with any good, joy.[69] The soul could only become good, however, by turning to a good outside of itself when it loves, desires, and acquires.[70] Augustine himself had made a critical move toward acquiring these goods when he seized greedily upon the scriptures, and especially the apostle Paul.[71] In the scriptures themselves, texts such as Mark 10:30 promised that the disciple might hope to receive or possess eternal life.[72]

But the question of *how* to acquire remains, even if the apologist and the philosopher agree that when we acquire the Supreme Good we are blessed, while when we lack it we are wretched. Creatures created with capacity to acquire (*adipisci*) or hold onto (*capere*) the blessing of clinging to God as their highest Good still could not do so by themselves, precisely because they were "created out of nothing, [and] receive [their blessedness] from the one who created them." Thus, as soon as Augustine thought he might have consensus that "eternal life is the Supreme Good, and eternal death the Supreme Evil, and that to achieve [*adipiscendam*] the one and escape the other, we must live rightly," he quickly added:

> That is why the scripture says, "The just man lives on the basis of faith." For we do not yet see our good, and hence we have to seek it by believing; and it is not in our power to live rightly, unless while we believe and pray we receive help from him who has given us the faith to believe that we must be helped by him.[73]

And God?   Ultimately, we could not call eternal life the Supreme Good except that it participates in the life of God, whom we most properly call the Supreme Good, and who shares God's own life as a gift. But is one to grasp or have or contain God? Surely one should not be concupiscent toward God.

While biblical language in texts such as the Psalms allowed Augustine the possibility that God could in some way be one's "portion," "inheritance," or possession,[74] Augustine remained circumspect. The great mystery of the opening chapters in the *Confessions* was the question of what or who could know, call upon, and contain (*capere*) God.[75] Yet everything in the work—from Augustine's autobiographical details, to his failed mystic ascents, to his affirmations of the need for a mediator, to his closing exegesis of Genesis 1—conspired to reverse the question: How, rather, does God call and grasp us? As Augustine's narrative began in book eight to shift from his own frustrated questing to God's gracious saving, his prayer hinted that God would be the one to call, seize, and carry him back (*rapere*).[76] By book ten Augustine was making clear that no place within him could contain (*capere*) God's light, and no time could seize (*rapere*) God's voice.[77] As the final book of Augustine's *Confessions* opened, the answer to the question with which he had begun was finally becoming clear. Only through God's initiative could one's soul somehow accept God within:

> I call upon you, my God, my mercy, who made me, and did not forget me, although I forgot you. I call you into my soul [*invoco te in animam meam*], which you prepare to accept you [*ad capiendum te*] by the longing that you breath into it. Do not desert me now when I call upon you, for before I called upon you, you went ahead and helped me, and repeatedly you urged me on by many different words, so that from afar I would hear you and be converted, and call upon you as you called upon me.[78]

Before all else, God's initiative in sending God's own Son as Mediator is what makes it possible for human beings in some sense to obtain God. "For, remaining God with the Father, [Christ] was made human among human beings, that, through the One who was made human, you might become such as to obtain [*capit*] God." Human beings can see other human beings, but they cannot grasp or obtain God; even when seeing Jesus, his contemporaries could not really see God apart from the eye of the heart, which sees by faith. Augustine's exhortation, then, was: "Believe in Christ, made mortal for you, so that you might obtain [*capias*] the Immortal One."[79]

Could one then grasp Christ, the Word made flesh, the Mediator? Augustine preferred to speak of Christians as clinging to Christ, or as having Christ (*habeo*) and holding onto Christ (*teneo*). These are general terms that lack the manipulative connotation of verbs such as *-prehendo* or other words for grasping. *Habere* and *tenere* might even serve as synonyms for *haereo* verbs. Thus Christians could have Christ in their hearts, or have him as their foundation. And as they drifted down the river of time in their love of temporal things, then looked in desperation to Christ planted beside the river, they should indeed take hold of the tree. But Augustine's exhortation was this: "*Tene lignum. . . . Tene Christum.*" One could hold on to Christ, but not seize him by grasping.[80]

No, Augustine preferred rather to speak of God grasping hold of him. Thus he prayed in gratitude to God's mercy: "'your right hand has upheld me' in my Lord, the Son of man, mediator between you, the One, and us, the many . . . so that by him 'I may apprehend, in whom I have been apprehended.'"[81] Here he quoted the Apostle Paul's own hope in Philippians 3:12.

If the possibility that "I may apprehend" life's most important goods initially seems to deviate from the pattern of Augustine's grammar, closer examination shows the phrase to be an exception that proves the grammatical rule—showing just how conscious Augustine was that he must not claim to grasp God or eternal life or blessedness. The Pauline text rather than Augustine's own sensibilities suggested the phrase. But more than that, Augustine increasingly put Philippians 3 to use when the Pelagians in effect argued that human beings *could* grasp hold of eternal life through their own efforts. Again and again Augustine let Paul make his point: "Brothers, I do not judge myself to have apprehended." The hope of pressing "on toward the goal" and grasping "the prize of the upward call of God in Christ Jesus" was only realistic insofar as one is "also grasped by Christ Jesus."[82]

Augustinian *caritas* is therefore not acquisitive in the way that Nygren argued. For from the beginning any acquisition is God's work, and at the end of God's working the love acquired is mutual. No one can have a right relation with God except as a gift—which is *not* to have it in a manipulative, controlling, way.

The Grammar of Clinging

"For me to cling to God is the good." In quoting Psalm 73(72):28 as he so often did, Augustine tended to interchange a series of Latin verbs with *haereo* at their root.[83] In all its forms, and in many settings, the complex of verbs that appear in English translations as "clinging" consistently contrasts with that for "grasping."[84] Human beings cling to

God by loving God, in recognition that God is their supreme good; such clinging is basic to the love that enjoys rather than uses, for "To enjoy something is to cling to it with love for its own sake."[85]

To cling to God is also the only way to love ourselves rightly, "for if I do not abide in him, neither will I be able to abide in myself." Clinging to God brings spiritual health, everlasting joy, virtues, and unity among believers. Thus, it is what repentant sinners must do, what the unconverted Augustine knew that he had to do, yet also what he knew he could not do on his own. Even as a Christian, to cling to God was Augustine's constant prayer. After all, to cling to God with robust affection does not come naturally; people never cling so devoutly that they can be confident that their affection for God will sustain either them or their self-denial in extreme situations such as torture.[86]

Augustine also spoke of clinging to Christ, though less often. To cling to Christ perseveringly was a key element in Augustine's definition of the Christian life. For the first disciples, to follow Christ meant relinquishing all else and clinging to him as Master and Teacher. By implication, Christians must continue to do likewise, for during the sack of Rome some who were weak in character had clung to worldly goods in preference to Christ. Jesus Christ, after all, is the mediator to whom Christians must cling tenaciously, the high priest through whom God enkindles the love by which they cling to God. *Confessions* 7.18.24 makes clear, however, that Christ's roles as Teacher and Mediator are anything but distinct; only insofar as Christ has first humbled himself through the incarnation, identified with the humble, and now "bring[s] them to himself," can human beings cling to him, learn of him, and enjoy God.[87]

Thus, Augustine told his listeners in one sermon that they should "Cling unto Christ, who by descending and ascending has made Himself the way. Do you wish to ascend? Hold fast to Him that ascends. For by your own self you cannot rise." The Church could only hope to possess God, clinging to the One by whom it is blessed, insofar as it receives the inheritance of eternal life "through our Lord Jesus Christ." As Augustine so often said, citing Romans 5:5, we love God and cling to God through the love that God pours into our hearts by the Holy Spirit who is given to us. Those who partake of Christ do so truly if they abide and are abode in, if they dwell and are dwelt in, if they cling so as not to be deserted. Human beings, then, cannot cling to the good except as God grasps hold of them through Jesus Christ.[88]

Augustine might also speak positively of clinging to other goods—the words of someone wise, the solidity of truth, the foundation of God's scriptures, the Church, and the common good.[89] One might *attempt* to cling to sin or pleasure, but of course should not and finally could not.[90] If one related to temporal goods in such a way that one clung to them, they clung back, and one sinned thereby.[91] To cling wrongly to a thing or person, as Augustine described the action of his heart when "the woman with whom I was wont to share my bed was torn from my side," could eventually result in the deepest and most wounding of pains.[92]

Yet when human beings rightly love their neighbors, friends, and fellow Christians in God, according to Augustine, they also cling to one another rightly. In contrast to the self-serving and manipulative way that Augustine had loved his unnamed friend in book four of the *Confessions,* a friendship could only be true where "you [God] glue it together among those who cling to you through charity."[93] Mutual clinging to God then joins believers together in mutual clinging to one another.[94] Even before Augustine and Alypius were Christians, they were in some sense "carrying one another up to God," and thus, Augustine could speak of Alypius as one who clung closely to him.[95] Among the narratives in book eight of the *Confessions* that contributed to Augustine's own conversion was the story of two ambitious Roman friends who agreed to bond or cling together (*adhaerere se*) as comrades in service to God.[96] On a larger scale, all those who share in the good of clinging to God "have holy fellowship with [God] to whom they adhere, and also among themselves"; such mutual adherence, whether on pilgrimage yet on earth or at rest together with the holy angels, constitutes the one City of God.[97]

The City of God does not live at all, however, except as it receives its very life and all of its light as a perpetual gift of God's love; to cling to God is to receive God's gifts in trust. Years before he wrote *City of God,* Augustine had identified the city of those citizens who comprise God's house in a single "pure mind, most harmoniously one by the established peace of holy spirits," as the "heaven of heavens."[98] Though at one level Augustine's interpretation of the Latin Hebraicism "*caelum caeli*"[99] in book twelve of the *Confessions* was highly Platonic, Augustine used the Platonic idiom to undercut the very presumption of Platonic questing that Nygren thought the *Confessions* represents singularly well.[100] For Augustine this "heaven of heavens" was the archetypical—

and archetypically faithful—creature, whose very faithfulness means looking to God as its only source of light and nourishment, thus clinging to God so fully, so joyfully, and so continently, that it almost shares in God's own immutability.[101]

Metaphysical speculation aside, Augustine's discussion here offers a kind of limit case for the possibilities and limitations of all creatureliness. For the "heaven of heavens" supplied the ultimate standard against which Augustine might measure himself as a creature. Unlike God's most perfect creature, which had never departed from God, Augustine had fallen away to the love of material things, and out of God's light. Alienated from God, he had heard a distant voice beckoning him to return, so that he burned and yearned for God's "fountain." The lesson was not, however, that such "erotic" longing itself might lead to God, but precisely the opposite: "Let me not be my own life: badly have I lived from myself: I was death to myself: in you I live again. Speak to me, speak with me." Thus, it is the voice of Paul, not Plato or Plotinus, that emerges with the final word in Augustine's Confessions— Paul confessing that "it is no longer I who live, but it is Christ who lives in me" by faith, Paul insisting that "faith comes from what is heard, and what is heard comes through the word of Christ."[102]

What Augustine as a creature must therefore learn (but must necessarily learn through God's grace) was what the archetypically faithful creature had never forgotten: No creature could ascend through its own agency, or control its own destiny, or create itself, but each must recognize its entire life and self as an undeserved gift of God's pure uncoerced love.[103] Even the highest lights or spiritual creatures of heaven did not have any light of themselves, but must cling to God in order to retain their light; this was true even for the heaven of heavens. All life and being owe entirely to God's grace. Any "ascent" by needy, fallen creatures is God's gift. Whether created or re-created, therefore, one's very creaturehood is an overflow from God's love.[104]

Having by Not Having

To say that the phenomenology of grasping and clinging formed part of the deep grammar of Augustine's thought is to indicate how the same can be true about continence itself. Here is where our word study bears fruit. The one who loves rightly opens "the hand of the soul" in order to cling to God. In so doing, he or she also clings mutually with others who cling to God as their common good. Thus loving "in God," those who love rightly receive even temporal goods as gifts, so long as they receive them in the right ecology of interrelationship which is the common good, rather than through strictly private possession of private goods. Therefore, "this whole rich world belongs" to the "person of faith, . . . who, by clinging to [God] whom all things serve, is as one having nothing yet possessing all things—*quasi nihil habens omnia possidet inhaerendo tibi.*"[105] Those who love in this way surely possess much—even "all things"—but they do so through a fundamentally nonegocentric, nonviolent way of acquiring. For they "acquire" by continently respecting. They recognize that "Everything which does not decrease on being given away is not properly owned when it is owned and not given."[106] They do not grasp; rather, they "have" by not having.

Continence is this trustful, nonmanipulative way of having a right relationship with the objects of one's love. Continence, then, is *caritas*'s operative mode, as it respects God's gifts and allows them their rightful place in God's ecological order. In other words, the movement whereby love, as "the hand of the soul," clings to God is the same movement by which it continently refrains from grasping at all those smaller goods it might dream of closing in upon and manipulating for itself. Mundane grasping by the actual hand of the body is basic to temporal survival, of course. Yet even here, to grasp things as though they were anything other than temporal is illusory, for such grasping ultimately destroys both the thing grasped and the person grasping. Meanwhile, some goods one may not "have" or "acquire" or "possess" at all through grasping at them, but only through respectful continence: friendship, marriage, one's very life, a relationship with God, along with joys and pleasure appropriate to each. To attempt to manipulate and control the friend, the spouse, the destiny, or the divine, inevitably means to treat the goods that one claims to love as something less than they truly are, thus degrading either the object of love, or the one loving, or both. Moreover, if the alternate way of "having" such goods is continence, the virtue of continence itself must necessarily be "had" continently, through faith not willpower, as a gift of God. Both the logic of Augustinian continence, and the controversies that Augustine's prayer for such continence provoked, would drive him to clarify that crucial point, as we will see.

Concupiscence or lust is the operative mode of wrongful love or *cupiditas*. It has not just desired, but begun to grasp, or to contemplate grasping, the object of its desire as its own private good, and thus to disrespect and violate the true good of what it allegedly loves. In Augustine's view, of course, concupiscence must ultimately be self-defeating; while the grasping by which we attempt to possess privately often chokes the object of our grasping, rejection of the common good always leads to our own alienation and destruction. The very hubris by which we grasp at goods as though we could secure them for ourselves forever expresses a "perverse appetite for exaltation."[107] At the deepest level, what we have really loved is not so much the goods we claimed to want to enjoy, but domination for its own sake.[108] It is this kind of love of self that distinguishes the earthly city from the City of God; when human beings have tried in their pride to be self-sufficient, to make themselves "their own ground," and to aim at something more than obedient "participation in the true God," they have overstretched their reach and had nowhere to go but "down."[109] The "poverty-stricken kind of power" by which human beings (like the false gods they emulate) then "scramble for their lost dominions" at best creates an alienated relationship even with those temporal goods that they tenuously possess, and at worst exacerbates all the human suffering against which they sought to secure their safety.[110]

In the context of Augustine's phenomenology of love and continence, statements that express the paradoxes of self-love and self-denial now turn out to be far less paradoxical. Though in one sense "no one hates himself," the perverse self-love that claims God's prerogatives "is better called hate," or self-hatred.[111] Inversely, a person uses power most rightly to conquer his own vices, thus acting "in an odd way against himself for himself." Likewise, Jesus' evangelical call to follow him and to deny oneself translated into the homiletic exhortation to prefer God's will over one's own will, and to "learn to love yourself by not loving yourself"; after all, "if by loving himself man is lost, surely by denying himself is he found." Finally, those who know, with Paul, that "it is no longer I who live, but it is Christ who lives in me" (Galatians 2:20), actually find their truest, most fulfilled self: "For where not I, there more happily I."[112]

In all of these cases, much of what looks like paradox results not so much from contradiction—or even rhetorical flourish by Jesus, Paul, or Augustine himself—but from the limitation of words. All involve some kind of having or acting or acquiring that is only possible through some other kind of not having or not acting or not acquiring. Each involves a movement of human agency that, like the *caritas* or *cupiditas* from which each springs, could hardly be more dissimilar in one sense, yet in some other way is still so similar that we easily apply the same word to it as we do to its contrary.[113]

The closest thing to a real paradox is the nearly insoluble mystery of continence itself. If the phenomenology of Augustinian love requires human beings to "have" only in continent ways, then they must have continence itself in a continent way. Though they must control their wills, they cannot do so through their own willpower. To attempt self-control through their own willpower actually acquiesces to the greater incontinence of uncontrolled pride. Whether paradoxically or expressing the mystery of God's grace, true self-control is not possible through one's own self-control, therefore, but is the gift of God.[114]

Such was the burden of Augustine's argument when the Pelagians forced him to write *On Continence,* his most systematic treatment of the subject. Because Augustine had been using the problematics of human sexuality as evidence for original sin, and had been appealing to original sin to demonstrate that humans no longer had wills that were free and strong enough to perfect themselves, the Pelagian bishop Julian of Eclanum had begun accusing Augustine of blaming the material flesh or created human nature for sin and thus returning to a covert Manichaeism that saw flesh as evil. The accusation forced Augustine to clarify what had long been implicit in his writings, namely, that sexual continence is only one instantiation of a higher continence of the heart. There, within the heart or soul, lie the roots of all actions, and if one has continence of heart, one will be continent in both word and deed.[115]

To recognize the need for continence at all, however, is to recognize that one is still struggling against sinful desires, Augustine continued in his treatise *On Continence.* When the New Testament identifies these desires with "the flesh," it refers not to the body but to the soul's choice to live according to the standards of the flesh, thereby making bodily pleasures and bodily self-preservation its highest purpose. No one is so perfect that they cease to struggle against the wrongful desires in this life; the most one can hope for is the continence that refuses to consent to them, so that one desires not to desire or wills not to will. This continence, however, must come from the Holy Spirit, who gives the grace human beings need to escape the reign, if not the presence, of sin. Even those struggling most valiantly against sin, Augustine noted, are still to pray "Forgive us our debts," for though they are warriors whose purpose is firm, they suffer wounds.[116]

Hence, those who have overcome overt sins still need "a more cautious continence," which restrains pride itself—the appetite whereby a person "is self-pleased, and unwilling to be found worthy of blame, and disdains, when he sins, to be convicted that he himself has sinned." Such a person lacks the "healthful humility" to take on self-accusation, "but rather with fatal arrogance [seeks] to find an excuse." To have the continence to restrain such pride we must, like the Psalmist, seek it from the Lord, not ourselves; to attempt to excuse or justify ourselves only increases the evil of our deeds. We need continence to deal with *all* sins, therefore, and not just sexual lust, for in every case we most of all need continence to avoid proud self-justification. After all, "that continence which is true, coming from above, wills not to repress some evils by other evils"—in other words, it does not restrain some sins by exercising the fundamental sin of pride—"but to heal all evils by goods." We dare not take credit for human works that we ought rather call the works of God, "who is at work in you, enabling you both to will and to work for his good pleasure." Just as the essence of wisdom is insight into whose gift wisdom is (Wisdom 8:21), so continence is only continent if it recognizes itself as God's gift. Thus, the work of continence is not simply to refuse consent to those evil inclinations that remain within a Christian, but above all to confess that whenever one either resists evil or does good, it is Christ, "not I," who now lives one's very life. "Continence is the gift of God"; so too is the patience that endures great suffering for God's sake. "What does not have faith, therefore, is not to be called continent."[117]

Continence as the Work of God

At least two objections may have surfaced by now. Both would suggest that in seeking to discern the underlying grammar of Augustine's thought on continence, we may have slipped back into an ancient though fallacious way of reading him. Before modern methods of historical and textual criticism allowed for a generally confident dating of Augustine's writings, scholars tended to flatten them out into one vast *auctoritas* from which to draw propositions and positions that all stood on the same plane, without regard for chronology, development, setting, or genre.[118] If we have accurately discerned the grammar of Augustine's thought, that structure may well have been more stable—because less self-conscious—than were any explicit theological formulae that he continued revising throughout his career. The notion of a grammar is helpful precisely because it allows for both continuity and development in Augustine's thought.[119] Facing questions about the development of Augustine's thought actually underscores what is at stake in the recovery of Augustinian continence.

Continence by Faith Alone

The first objection is that Augustinian continence did not really imply the need for faith—faith as trust in God's unmerited love—until late in Augustine's theological career, after the Pelagians goaded him toward this realization. Nygren would certainly raise just this objection, and find support from Luther.[120] If they were right, then what we have claimed was basic to the structure of Augustine's thought would have obtained only for the later Augustine.

Perhaps the objection has a certain validity; controversy usually forces theologians either to construct their positions or draw out the implications of their thought, and virtually everything Augustine wrote engaged one debate or another. Yet if the objection implies, as Nygren did, that theologically there were really two Augustines—what we might call the early "Catholic Augustine" whose "*caritas* synthesis" laid the basis for a medieval spirituality of questing for God, in contrast to a later "Lutheran Augustine" whose struggle against Pelagian works-righteousness made him a precursor to the Reformation—then much of what we have seen in this chapter has already tended to refute the objection.[121] Tracing the underlying logic of continence as a non-acquisitive way of relating to God and all other goods has already shown us that the *Confessions* aimed to reverse the question of how humans might acquire God; that Augustine's Platonic ascents failed when they were his doing; that the "heaven of heavens" was his model of creaturely recognition that one's very life and self are an unmerited gift of God's love; that he recognized God as having taken the initiative in sending the Mediator after human beings fell away from the kind of vision and faith that the "heaven of heavens" models; and that through all of this, God's love has priority over every human quest to love rightly, such that the continence which recognizes all of God's gifts *as* gifts is itself a gift of God's love.[122]

In other words, the study of Augustinian continence as a critical element in Augustine's doctrine of love shows that the structure of his theology was in place at least from the mid-390s and remained stable thereafter. That was when he reread Paul, resolved his understanding of the will, and recognized that salvation, conversion, works of love, and continence must all be gifts of God's grace alone.[123] Surely his thought continued to develop, correct itself, and encounter new problems, but the Pelagian debate mainly provided an occasion for him to draw out the implications of what he had already begun to say by the time he wrote the *Confessions*. Augustine's understanding of continence, then, was itself a critical element to the foundation upon which he eventually built his anti-Pelagian arguments.

Apparently, Pelagius himself recognized this. For what we now call the Pelagian controversy did not begin when Augustine learned the views of Pelagius or his followers, but rather, when Pelagius encountered the prayer Augustine had repeated three times in book ten of the *Confessions*: "Give what you command, and command what you will." Pelagius had initially appreciated the *Confessions* as an eloquent testimony to conversion, but grew annoyed at the suggestion that baptized Christians did not already have within them the power to do as God commanded. And just what did God command? At every one of the passages in *Confessions* 10 where Augustine had asked God to "give what you command," he made clear: "You require of us continence."[124]

But in a way, the need to have continence *continently* had been shaping Augustine's thought even before the mid-390s. Although we must rely on Augustine's own hindsight after the mid-390s, we cannot dismiss the claim that his conversion account represents. Although Augustine chose to portray his conversion in a highly stylized way, his very choice of literary device itself makes a claim at once autobiographical and theological about what made his conversion possible. At ground zero in his conversion, he said, he had a vision of Continence.[125] She stood outside of him, addressing him, shaming him, challenging him, for her virtue was not his own.[126] Though he needed her desperately, he could not have her by grasping and thus violating her, for he would thus have marred the very beauty of her "alluring" virtue and stolen her name, yet he would not then be any more continent himself. No, he must have a relationship with such a woman through respect, joining with her and all her children in a chaste "embrace," which Augustine elsewhere identified with the act of clinging to God and thereby to other Christians. However many years it took him to articulate intuitions from August 386 in the garden of Milan, the very impasse he had reached by that point was an impasse he could only cross over *then* because God, not he, did the work of making him continent.

Having examined the historical and textual evidence for why Augustine sensed such a deep need for the continence to embrace "neither wife nor ambition," we can hardly reject as implausible his claim that there, in Milan, Augustine also recognized that he must receive it as a gift from God. He was no different from other simpler folk who had already embraced continence. "Or can these youths and these maidens do this of themselves, and not rather in the Lord their God?" asked the lady of the vision. "The Lord their God gave me to them. Why do you stand on yourself, and thus stand not at all. Cast yourself on him. Have no fear. He will not draw back and let you fall. Cast yourself trustfully on him: he will receive you and he will heal you."[127]

Seeking Not One's Own

A second objection would engage the latter part of Augustine's career. The critic might recognize continuity between the Augustine of the *Confessions* and the later anti-Pelagian Augustine, or even concede that the abiding structure of his thought was in place by 396 or 397. But the critic might turn the question of continuity on its head and insist that the later Augustine failed to break with the Platonic framework of his early theology. Perhaps the critic would recognize the weight of Augustine's long but deepening critique of Platonism; already in the *Confessions* he had used its own language against its pride. But the critic might still object that Augustine never shook off eudaemonistic or teleological assumptions that undermine specifically Christian understandings of love as self-giving and self-denying.[128]

True enough: Augustine never did abandon teleology, or the confidence that human beings can orient their lives around an end that they expect will ultimately hold the key to their own happiness, blessedness, flourishing, or good. Augustine was not simply taking homiletic license when he appealed to the ultimate self-interest of listeners and readers as motivation to obey God's will and do their duty: "God's intention" in giving a command to the first humans "was to impress upon this created being that he was the Lord; and that free service was in that creature's own interest [*salubritatem*]."[129] Even Jesus, in speaking a "hard saying" to the rich young man of Matthew 19, did not *really* ask him to lose anything of importance. Only the covetous think in this manner, for if we properly understand, piously believe, and devoutly receive the word of the Gospel, we see that "He has not enjoined us to lose, but rather shown a place where we may lay up" true and lasting treasure.[130] Likewise, Jesus' word to follow him by denying oneself might look hard and grievous, but in fact his "yoke is easy" because charity makes easy whatever seems hard; if those who love money, honor, or women endure great hardships for the things they love, Christians should not wonder "if he who loves Christ, and who wishes to follow Christ, denies himself for the love of Him."[131]

To critics from various perspectives, the teleological framework into which Augustine has placed evangelical self-denial seems to present a conflict. For Nygren, any teleological motivation at all must contaminate Christian love, especially God's love for sinners.[132] In his concern to protect the authenticity of Christian love for neighbor as well, Nygren stood firmly with Kantian moral theory. For moral theorists in the deontological or duty-based philosophical tradition of Immanuel Kant, the grounding of duty in any motivation other than duty itself invites people to abandon their duties as soon as some stronger desire presents a competing motivation. And in fact, Augustine signaled his own awareness of the problem of mixed, inauthentic motivation when he chastised his congregation for wanting good things without *being* good themselves: "Who is there that does not wish for [eternal] life?—and yet who is there that *does* wish to keep the commandments?"[133]

Yet to Augustine's defenders, his teleological framing of self-denial may present not so much a conflict as a clue. Burnaby has noted that even for the very early Augustine writing *The Morals of the Catholic Church,* such tensions as came with his neophyte attempt to introduce the two great love commands of a Christian ethic into a Neoplatonic system soon impinged upon Platonic desire itself: The source of happiness turned out to be a power that claims allegiance; any attempt to love God according to the first commandment must change the character of eros itself. After all, as Burnaby concluded, if God's own self is the only true fulfillment of human longing, then God will hardly allow our desires to go unchanged: "For God will not reward our service by becoming the servant of our desires. God will be eternally Himself, eternally to be worshipped, the King and not the Kingdom. The 'possession' of God is the knowledge of Him and the love of Him as He is, not as we in our sinfulness might wish Him to be."[134]

Augustine did not have to abandon teleology in order for his doctrine of Christian love to sustain evangelical self-denial. For if continence is the operative mode of love, we may understand love teleologically, as the desire to enjoy and participate in the supreme and common good, yet also insist that desire and duty, self-love and self-denial, are so inextricably integrated that neither loses out to the other. Even Christ, we may note, endured the cross "for the sake of the joy that was set before him"[135]—for the joy of a restored creation united in mutual love, for the joy of a people bearing the first fruits of that love already in history, for the joy of our own participation with him as his "body" in the very trinitarian life of God[136]—yet Christ himself did not *have* by *grasping*.[137] One cannot truly or rightly have any lasting good through that grasping, prideful control which subjects the object of one's love to one's willful desires. One must instead subject one's desires to the good of that which one loves. In an Augustinian teleology of Christian love, the desire that seeks to participate in the good must, therefore, necessarily be desire that respects.

Evangelical self-denial not only has a secure and integral place in Augustine's account of Christian love, but may actually require a teleological ordering if it is to remain evangelical at all. Augustine's argument to this effect appears in a neglected treatise *On Patience* that is almost surely a companion to his treatise *On Continence,* but that actually clarifies certain aspects of Augustinian higher continence that the other does not.[138] Just as a misdirected love is not *caritas* but *cupiditas,* patient suffering or self-denial at the service of some lust for a wrongful object is not, according to Augustine, true patience at all.[139] As we now might explain, delayed gratification alone is no virtue, for the delaying alone is not evangelical self-denial or loving self-sacrifice unless it is for the sake of that good which the gospel announces and promises. What looks like the most costly and self-sacrificial *benevolence* must, in other words, actually be *beneficent.* This, we may recall, is precisely the reason Augustine distrusted any "love of neighbor" on the part of those who had not first learned to love themselves rightly:[140]

if they did not know that their own good lay in clinging to God as their highest good, their well-meaning efforts to love their neighbors might only deceive and mislead.[141]

The teleological ordering of self-denial in Augustine's thought appears in a revealing way at points where Augustine explained the New Testament exhortation not to seek one's own. Nygren tried to insist that Augustine's "primary definition of love" as the seeking of one's good excludes Paul's statement in 1 Corinthians 13:5 that "Love seeks not its own."[142] Standing by itself, this phrase implies that New Testament love *in turn* implies a freestanding duty not to seek one's own good. But Augustine noticed what Nygren apparently overlooked. For when Augustine thought of this phrase he associated it with a trio of other texts that place Christ-like self-sacrifice in the context of Christ's larger purposes. Those texts are (1) John 10:11–15, which contrasts the way that Jesus as the good shepherd lays down his life for the sheep who are his own, while mere hirelings care nothing for them and flee; (2) Philippians 1:15–18 and 2:21, which speak of pretenders and church workers who "are seeking their own interests, not those of Jesus Christ"; and (3) 2 Timothy 3:2 ff., which identifies the worst of such pretenders as those who love themselves or love money but do not love God at all. In such a context Augustine exhorted: "Let us, then, love not ourselves, but Him; and in feeding His sheep, let us be seeking the things which are His, not the things which are our own." Seeking not one's own did not mean for Augustine that one should not seek any good whatsoever nor dare to imagine one's own participation in that good. Rather it meant that instead of seeking a private good, one seeks a common good, the cause of Christ, which is itself the participation of all things in the mutual love of God.[143]

The Trinity of Love

If Nygren shrank from the notion that God's self-giving love in Jesus Christ could spring from a divine motive to draw creatures into the mutual love of the Trinity, then we have come once again to the irreducible point of difference between Augustine and Nygren. The latter was certain that to ascribe any motive to God's love tainted God's own sovereign, spontaneous, and overflowing love for sinners with acquisitive self-love. The former saw the sovereign majesty of God's overflowing love precisely in God's uncoerced will to share God's own trinitarian life of mutual love with sinful creatures whom that life must necessarily transform. Some of the distance between these two views may result from what John Burnaby identified as a "fatal defect in [Nygren's] whole construction," the neglect of *philia* or mutual love.[144] But surely not all. For no one will be able to adjudicate between these positions without drawing on some metaphysical presuppositions.

Nor will we be able to appropriate Augustine's notion of continence without some kind of metaphysic, for like any virtue (according to Augustine), continence must both acknowledge itself as God's gift and aim at the right end if it is to be true continence at all. And to identify which end is right requires a right appraisal of the order of good. We cannot do this without making metaphysical presuppositions. We *can*, however, do without a full and incontrovertible metaphysic. Short of a detailed metaphysical system, this order of good is already apparent in the good of mutual love, and that good is visible in the work and character of Jesus Christ.

For Augustine, even the sinful love of cupidity has a triadic structure,[145] while the right love of *caritas* has a trinitarian structure.[146] Whenever a lover loves a beloved, their very relationship comprises a third subsistent, love itself. To translate somewhat: Even where human love moves only in one direction without yet reaching mutuality, it is *a priori* impossible for the subject not to love love itself—impossible not to be drawn toward the good of right relationship itself—even before the beloved responds in kind or even after the beloved spurns that love.[147] In the fullness of mutual love, each lover continues to give self-sacrificially, for the fullness of a mutual relationship fully exposes each to the vulnerability *of* the relationship, and neither may grasp at the relationship controllingly lest it become something less than mutual. So while the trinitarian nature of love is clearest where mutual love has come into being, unidirectional sacrificial love also moves toward the *telos* of mutuality, when it risks and suffers the cost of creating the good and mutual relationship that it allows the loved one freedom to reject. Thus, to translate Augustine's trinitarian thought more freely still:

- In the love of love we see desire at work, the teleology of the Holy Spirit seeking to bind all things together joyfully in God.
- In respect for the dignity of those loved we see duty, the deontology of the Christ who learned obedience through what he suffered,

even while enduring the cross for the joy set before him (Hebrews 5:8 and 12:2).

- And in the source of all joy we see the ground of both, the gracious self-giving of God that makes all mutual love possible.

Desire for the *telos* of mutual love only seems to undermine "agapeic" sacrificial love when we confuse it with a mere contract of reciprocity. God makes covenants, not contracts. If the difference seems slight in human affairs, the scriptural account of salvation history fills up the meaning of covenant: when human beings break covenant, God takes the initiative to restore relationship. Whatever the insoluble mysteries of how God relates to time from eternity, in Jesus Christ we see that God always "goes first," risking and suffering to effect a loving relationship with creation even while creatures spurn to the point of crucifixion that communion which God offers.[148] As Augustine noticed when he preached on John 13:34 and Jesus' new yet old commandment "that you love one another," mutual love is only possible and true because "I have loved you." It is the love by which Christ loved us that ever renews God's people, so that "the members thereof have a mutual interest in one another," suffer and rejoice with one another, and God leads them to the goal of eternal blessedness, "when God will be all in all."[149]

———

For Augustine, mutual love in the body of Christ is the highest earthly good. Through such love Christians begin to participate in the very life and mutual love of the Trinity, thus anticipating the eschatological order wherein all creatures will be in right relationship because "God will be all in all." While human beings cannot perceive the good of the whole creation in coordination with all its parts, in Jesus Christ we can learn the character of God's good will, and begin to love what God loves in the way that God loves. According to the trinitarian shape of Augustine's doctrine of Christian love, Christ teaches the obedience which he himself learned through suffering—that "the joy set before him" and before us is one realized by risking love even without guarantee of reciprocal response. A joy *is* in fact set before us, and continence is the operative mode of that *caritas* which realizes this joy. Continence is thus the mediating concept that shows how Augustine affirmed a kind of right self-love yet built self-denial into his account of how human beings must pursue their good—by receiving God and all good things continently, in trust, rather than through coercive manipulation. In the grammar of Augustine's thought, continence is necessary if one is to have any higher good in a way that is not acquisitive in Nygren's pejorative sense.

Theologically, then, we see how the grammar of continence could allow Augustine to sustain evangelical self-denial. But did it in practice? Coming chapters will test Augustine's practices in various ways, by sampling how he applied his notion of *caritas*-working-through-continence when either his own life situations, or theological controversies, or the lectionary reading before him in the pulpit, or pastoral circumstances led him to address the Gospels' call to self-denial. Arguably, his record proves mixed. The requirements of continence will force us to read Augustine against himself, insofar as Augustinian continence must judge some of Augustine's most portentious ethical judgments to have been incontinent. Still, the very possibility of such an internal critique suggests the cogency of Augustine's underlying thought and the potential it continues to have for sustaining evangelical self-denial.

CHAPTER FOUR

Augustinian Continence as a Response to the Gospel Imperative

For you had converted me to yourself, so that I would seek
neither wife nor ambition in this world. . . .

Augustine, *Confessions*

Augustine certainly believed that his own conversion and subsequent Christian life were a direct response to Jesus' own hard sayings recorded in the Gospels, calling would-be followers to deny themselves and ultimately to share his cross. Augustine placed himself quite explicitly in a direct lineage of responsive discipleship. As book eight of his *Confessions* portrays the days and weeks leading up to his conversion in a garden of Milan, a series of vivid narratives had mediated to him the way of continence and humility that he must follow, as well as something of the grace he needed to do so. Among these narratives was the story of St. Anthony, who had been among the first Egyptian monks to go into the desert a century prior to Augustine's conversion.[1] As Augustine struggled amid the throes of uncertainty over whether he might embrace both continence and God's offer of grace, thus to love God stably at last, he heard the now-famous words of a childlike chant, "*Tolle, lege*—take up and read."[2] He paused briefly to puzzle over the source of the chant. But he did not hesitate at all to associate the course to which it called him with a life-changing moment in the life of Anthony.

> I checked the flow of my tears and got up, for I interpreted this solely as a command given to me by God to open the book and read the first chapter I should come upon. For I had

heard how Anthony had been admonished by a reading from the Gospel [*ex evangelica lectione . . . admonitus fuerit*] at which he chanced to be present, as if the words read were addressed to him: "Go sell what you have, and give to the poor, and you shall have treasure in heaven, and come, follow me," and that by such a portent he was immediately converted to you.[3]

Though the book of the New Testament that Augustine had within reach was Pauline, and though the text he encountered seemed to call him more explicitly to sexual than to economic continence,[4] Augustine no doubt interpreted these variations as a personalizing of the Gospel imperative for his own time, place, and situation. In fact he did go on, like Anthony, to renounce not simply marriage to a wife but also "ambition in this world."[5] Romans 13:13–14 empowered him *not* because it told him he should be continent and avoid fleshly concupiscence—this he already knew. Rather, it promised that he *could* do so as he "put on the Lord Jesus Christ." And to put on Christ is discipleship in a Pauline idiom.

To heed Jesus' words meant, for Augustine, to do so by following the exhortation of Paul and the example of Anthony. If Augustine was in continuity with the disciples who first responded to Jesus' words, he also continued a tradition that the first Christians had begun in the weeks and decades after Jesus' ascension, according to New Testament records. That was a tradition of *adapting* in order to *adopt* the gospel imperative. Many New Testament passages,[6] no less than later postcanonical works,[7] show Christian communities struggling to remain faithful to Jesus' life, teachings, and sacrificial death in new life situations. While postcanonical examples and exhortations cannot have the same authority as canonical texts, the continuing tradition witnesses with equal authority in at least one way: It reminds successive generations of Christians that they too must translate Jesus' teachings and hard sayings into their own contexts if they are to appropriate them at all.

Not only as a new convert, but later as a teacher and preacher, Augustine believed himself to be sustaining the vitality of Jesus' evangelical call to participate in the joyful beatitude of God's Reign, through lives and actions marked by self-denying or continent love. His self-perception might not coincide automatically with the judgment of history, of course, but that judgment must coincide with the complexity of Augustine's development. When a hard saying of Jesus evoked what we would now call cognitive dissonance—as when Jesus said not to resist evil or suggested hatred of one's wife—Augustine's first instinct, especially as a new preacher, was to draw on the eclectic philosophical resources of Neoplatonism and Stoicism that he had accumulated in order to make sense of both the hard saying and the life situation with which it seemed to clash. Such efforts sometimes produced premature solutions that he might later renounce or simply ignore. But even where he was least critical of his philosophical heritage, one constant is evident throughout his theological career. That constant was a commitment to marshal philosophy for the cause of faithful scriptural interpretation. This, in his memorable phrase, was to do what God had told the fleeing Israelites of Exodus to do—to carry off the "gold of Egypt."[8]

To be sure, gold can corrupt the loyalties of those who bear it with even the best of intentions. But at least Augustine set out to make the gold of Egypt serve rather than master the gospel. We may observe this pattern by analyzing the role that continence played in his initial and theologically formative response to the gospel, by inductively sampling expositions on Gospel texts that include some of Jesus' hard sayings, and by noting how he sought to sustain evangelical self-denial at critical points in his life and career. A sampling of Augustine's biography and sermons cannot be adequate to *prove* conclusively that Augustine sustained evangelical self-denial in practice. But it can demonstrate the possibilities within his theology for doing so, even while encountering some of the challenges that obstructed his best-intended efforts.

Augustine's First Response: Continence, but Why?

"For you had converted me to yourself," wrote Augustine as he closed the decisive eighth book of his *Confessions,* "so that I would seek neither wife nor ambition in this world. . . ."[9] From the time of his conversion on, continence meant much more to Augustine than sexual abstinence. As we saw in chapter 3, sexual continence was only one part of a more general phenomenon by which one comes to love rightly by relating to the objects of one's love without grasping manipulation, but rather with the trust that clings to God as one's good, who gives all other goods. Preoccupation with sexuality has in fact distracted many readers through the centuries from noticing this underlying pattern to

Augustine's thought. His experiences of sexuality were, however, a source of insight into the larger phenomenon of concupiscence and control that God's gift of continence should heal. Even if we no longer allow sexual continence to distract us from attention to general continence, therefore, the formative role that Augustine's option for celibacy played in his thought does warrant attention.

Augustine's belief that for him to become a Christian at all he must also become celibate, or sexually continent, has puzzled many of his readers.[10] Even sympathetic readers have found Augustine's conflation of commitments idiosyncratic. More critical readers have thus found reasons to judge him as having saddled the Christian tradition with his own merely personal sexual preoccupations, encouraged disdain for the body, and contributed to the tradition's wariness if not misogyny toward women.[11] What has puzzled many is that Augustine never insisted or even intimated that others must embrace celibacy in order to become fully and authentically Christian—so why did he assume this of himself?[12] As Confessions 8.1.2 portrays the period in which Augustine wished, yet hesitated, to become a Christian, he already knew from 1 Corinthians 7:27–35 that "your apostle did not forbid me to marry." Yet the reason he gave for his failure to love God, despite his longing to enjoy "your sweetness and the beauty of your house, which I loved," was that "I was still tightly bound by love of women." Thus, when the apostle Paul "exhorted me to something better" than marriage, Augustine took that exhortation as a positive command. Somehow, even though he was now engaged to marry a young Catholic girl,[13] he was sure that he would marry for wrong reasons. For him, the Pauline middle course of Christian marriage would itself be incompatible with his anticipated life as a Christian.

The text of Augustine's Confessions suggests additional clues as to why Augustine became sexually continent. That decision actually points beyond itself toward a larger role for continence, in relation to far more than sexuality alone.[14] Chief among these clues is Augustine's regular juxtaposition of sexual issues with issues of power and ambition.[15] Early in the Confessions Augustine noted that even his pious Christian mother Monica had discouraged him from marriage because a wife (particularly one of his own class, we may assume) would have held back his rise into the ruling class by way of a career in rhetoric. Precisely when such hopes bore spectacular fruit in an upward mobility that led all the way into the emperor's summer court at Milan,

Monica (and perhaps Augustine himself) found it convenient to send away the lower-class mother of Augustine's son and arrange a suitable marriage for him into an upper-class Milanese family. Once Augustine tasted worldly success, he claimed in 8.1.2, his desire for honor and wealth fell away first, leaving an unvarnished desire for women as the last shackle holding him back from a stable love for God. Yet if the very juxtaposition of ambition and sexuality in this paragraph does not hint that matters were more complex, Augustine's later confession must: Once he actually committed himself to a life of sexual continence, he discovered that the desire for recognition and influence, honor and power, resurfaced to become his most intractable temptation, which could dog a Christian bishop in relentlessly subtle ways.[16]

Glimpses into actual Roman bedrooms are relatively rare in ancient literature, but the ones that Augustine left in his texts consistently show that the pathos he saw there had less to do with the allure of sexual pleasure per se than with a drive for domineering power that used other people in a way wholly incompatible with Christian love. He once called his own relationship with the mother of his son "the bargain [pactum] of a lustful love," even though he had been "faithful to her bed" for some fourteen years.[17] Such an evaluation may have repressed as much truth about the relationship as it revealed, for his love for this unnamed woman was probably more mutual, respectful, and tender than Augustine would later know how to admit to himself.[18] What is certain, however, is that power in Augustine's relationship with the woman was quite unbalanced. In this sense it was more of a bargain for him, in fact, than it was a pact between the two. As deep as his love for her might have been—deep enough that this most introspective of men may himself have never fathomed its good and life-giving qualities—he still could conspire all too easily in her summary dismissal.[19]

Augustine provided glimpses into other Roman bedrooms and households as well; their images of power, domination, and abuse show less chiaroscuro, but are still quite haunting. His own parents' household is itself an example. Augustine's mother was astute about the fact that Roman marriage contracts amounted to "legal instruments making [women] slaves." Wife-beatings were clearly the norm among Monica's friends, who were surprised that with a "sharp-tempered husband" such as Patricius, Monica neither divulged nor showed signs of beatings. Her advice to them was a prudent policy of controlling their tongues and waiting to challenge their husbands until their anger subsided. Yet a woman who knew how to hold her tongue in this way might not be revealing everything; Augustine characterized his father's anger as *"fervidus"*—boiling, seething, or perhaps (as John Ryan translated the word) openly "violent." One thing at least is clear. Even if Monica managed to avoid provoking dangerous quarrels with her husband, she certainly "endured offenses against her marriage bed."[20]

Of course, women of all centuries have endured the unfaithfulness of husbands, if that was the allusion, but danger and degradation were present in marriage chambers too. In book six, chapter nine of the *City of God* Augustine inadvertently showed us what might happen on a Roman wedding night.[21] Just look, jeered Augustine, at how many gods the Romans must invoke for a new husband to complete the business of overcoming and "ravishing the virginity" of his bride. Though she might be a girl as young as fourteen who "feels the weakness of her sex and is terrified by the strangeness of her situation," and though he was usually a much older man, the Romans needed three different gods just to get her into the bedroom, and at least five more to undress, subdue, press, and penetrate her. Most of these gods were minor bureaucrats in the pagan system of divine administration, yet they acted in league with that whole pantheon of idolatry, deception, and lust for domination which, according to Augustine's larger argument in *City of God,* founds and upholds the "earthly city." As the name of the goddess Venus allegedly and fancifully implied, "'not without violence' (*vi non sine*) can a woman be robbed of her virginity." Venus alone could have offered adequate aid to do the deed. But the lust for domination, apparently, is nothing if not excessive. All these gods had their part to play in upholding the empire, and that part was to legitimate and conspire in the legalized rape of a frightened fourteen-year-old girl.[22]

If these were the violent associations that sexuality carried for Augustine, we need hardly wonder that he could never bring himself to see even the most faithful and tender sexual pleasure of married Christians as entirely pristine and without taint. Had Adam and Eve not sinned, Augustine eventually surmised, spouses would have joined together in "a faithful partnership based on love and mutual respect." With "a harmony and a liveliness of mind and body" they would have relaxed in one another's arms tenderly and peacefully, without their passions and sexual organs exercising a will of their own. Now, however, even a man who fulfilled the New Testament command to mate "in holiness and honor" would have to do so by turning to good use the evil of concupiscence, bridling and restraining that "rage" which "works in inordinate and indecorous motions."[23]

While any answer to the question of why Augustine embraced celibacy must finally involve an element of speculation, a simple explanation may be best. Whatever the case for other men, Augustine had come to know himself well enough to recognize that he simply could not get sex right. Everything we know about Augustine tells us he was a passionate, domineering personality. With his rhetorical flare, he could roast his opponents and charm his friends. Even when he thought he had renounced worldly ambition and accepted humble anonymity in backwater cities of provincial North Africa, he always ended up at the center of a well-connected circle of friends and correspondents.[24] If even the best of human friendship remained for him a problematic, lifelong mystery,[25] then he must certainly avoid the uncertainties of that most potent human relation, sexual coupling, which could be as devastating as it could be creative. All the more, when it carried so many violent associations.

It is pointless to try to decide whether Augustine's experiences determined his theological insights, or whether his theology gave him insights into his experiences. At one level, Augustine had ample biblical precedent for using sexuality as a metaphor for unfaithfulness to God; Psalm 73(72):27–28 in particular told him that clinging to God was the answer to the philosopher's ancient question about what comprised the human good, even as it contrasted such clinging with fornication against God. At another level, he may well have seized upon this text because it made sense of his own experience with sexuality, which had dissipated his very sense of self so that his only chance of personal reintegration was a newly unified, single-hearted love for God.[26] Must such an analysis mean that everything he said in his massive critique of Roman self-assertion had roots in his sexual experiences? Perhaps so—yet it is far too easy for modern readers to assume that once they have traced the genealogical roots of his ideas, they have exhausted the insights that drew on them. Roots nourish fruits, but fruits bear within them the code for sending out new roots and thus nurturing further insights.[27]

In fact, to ask whether theological insight or life experience came first may well be to miss Augustine's point, where continence and concupiscence are in question. In the fallen human condition that poses such questions, errant sexuality is both an effect and a cause, according to Augustine. In his theory of original sin, sexual concupiscence exemplified the much larger drive for control and domination that simultaneously generated rich creativity and harsh injustice in human society. But sexuality was such a ready example precisely because that drive in turn expressed itself so poignantly and inextricably in human sexuality. When modern readers allow Augustine's theory of original sin to repel them, they often miss this lesson. Yet it was never lost on Augustine himself, even amid his more arcane debates with the Pelagians. Self-assertive pride, not sexual pleasure, was *the* original human sin. To be sure, for every generation after the first, sexuality conspired within the complex of original sin. And once such a cycle sets in motion, it becomes pointless to ask whether lust for bodies or lust for power comes first; each expresses and generates the other. Although we must resign ourselves to reading each in light of the other, we must not lose sight of insights into human domination that may well have been the real import of Augustine's analysis of sexual concupiscence. Even as he committed himself to a life of celibacy, Augustine was beginning to recognize the general role of "*higher* continence" in the practice of *all* love.[28]

A Premature Solution: Interior and Otherworldly Self-Denial

In 394 Augustine preached and wrote his only complete commentary on Jesus' Sermon on the Mount as it appears in Matthew 5–7. He was a year or two away from elevation to the bishop's chair; theologically, he was also about to enter a crucial time of transition. The commentary thus reflects Augustine's approach to biblical interpretation and to morals as fully as it had developed in his early period, prior to his fresh reading of Paul, to his initial writing *On Christian Doctrine,* and to his *Confessions.* It thus suggests how he first attempted to sustain evangelical self-denial not just as he responded to the gospel call in his own life, but as he began to commend it to other Christians through exposition of the biblical texts before him in the pulpit.

Augustine's preached commentary *On the Lord's Sermon on the Mount* suggests that an eclectic blend of Stoic and Neoplatonic habits of mind had shaped his initial approach to evangelical self-denial. As he portrayed Jesus' sermon in the opening chapter, it presents "the highest morals, a perfect standard of the Christian life," and it contains "all the precepts which go to mold the life" of the wise. According to his interpretation of the beatitudes, they marked an ascent from a God-fearing humility that is the "beginning of wisdom," through the meekness of those who do not "quarrel and fight for earthly and temporal things," and on to a highly interior, Stoicized conception of what it means to be a blessed "peacemaker." The perfection of peace, he was sure, is free of conflicts and opposition; peacemakers therefore are those who bring order to the motions of their souls, subjecting them to reason and subduing their carnal lusts. "And this is the peace which is given on earth to men of goodwill; this is the life of the fully developed and perfect wise man." An early tendency of Augustine toward perfectionism would appear repeatedly in this work, and come back to haunt him amid the Pelagian controversy. An abiding tendency to interiorize the ethic of Jesus would also appear most markedly in this work, and come back to haunt later traditions of Augustinian Christianity.[29]

In fact, what may be the most radical statement of otherworldliness in Augustine's entire corpus appears midway through his discussion of Matthew 5. It came as he sought to explain why, if Jesus taught his disciples not to put away their wives, he also commended hatred of wife in Luke 14:26.[30] This hard saying required explanation precisely because it caused a certain cognitive dissonance among average pious Christians, or as Augustine put it, tended "to disturb the minds of the little ones, who nevertheless earnestly desire to live now according to the precepts of Christ." Augustine's answer was that if Christians want to aim for the life of God's kingdom, they are not to hate the persons themselves, but the "temporal relationships" that constitute this "transitory . . . dying" life. In Christ there is neither male nor female, he noted, and marriage will not be part of the resurrected life. Thus, "if I were to ask any good Christian who has a wife . . . whether he would like to have his wife in that kingdom" which is incorruptible, he would vigorously reply in the negative—but if one asked the same Christian whether he would like his wife to undergo an angelic transformation and join him in that life, he would reply just as vigorously in the affirmative. "Thus in one and the same woman a good Christian is found to love the creature of God, whom he desires to be transformed and renewed; but to hate the corruptible and mortal conjugal connection and sexual intercourse: *i.e.* to love in her what is characteristic of a human being, to hate what belongs to her as a wife."³¹ Read in isolation, such a formula would seem only to confirm the suspicions of those who see in Augustine's thought the tendency of Stoic and Neoplatonic influences to produce a callous lack of love for neighbors amid their mundane neediness, at best, and an otherworldly hatred of all things temporal and bodily, at worst.

The effect such a formula would have on Christlike love of enemy was unclear. For parents, kin, and enemies alike, "the disciple of Christ should hate these things which pass away," out of the disciple's very desire that they too will "reach those things which shall forever remain." In fact, "the more he loves them," the *more* the disciple should hate those passing things. Augustine was consistent enough, for just as he expected a good Christian both to love and to hate his wife, "So also he loves his enemy, not in as far as he is an enemy, but in as far as he is a man," wishing that the enemy like himself might enjoy such "prosperity" as will come when both "reach the kingdom of heaven rectified and renewed."³² Insofar as this formula allows Christians to distinguish persons from their roles so as to retain respect for them as human beings in every circumstance—or insofar as it encourages Christians to hold less violently to their own temporal goods and bodily preservation—the formula may raise no ethical objections. Yet Augustine had said nothing here about wishing one's enemy any good on earth, or any earthly prosperity, or even the fulfillment of basic needs such as Paul had listed in Romans 12:20. Too sharp a distinction between person and role, or soul and body, could thus help rationalize repressive policies against heretics or schismatics for the sake of their eternal welfare.

When Augustine came to Jesus' call for enemy love in Matthew 5:38–48, he began by laying out a logical continuum of human responses to injury. At one end are those many people who are inclined to avenge any blow with even greater force. In the middle is the "lesser righteousness of the Pharisees," who insist upon a measured response, eye for eye, tooth for tooth; "this is the beginning of peace: but perfect peace is to have no wish at all for such vengeance." At the other end, Jesus urged his disciples to move beyond a response of reduced violence or a merely passive turning of the cheek, according to Augustine, and on to the active preparation of one's heart to do good. "For many have learned how to offer the other cheek, but do not know how

to love him by whom they are struck." As salvation history unfolded—
or "according to the distribution of times"—God had been seeking to
move people toward a higher perfection, "from the highest discord to
the highest concord."[33]

Did this mean that the beatitude of the peacemakers applied to
those who made peace among human beings, rather than simply
within themselves? Perhaps, yet for the most part Augustine still wrote
of enemies as though they merely offered an especially apt training
ground for the virtues one needed for one's own moral perfection. For
example, a righteousness that surpassed the Pharisees required that a
Christian do more than love neighbors while yet hating enemies, for
"in the kingdom of Him who came to fulfill the law, not to destroy it,
[a person] will bring benevolence and kindness to perfection, when
he has carried it out so far as to love an enemy."[34]

For the problem of how, in light of Jesus' call for nonresistance, to
correct or punish wrongdoers, Augustine's tendency to interiorize
Jesus' ethic provided him with a ready answer. Being "prepared to endure more at the hand of him whom [one] wishes to set right" does
not preclude "inflicting such punishment [*vindicta*] as avails for correction, and as compassion itself dictates." Matthew 5:45 makes clear
that the perfection of love in love for enemies reflects the very perfection of "the Father Himself," yet the Lord corrects and even scourges
those He loves. Weight from the gospel imperative remained in Augustine's insistence on interior readiness to suffer, on compassion, and
on a heart free of vengeance—for "no one is fit for inflicting this punishment except the man who, by the greatness of his love, has overcome that hatred wherewith those are wont to be inflamed wish to
avenge themselves."[35]

Yet just how weighty did the gospel imperative then remain? Interior disposition is of great importance, and in the Sermon on the
Mount Jesus himself took pains to move his disciples beyond a merely
external and legalistic righteousness. Moreover, the New Testament itself expects that the church will enact certain social sanctions as part
of its own redemptive discipline or fraternal correction.[36]

Still, the more interior the purview of criteria for ethical action,
the less they remain measurable.[37] A demand for good intentions may
itself become no more than a platitude. Augustine might later in-
struct a general such as Boniface that he should make peace his only
desire even in war.[38] But Augustine himself believed that all creatures,

including monsters and robbers, seek peace anyway, so that the sole normative content in Augustine's instruction to Boniface lay in the word "only." Applied stringently, Augustine's criterion of right intention would require soldiers and policymakers to become saints free of all hatred and desire for vengeance before they were "fit for inflicting . . . punishment." But was that really workable?[39]

Interiorization alone could hardly sustain Jesus' evangelical imperatives. For alone, without attention to concrete exterior actions, interior criteria are not only vague and platitudinous but incoherent. About six years after preaching his commentary on the Sermon on the Mount, Augustine suggested in a debate with the Manichaean Faustus that "[t]he real evils in war" are not the deaths of those who would die anyway, but "love of violence, revengeful cruelty, fierce and implacable enmity, wild resistance, and the lust of power." The statement is a classic of Augustine's interiorization—yet none of these evils can really be evil unless the sufferings they inflict are also real. And if pain and death and social conflict and domination are "real evils," they must be the concern of Christian teaching after all.

Apparently Augustine came to recognize this. Few have written more eloquently of the concrete sufferings of human life than Augustine would eventually do in the closing pages of *City of God*. Though he looked toward eschatological release from human misery in the heavenly city, he could not have written such words if earthly pains were not overpoweringly real to him. In the end, even in heaven, only a resurrected body could compensate for such suffering, not a bodiless resurrection.[40]

In any case, while Augustine always retained a certain suspicion of love for temporal goods and relationships, he would not continue to state his suspicion in terms as radical as he did when he sought to explain why Jesus had told disciples to hate their wives. Thoroughgoing otherworldliness of the sort that despised all things temporal was a false solution that he himself came to reject.[41]

A Conflicted Return: Concrete Demands Again

Of course, frank worldliness would hardly sustain evangelical self-denial any more than interior or otherworldly self-denial. For over three centuries Christians had gradually come to face a problem they sometimes sensed but usually struggled to name—the mixed blessing of social toleration.[42] Further, for over eight decades now many had embraced this blessing in the form of the Emperor Constantine's legal toleration of Christianity. When the "blessing" became official in the 380s, as Emperor Theodosius made Christianity the religion of the empire, the mixture of imperial and churchly interests and tensions that some call "Constantinianism" only grew more potent. Church leaders who enjoyed a new intimacy with political power and intrigue might still express unease when problems grew up in their own communities that (in hindsight) the very climate of toleration and then prestige seems to have nurtured. Across the Mediterranean a contemporary of Augustine's, John Chrysostom, would exert great influence on events in Antioch through his preaching during a time of crisis, and later become bishop at the political center of the empire in Constantinople, though against his will.[43] Yet without crisis even Chrysostom's powerful preaching barely altered the lifestyles of his congregation, which now differed little from those of non-Christians. Even the salutary moral impact of an earthquake might only last a few days, he once lamented.[44]

Augustine has a reputation as both a more astute politician and a less rigorous moralist than Chrysostom. Yet Augustine too struggled against some forces that Constantinian tolerance had brought to the church, even as he sought to harness other such forces on its behalf. For all the fame as an opponent of perfectionism that Augustine's polemics against the Donatists and the Pelagians have brought him,[45] Augustine never entirely loosened the tension in Christianity between a forgiving inclusivity that takes its extreme in moral "laxism" and a demanding exclusivity that takes its extreme in moral "rigorism." Augustine the novice theologian had portrayed salvation as an ascent toward moral perfection, yet his earliest works against the Manichaeans were quick to criticize the moral elitism of the Manichaean inner circle.[46] Augustine the mature theologian would be even quicker to criticize what he regarded as the moral presumption of Pelagians who thought perfection possible in this life,[47] yet even the anti-Pelagian Augustine refused to relinquish the conviction that God's grace must ultimately transform and sanctify sinful human beings so that they merit or become fit for that very salvation which is a gift.[48] Midway through his career Augustine preached on Jesus' healing of two blind men in Matthew 20:29–34, in a sermon now catalogued as number 88 and dated around the year 400. In it he attempted to negotiate these forces by marking out a position somewhere between the moral rigorism of North Africa's Donatist Christians, and the moral laxism within his own congregation.

Matthew 20 recounts the story of two blind men who heard Jesus passing along the road and cried out for mercy and for sight, only to receive a rebuke from the crowds who told them to be silent. In this story Augustine found a mirror for tensions in his own Christian community. However intermixed with worldly society his church was becoming as a result of Christianity's new official status, it was not so established that it ceased "to give birth to" new converts "such as these" two men. They had a zeal to see God and to be healed. They began "to live well [i.e., righteously], to be fervent in good works, and to despise the world." But this exposed them to the criticisms and contradictions of "cold Christians"—the "many Christians in name, and in works ungodly," the "wicked Christians," the "sinners, and sensual men, . . . lovers of the vanities of the world."[49]

The flash point at the moment for tensions between younger ardent Christians and older colder ones was attendance at public shows. If none except "heathens and Jews" ran to the shows, so few people would be there that a Christian would leave in shame; but no, "Christians run thither also, bearing the Holy Name only to their condemnation" and amassing crowds that compared all too well with the rude ones who had followed Jesus on the Palestine road. "A good Christian," meanwhile, "has no wish to attend the public shows," but instead is continent: "In this very thing, that he bridles his desire of going to the theater, he cries out after Christ, cries out to be healed." Yet the shows were *only* a flash point. The community's real tensions ran deeper still, involved more fundamental social and economic issues, and raised fresh questions about how to respond to Jesus' own ethic.[50]

Each part of the community was "crying out," after all, though in different ways. On one hand, those who cried out for healing from their blindness did so by despising the world, despising its pleasures and saying not only with their tongues but with their lives that the world was crucified to them and they to the world. Specifically, those who "have distributed freely, [and] given to the poor" were those who cried out to Christ through their very works.

> For let him that hears, and is not deaf to the sound, "sell what you have, and give to the poor; provide yourselves bags which do not grow old, a treasure in the heavens that does not fail"; when he hears the sound (as it were) of Christ's footsteps "passing by," let him cry out in response to this in his blindness—that is, let him do these things. Let his voice be in his actions. Let him begin to despise the world, to distribute to the poor his goods, to esteem as nothing worth what other men love, let him disregard injuries, not seek to be avenged, let him give his "cheek to the smiter," let him pray for his enemies; if any "one have taken away his goods," let "him not ask for them again"; if he "have taken anything from any man, let him restore fourfold."

On the other hand, those who had been in the church longer were crying out with accusations that every fresh generation of Christians must probably hear at some time, the charge that they are naive and fanatical when they try to live according to Jesus' teachings. For when such a Christian begins to do these things,

> all his kinsmen, relations, and friends will be in commotion. They who love this world, will oppose him. What madness this! you are too extreme [nimius]: what! are not other men Christians! This is folly, this is madness. And other such things do the multitude cry out to prevent the blind from crying out.

So it must go, predicted Augustine, until the end of the world.[51]

Though Augustine's acumen here did not require modern sociology of religion, he did struggle to name the trends he was in some ways bucking, though in other ways abetting: "Brethren, do you see my meaning? For I know not how to speak, but still less do I know how to be silent. I will speak then, and speak plainly." After all, the New Testament supplied him with its own vocabulary: "Evil and lukewarm Christians hinder good Christians who are truly earnest [studiosos], and wish to do the commandments of God which are written in the Gospel." Yet a false "authority of numbers" might mislead them into presuming that "those who become Christians before them" offer models to imitate. In fact, prevailing models of "Christian" life ran counter to the Gospel. So the "good Christians" should not say,

"Let us live as all these others live." Why not rather live as the Gospel ordains? Why do you wish to live according to the remonstrances of the multitude who would hinder you, and not after the steps of the Lord, "who passes by"? They will mock, and abuse, and call you back; you must cry out until you reach the ears of Jesus. For those who shall persevere in doing such things as Christ has enjoined, and regard not the multitudes that hinder them, nor think much of their appearing to follow Christ . . . shall on no account be separated from Him, and Jesus will "stand still," and make them whole.

Repeatedly Augustine exhorted the earnest Christians to persevere in crying out. For the cry of both their righteous works and their protest would not only be a prayer to God but a witness to the crowds.[52]

Eventually, hoped Augustine, those who first rebuked would come instead to respect the perseverance of earnest Christians and honor them, just as in a Markan parallel the crowd eventually acknowledged to the blind man that Jesus "is calling you."[53] Whatever temptations the crowd of rude and "lukewarm" Christians inflicted, the crowd remained precisely the place for earnest followers of Christ to speak and act: "Cry out amidst the very crowds, despair not of reaching the ears of the Lord. For the blind men in the Gospel did not cry out in that quarter where no crowd was" so that Christ might hear them without impediment; likewise, "Go not to another quarter to cry out unto the Lord, go not to the heretics, and cry out unto Him there." After all, Christ's call was that those who labor should come unto him, and this must apply to everyone in the world, where all labor with their sins. When Christ beckoned "Come," the invitation was to a house that was not so narrow as to exclude any. In a mysterious way, claimed Augustine, the Matthean passage indicated plainly what other texts in the sacred books expressed, "that there are within the Church both good and bad, as I often express it, wheat and chaff."[54]

Here then, with a measure of both hope and resignation, Augustine labored against the schismatic rigorism he saw in North Africa's Donatists even while struggling against the growing worldliness of his own congregation. Augustine's admittedly frequent appeals to the image of wheat and chaff might rationalize this worldliness (along with the Parable of Wheat and Tares). No one should separate from the unity of the church, he believed, for that would be to "leave the [threshing] floor before the time" of final bodily separation in God's "barn" of harvested grain. Until then, the wheat must "bear with the chaff in the time of threshing" and do this nowhere except on "the floor." Continuing his attempt to strike a balance, Augustine added: "In heart be always separated from the bad, in body be united with them for a time, only with caution."[55]

To his credit, Augustine's motive was not simply to rationalize the presence of "the bad" within the church. It was also to retain the witness of "the good" within the church, in the hope that they would yet contribute to a miraculous conversion of chaff into wheat. To earnest Christians in his midst Augustine's exhortation was that they not tire of applying fraternal correction. In this sermon at least, the need for "admonition," "instruction," "exhortation," and even "threats" so as to correct the erring "in any way you can" applied more to worldly Catholics than to schismatic Donatists.[56] The wheat should not leave the threshing floor before the winnower came; only in spirit and heart should they be separated from the chaff for now, while "in body [they remained] united for a time, only with caution." And during this intermediary, intermixed period the wheat must continue to correct most sternly:

> Yet be not negligent in correcting those who belong to you, who in any way appertain to your charge, by admonition, or instruction, by exhortation, or by threats. Do it, in whatever way you can. . . . In two ways the bad will not defile you: if you do not consent to him, and if you reprove him; this is, not to communicate with him, not to consent to him. . . . This the Apostle teaches us, when he says, "Have no communication with the unfruitful works of darkness." And because it was a small matter not to consent, if negligence of correction accompanied it, he says, "But rather reprove them." See how he included both at once. . . . What is, "Have no communication"? Do not consent to them, do not praise them, do not approve them. What is, "But rather reprove them"? Find fault with, rebuke, repress them.[57]

Still, Augustine had clearly resigned himself to the fact that a majority of Christians in the church that now represented official religion in the Roman Empire would fall so far short of lives such as "the Gospel ordains" that the name "Christian" applied to them only with adjectives like "evil" and "lukewarm." And when, in just a few more years, Augustine turned to the imperial apparatus for help to consolidate the church's own hegemony and "correct" the Donatists through the state's coercive sanctions, he would further consolidate that very situation to which he was both resigned and opposed.

Nevertheless, Augustine's sermon around the year 400 on Matthew 20:29–34 marks development in directions that some of his modern critics might consider more positive contributions within a mixed legacy of Augustinianism. First, the temporal economy and temporal relationships now had an increasingly positive role to play in Augustine's theology. Although Augustine's notion of the "threshing floor" converged with a contestable (though widely received) interpretation of the Parable of Wheat and Tares, it does imply that the arena of temporal life and bodily relationships is one to which God calls Christians not just for a hateful time of testing, but also for a positive witness on behalf of others. Likewise, the healing of the blind men's eyes, as well as our own, may not be complete until we "attain to the knowledge of Him as 'standing still' in His unchangeable Eternity"—yet healing *does* begin "by faith [as] we perceive Christ 'passing by' in the temporal economy [*dispensatione*]." "All the things which were done by our Lord Jesus Christ in time graft faith in us."[58]

Second, Augustine's deepening reflection on Christ's incarnation continued to loosen his dependence on Stoic and Platonic categories of interpretation. "We believe on the Son of God," he noted, "not on the Word only." For although all things were made through the immutable Word, according to both Greek thought and John 1, it is through the Word made flesh in birth to the Virgin Mary that the blind are able to hear Jesus "passing by" in the mutable world and cry out for healing. And that cry too is concrete, through "their life exemplifying the profession of their faith."[59]

Third, Augustine was finding a way to retain a place for this life of good works modeled on Jesus' own, even as he rejected the presumption of perfectionism and the possibility of salvation by merit. Though one could not merit salvation, nor would one's healing be complete in this life, nor could one be either saved or healed except by God's grace, Augustine could not conceive of a salvation that did not begin transforming the human person within time. Elsewhere he would hold these notions together by speaking in various ways of human beings being *made* to merit a life of eternal communion with God.[60] Here, Augustine clarified the place of works with the explanation that while good works are a way of crying out for healing, these works are still only a way "to correspond [*congruere*] to the grace of Christ," which must surely be prior to all human working.[61]

Finally, in all of this, Augustine was showing that although he still retained a Neoplatonic tendency to spiritualize (and occasionally allegorize) the meaning of scripture, he could also use this method not only to interiorize but to concretize the demands of the Gospel. The text before him, after all, did not require him to interpret the blind men's cries as works—much less to specify works that involved giving to the poor, despising wealth, rejecting vengeance, turning one's cheek, praying for one's enemies, and forgiving injustices to oneself, all while correcting injustices one had committed.[62] But his pastorate apparently did so require, while his theology at least so allowed.

If Augustine's theology did not consistently sustain evangelical self-denial, that may be due to another variable. Augustine knew the church to be on pilgrimage, living between Christ's efficacious self-sacrifice on the cross and the eschatological fullness of mutual love. Yet he never fully fleshed out his ecclesiology for a pilgrim church with sociological specificity.[63] His conception of continence might have reminded him not to grasp after a fullness for which pilgrims must still patiently trust. Instead, ecclesiological impatience might bring an incontinence that rendered evangelical self-denial unsteady.

What Kind of Cross? For What Kind of Church?

It has been a perennial question for Christians since the first century: Since Christ has tarried and with him the eschaton, how shall we live in time, in the world, yet live according to God's eternal purposes as Jesus incarnated them? Augustine may have done much to shape how the question has come down to Christians in the West. Yet a question it remained to the end, even for him.

By 417 Augustine had written roughly half of the *City of God*—his massive exploration of the relationship between the heavenly city of creatures who were faithful to God's will in heaven or who were still on pilgrimage toward such faithfulness, and the earthly city of those who disdained God's will with a proud self-assertion that culminated in imperial domination such as Rome's. Not for nine more years would

Augustine write book nineteen of *City of God,* his most nuanced statement of how God's pilgrim people should live amid the fallen earthly city, which offers a useful but quite imperfect kind of peace. But even this memorable statement would not offer a definitive solution to the perennial problem of how to live in time. Rather, at most it would define the ongoing tension for those who, like Jeremiah's exiles, seek and "make use of the peace of Babylon," without either rejecting it entirely, or loving it as an end they might possess eternally.[64]

By 417 Augustine had, however, written as far as book eleven of the *City of God* and had promised to outline "the rise, the development and the destined ends of the two cities" that are "interwoven, as it were, in this present transitory world, and mingled with one another." The underlying dynamics of the two cities were becoming clearer as Augustine explored the contrasting forms of power that the angelic components of each city exercised at the service of their contrasting loves and objects of worship. And within a year or two Augustine would conclude book fourteen with the summary statement that "the two cities were created by two kinds of love; the earthly city was created by self-love reaching the point of contempt for God, the Heavenly City by the love of God carried as far as contempt of self"; thus, the earthly city glories in itself, lusts for domination, loves its own strength, and proudly follows its own wisdom, while the Heavenly City "glories in the Lord," its members serve one another in love, it loves God as its true strength, and its wisdom is to worship God alone.[65]

But what might this transhistorical panorama of cities, angels, powers, and loves mean for an individual Christian or a single Christian community in ordinary days and weeks? Around 417 Augustine preached a sermon on Mark 8:34—"If any want to become my followers, let them deny themselves and take up their cross and follow me."[66] If the Heavenly City loved God with a love "carried as far as contempt of self," then Augustine's doctrine of love must show itself able to bear fruit not only in a panoramic theology of history, but in a mundane continence among Augustine's listeners that sustained living continuity with Jesus' evangelical imperatives. Augustine's sermon on Mark 8:34, now catalogued as number 96, certainly shows that he felt the tug of Jesus' own ethic of self-denying love, and expected all Christians to feel that same tug. Though we may ultimately conclude that some of Augustine's ethical judgments and ecclesial policies failed to sustain evangelical self-denial, the question of whether or not his theology in its basic structure contributed to such a failure should at least remain an open one. For in a sermon such as this one, Augustine's theology had opportunity to bear fruit by making Jesus' words live among, call out, and empower Christians afresh within new life situations that inevitably differed from those of Jesus' first disciples.

Wherever this happened, in fact, Jesus' evangelical imperatives might not actually be "hard sayings" at all. Convention has provided this handy label for those statements by which Jesus anticipated that his disciples would suffer or deny themselves vis-à-vis their families, in relation to their possessions, in love for their enemies, and at cost to their very lives. But to label Jesus' words as "hard" may say more about those who do the labeling than about the sayings themselves. As Augustine began Sermon 96, he suggested as much.

"For whatsoever is hard in what is enjoined us, charity makes easy." Jesus' charge to follow and deny oneself in Mark 8:34 looks hard and grievous, Augustine observed, yet Jesus himself helps us do what he has charged. Jesus' "yoke is easy" precisely because love makes it easy, Augustine assured. "We know what great things love itself can do." Even an impure love empowers men to endure great sufferings and indignities for the sake of the money, honor, or women that they love impurely; in their great "love" they may not even be conscious of their labors. Augustine made two points. First, most people "are such as their loves are," and so the most critical choice in regulating our lives is "the choice of that which we ought to love." A further implication is that if Jesus' sayings seem hard to us, that may bespeak the character of our love and thus the people that we are. Augustine's second point, after all, challenged his listeners to self-examination: "why do you wonder, if those who love Christ, and who wish to follow Christ, deny themselves for the love of Him?"[67]

In any case, all this had roots in the apparent paradox of self-denial as the Gospels themselves had stated it: "For if by loving himself man is lost," Augustine paraphrased, "surely by denying himself is he found."[68] Yet it also had roots in Augustine's own experiences of continence, years of theological reflection, and the spirituality that resulted from both. When Augustine assured his listeners that Jesus himself was helping them do what he charged, for example, he was drawing on the same reflections that years before had led him to pray,

"Give what you command and command what you will."[69] Two things can happen when roots intermingle. One set of roots can choke off another, as with weeds. Or one set of roots can nourish another, as with the legumes that some gardeners plant amid their nutrient-depleting corn stalks. The biblical witness and Augustine's theology of Christian love seem in many ways to have nourished one another mutually, yet the sprouts that some critics might consider weeds also appeared—and in poorer soils these might come to thrive. Weeds or not, Augustine's way of sustaining evangelical self-denial did admit certain ambiguities.

First of all, to compare the self-denial of Christian discipleship with the sufferings of those who love illicit objects risked reducing it to mere delayed gratification. Elsewhere Augustine might take pains to distinguish Christian *caritas* from delayed gratification,[70] yet in the pulpit his rhetorical interests apparently led him to ignore such distinctions.[71] The technique was akin to Augustine's appeals to a universal desire for happiness; amid philosophical debates, his interlocutors must acknowledge this common point and might even find grounds for conversion. Earlier, we outlined replies to critics of Augustine's eudaemonism, and those replies also apply to Augustine's treatment of natural human love: he avoided an egocentric account of both self-love and self-denial by showing that Christianity did not simply promise a better way to reach ends that all people might desire or define for themselves. Rather, it required change, refinement, and training of human desire so that one loved in accordance with God's will for human existence. So with Mark 8:34 before him, Augustine insisted and exhorted that "The first destruction of man, was the love of himself. . . . For this is to love one's self [perversely], to wish to do one's own will. Prefer to this God's will; learn to love yourself [rightly] by not loving yourself."[72] In light of the travail, pain, and fear of earthly life, everyone would want to follow Christ to supreme happiness, peace, and security, if following did not mean taking up the cross of dishonor, scourging, mockery, and death. But Jesus was explicit: deny yourself by taking up the cross and following; in this way, "follow on."[73]

Even if Augustine himself avoided reducing evangelical self-denial to delayed gratification, Christian thinkers in the tradition that followed from Augustine have not always been so careful. Certainly many have been even less careful to prevent another ambiguity in the way that Augustine sustained evangelical self-denial, one which risks diffusing such self-denial. Over the centuries the tendency has been to keep cross-bearing alive by associating its meaning with more and more kinds of general human suffering.[74]

Second, then, Augustine was already demonstrating a certain tendency to transform "the cross" into *any* of life's nagging irritations and troubles. What cross is the disciple to take up? asked Augustine. "Let him bear whatever trouble he has; so let him follow" Christ.[75]

In context, Augustine did have certain kinds of troubles in mind. They were precisely the troubles that resulted from commitment to Christ's cause: "For when he shall begin to follow Me in conformity to My life and precepts, he will have many to contradict him, he will have many to hinder him, he will have many to dissuade him, and that from among those who are even as it were Christ's companions." Augustine had not forgotten about the blind men and the crowds of Mark 10, on which he had preached years earlier, for again he noted that those "who hindered the blind men from crying out were walking with Christ." Whether these less-than-faithful Christians offered "threats or caresses" or other hindrances, anyone who wished to follow Christ in truth must "turn them into [their] cross, bear it, carry it, [and] not give way beneath it."[76]

Thus the words of the Lord contained an "exhortation to martyrdom" even for those who must witness in times that proffered a new set of obstacles. These were subtler temptations than the outright opposition of earlier times, precisely because they now came on the lips of those who bore the name but not the cross of Christ, and who followed after his renown but not his cause. If Augustinian continence was an appropriate way both to translate and to sustain evangelical self-denial within this new context, that was because subtler temptations required subtler resistance. Now that external opposition to Christ seemed to have subsided, internal preparation to follow Christ must receive greater attention. That would be interiorization at its best—not avoiding but preparing for external practice. Though Augustine did not use the term here, continence was in fact what prepared the heart to sustain faithfulness in the face of new forms of persecution by diminishing contrary desires through the tenacity of a greater love for the greatest good: "If there be persecution, ought not all things to be despised in consideration of Christ? The world is loved; but let Him be preferred by whom the world was made." Great, fair, and sweet is the world; but greater, fairer, and sweeter is the one through whom God made the world. So too, "Evil is the world; and good is He by whom the world was made."[77]

Yet here was a third ambiguity, the meaning of "the world" in Christian thought. Behind the perennial question of how Christians are to live in time and in the world lay another question—which world? The New Testament had spoken of "the world" in at least two ways: as the creation God loves and seeks to rescue from its sin and groaning, and as the despotic society actively resisting God's purposes and people. As he had done before, Augustine moved to explain this diversity of meaning in order to answer the question, "How then is the world evil, and He good by whom the world was made?" The good world was "the heaven and earth and all things that are in them," yet some of its inhabitants loved that good world more than its Creator and refused to recognize the One through whom the world was made. "So then the world [in the latter sense] is evil, because they are evil who prefer the world to God."[78]

Such an explanation was basic enough, but Augustine had noticed a third, arguably biblical, meaning for "the world." "For there is among men themselves a good world also; but one that has been made good from being evil." This is the world that is "holy, good, reconciled, saved, or rather to be saved, and now saved in hope"; it is "the Church which wholly follows Christ," spread throughout the whole physical world. "The condemned 'world' persecutes; the reconciled 'world' suffers persecution. The condemned 'world' is all that is without the Church; the reconciled 'world' is the Church." Augustine's surprisingly restrictive definition of the church in this sermon, as the body that "wholly follows Christ," was not a momentary accident of phrasing. For however else Augustine defined the true church in other texts, here he insisted that the call to follow Christ by denying self was "of universal application." In this regard at least, and in this sermon, Augustine explicitly ruled out the possibility of a two-tiered church of religious who lived according to "evangelical counsels" and of laity who need not:

> For it is not that the virgins ought to give ear to this, and the married women ought not; or that the widows ought, and the women who still have their husbands ought not; or that monks ought, and the married men ought not; or that the clergy ought, and the lay-

men ought not: but let the whole Church, the whole body, all the members, distinguished and distributed throughout their several offices, follow Christ. Let the whole Church follow him, that only Church. . . .[79]

The real ambiguity in Augustine's treatment of "the world," then, was an ambiguity in "the church." On one hand it would seem here that Augustine had an almost Donatist clarity of vision about who was within and who was without the true church. To be sure, Augustine hesitated to match that distinction with sociological or ritualistic markers as rigid as those of the Donatists. Yet even more clearly than the Donatists, with their insistence on marks of *ritual* purity, Augustine was distinguishing the true and faithful church according to criteria from Jesus' ethic—according to the marks of evangelical self-denial. Further, Augustine's reference to the catholic "world" of those who are "holy, good, reconciled, *saved, or rather to be saved, and now saved in hope*"[80] hinted at a way to continue holding up such a standard while avoiding a Donatist form of perfectionism. That was to sustain the New Testament's own eschatological tension between the "not yet" and the "already" of the redeemed and being-transformed Christian life.

On the other hand, however, Augustine could only project this church of disciples struggling toward faithfulness by momentarily ignoring the lesson of the rude crowd in Mark 10 as he had interpreted it years before and recalled it in this very sermon. The evil and condemned world that persecuted the good and reconciled world was not *just* "all that is without the Church" but was also present within the Church. So long as one does not insist on an altogether stark description of church-world relations, there may be various ways—all internally consistent with Augustine's theology—to work with the problem of a rude crowd of nominal Christians.[81] Augustine did not hold himself to the rhetorical simplification that one day's homiletic task required, as the complexity of a work like *City of God* attests. Likewise, we should not conclude from a single sermon that either Augustine's ecclesiology or his way of sustaining evangelical self-denial was contradictory or incoherent. Yet clearly, ecclesiology was an unfinished project within Augustine's thought.[82]

This much seems clear: For Augustine's ecclesiology or ethic to cohere in such a way that his theology would both avoid perfectionist pride *and* sustain perfectionist longing to participate fully in the high-est good, Augustinian theology would have to retain a markedly escha-tological tension.[83] Should anyone introduce a realized eschatology into his theology, by starting to identify God's Reign too closely and confidently with any historical human institution, the mere suggestion would begin to erode its coherence. Yet Augustine's own policy toward the Donatists threatened to do just that.

CHAPTER FIVE

The Judgment of Augustinian Continence

Lord, you who alone dominate over others without pride, for you
are the sole true God, you who have no lord, I ask you, has this
third kind of temptation ceased for me, or can it cease throughout
all my life, this wish to be feared and to be loved by men,
for no reason but that from it there may come a
joy that is yet no joy?

Augustine, *Confessions*

Whatever the cogency of Augustine's doctrine of Christian love, and however well his grammar of continence helps meet key theoretical objections to it, some of Augustine's specific ethical judgments and ecclesial policies still provoke deep suspicions about his entire theological project. The Church Father who provided Christians with an enduring rationale for participation in "just war," as well as a dubious rationale for calling on civil authorities to intervene coercively in church affairs, would hardly seem an apt resource for sustaining an ethic of love that heeds Jesus' Gospel imperative to "take up your cross and follow me," "love your enemies," and "turn the other cheek" in witness to God's own love. Of course, it is at least possible to argue that conscientious application of criteria that justify warfare can be a legitimate way to love the neighbor who suffers unjust aggression.[1] Christian thought thus divides over whether Augustine's launching of the Christian just war tradition betrayed or extended the New Testament ethic of love. Few thoughtful Christians, however, remain willing to defend in any unqualified way Augustine's support for imperial policies to suppress a rival church indigenous to North Africa, the Donatists.[2]

Augustine's controversy with the Donatists, however, provided the very context in which much of his teaching on Christian love emerged. For nearly a century the Donatists, rigorists at least in sacramental practice, had been claiming the region's true lineage of apostolic succession, which clerical betrayal had supposedly not tainted, even in times of persecution. Augustine initially opposed imperial measures against Donatism and always opposed harsh measures. His personal relations with some Donatist bishops were often surprisingly warm. Eventually, however, he not only consented to anti-Donatist sanctions but penned rationales for coercive "fraternal correction." Those rationales lived a tragic afterlife in defense of practices of inquisition and conquest that were far more gruesome and violent than any he had imagined.[3]

So did Augustine sustain evangelical self-denial? Can Augustinianism do so?

None can answer such questions without judgment. And judgment invites judgment. Not only does the harsh and unfair judgment to which Jesus referred in Matthew 7 invite the same. The virtue of judgment—*prudentia, phronesis,* practical reason—embeds scholars in the give-and-take of a continuous conversation between multiple sources of wisdom, both ancient and contemporary. In such a conversation, all reasonable parties must struggle to name and interrogate their presuppositions, even as they inevitably and simultaneously argue from their presuppositions. My own presuppositions derive from an interpretation of Christianity that commits me to a more thorough-going nonviolence than Augustine's. Fairness requires me, therefore, to acknowledge the nature and possible limits of my inquiry. So, in a way, does continence.

While I certainly hope that my interpretation of Augustine may stand as a worthy contender vis-à-vis others, my goal all along has not been to propose a definitive interpretation of Augustine so much as to offer a retrieval. Especially in the present chapter, then, I will be probing what I believe to be a fault line in Augustine's thought. Pacifist presuppositions no doubt lead me to scrutinize a few texts in the Augustinian corpus far more closely than do other Augustine scholars. And in order to gain the necessary leverage to open up the fault line I believe these texts reveal, I rely more heavily on psychological analysis than I myself would generally favor. Yet even as I probe and pry, I hope the point remains clear. That point is not to exploit uncharitably the fissure I see in Augustine's thought, but to suggest why it may provide an entree into Augustinian thought and debate, even for Christians who do not entirely share his views. I trust this to be an act of respect—the very kind of respect that makes conversation possible as it ranges between critique and appropriation. In any case, I cannot conceive any other way for a living tradition to proceed.

Continence, Conversation, and the Possibility of an Augustinian Retrieval

To maintain three-way, mutually enlightening conversation between scripture, tradition, and new life situations is the project of Christian moral discernment itself. Even as we ask how well one generation, community, or individual has done at sustaining a living continuity with Jesus' own ethic of self-denying love, we must admit that no biblical baseline for making such a judgment is knowable apart from the mediation of some intervening tradition. Nor is any engagement with either the Bible or tradition likely without questions arising in present community experiences and challenges. Any Christian community hopes that scripture and the best of the Christian tradition have shaped its questions and presuppositions. But its claims to that effect are most trustworthy when they are fittingly continent—subject to ongoing interrogation from scripture, open to testing through conversation with tradition, and vulnerable to challenges from new life situations or other traditions.[4]

To examine the role of one figure who did exceptionally much to shape the Christian tradition is to contribute to this conversation, not to supplant it. What such an exercise may contribute to our reception of the other two conversation partners is clarity about the tradition-mediated presuppositions that shape our communities' understandings both of the scripture and of their current ethical challenges. Still, we cannot understand a figure such as Augustine ("tradition") without also making some quiet working assumptions about both the biblical base-line ("scripture") and the ethical questions that interest us most ("new life situations").

Stated most simply, my own assumption is that the process of *adapting* Jesus' teachings to new life situations must always aim at *adopting* them in a renewed and fuller way—but that we must take care lest we adapt Jesus' teachings so thoroughly that we render them un-recognizable. The need for adaptation to changing situations is peren-nial and inevitable.[5] The ongoing Christian tradition is a "pedagogue" or servant-teacher whose insights into both scripture and situation we ignore to our peril. When the pressures of new situations tempt us to rationalize away Jesus' teaching, however, or when the tradition's theo-logical constructs teach us to call temptation by some other name, then the church's ethic may all too quickly cease being a *Christian* ethic. To be sure, a three-way conversation will hardly ever move forward without tension. But without Jesus' own voice as the Gospels ever communicate it to the church, the conversation will only mimic other conversations and may in fact teach Christians to turn elsewhere for ethical guidance.

In what sense, then, can we hope to learn how the gospel impera-tive of self-denying love fared in Augustine's hands? This much seems circumspect and fair: Even without an uncontroversial biblical base-line, we can nonetheless proceed to examine the ways that Augustine *thought* himself in continuity with a New Testament ethic, inquire into the internal plausibility of this self-understanding, and pay particular attention to the ambiguities (or outright contradictions) in his own theology. These ambiguities, after all, are likely to coincide closely with the very areas where problems arose for the later tradition as it appro-priated Augustine's theology in conflicting ways.

If we are still able, in spite of such ambiguities, to identify an un-derlying coherence and plausibility in Augustine's doctrine of Chris-tian love, that will be because Augustine's overall thought retains an explanatory power that allows us to account for what many consider his own failings—not according to some impossibly "objective" bibli-cal base-line, nor according to an anachronistic standard we impose from our own century, but according to his own insights into that love of which the New Testament speaks. We dare not assume that the teaching of any postcanonical theologian is normative in the way that the apostolic teaching is. To suspect that we may end up reading Au-gustine against himself, in fact, is to assume that nothing he said is nor-mative simply because he said it. Still, we may find that a classical theologian such as Augustine remains a helpful conversation partner and source of insight for our own project of moral discernment, for our self-critical reading of scripture, and for a fresh look at contemporary questions, to the very degree that his thought yields resources for its own self-correction.

There is, after all, this intriguing lead: In book ten of the *Confessions* Augustine anticipated that his most abiding temptation would fall within the third of the three categories of temptation in 1 John 2:16, *ambitio saeculi*. This temptation expressed itself as the "wish to be feared and to be loved by men," not from a benevolent desire to use this power to guide and correct them, but from a false joy and prideful "passion for self-vindication" and praise, disguised as benevolence.[6] Thus Augustine also anticipated the very problems and policies that are most likely to trouble Christians who believe that Christendom has been too quick to rationalize away Jesus' hard sayings and involve itself in uses of power that are barely distinguishable from patterns of domination in society at large. Rationalization always appeals to benevolent possibilities, after all, for the temptation of generally well-intentioned people is never to do evil *except* for the cause of good.[7] Augustine anticipated the contention of many other Christians when he argued that "by reason of certain official positions in human society, it is necessary for us to be both loved and feared by men."[8] Perhaps. But he also admitted in the very same paragraph: "Lord, you . . . alone dominate over others without pride."

Given Augustine's confessed uncertainties about the whole complex of pride, temptation, and potential for rationalization that the third category of temptation in 1 John 2:16 involved, it is worth pressing the question of whether Augustinian continence does not call into question Augustinian political "necessities."[9] Might some or even many of these "necessities" not be attempts to have the good by grasping, rather than by trusting gratefully in God's gift? Whatever Augustine did to consolidate the cooperation—or perhaps even the synthesis—of church and state that followed from Constantine, his doctrine of love and his theory of continence may nonetheless diagnose what Mennonite theologian John Howard Yoder has called the "Constantinian temptation" at its very heart, the temptation to think it our duty to make history come out right.[10]

My contention, then, is that the structure of Augustine's doctrine of Christian love remains sound (and may thus offer a structure for integrating accounts of self-love and self-denial) even for Christians who differ with some of his specific and most famous ethical judgments.

For such a thesis to hold, however, any selection of what we claim remains tenable in Augustine's theology must prove itself reasoned rather than arbitrary. Previous chapters have in effect argued for a principle of selectivity: *If the core of Augustine's theology is his doctrine of love for God and for all creatures "in God," then one may only participate consistently in such love insofar as one does so in a way that is also consistently continent.* We must now test this principle of selectivity as we continue to review ways that Augustine's doctrine of Christian love did and did not sustain gospel self-denial in the very first case—his own.

Trial Balance: Augustine and Evangelical Self-Denial

In the last chapter we sought to ascertain how Augustine attempted to sustain evangelical self-denial at various points in his career. At least four variables were at work:

First, Augustine's tendency to interiorize the demands of the gospel was strongest in the early part of his career, but never entirely absent from his theology either. At a later date of 412, Marcellinus, the imperial commissioner to whom Augustine would soon address the *City of God,* asked Augustine how he should reply to critics of Christianity who believed that teachings such as "turn the other cheek" had weakened Roman resolve. Augustine assured him that "these precepts pertain rather to the inward disposition of the heart than to the actions which are done in the sight of men, requiring us, in the inmost heart, to cherish patience along with benevolence, but in the outward action to do that which seems most likely to benefit those whose good we ought to seek."[11] The relative strength of Augustine's tendency to interiorize the hard sayings of Jesus is apparent in his casuistry of self-defense. Since Augustine never authorized personal self-defense, it is possible to argue that he only allowed exceptions out of charity for others, never one's own self-interest. Jesus' precepts still had force in Augustine's prohibition against personal self-defense, but beyond that—and for police, soldiers, or others with public responsibilities—such precepts serve only to "prevent us from taking pleasure in revenge, . . . but not to make us neglect the duty of restraining men from sin."[12] Jesus' precepts did carry some additional force in Augustine's insistence that all Christians exercise "readiness of mind"[13] to be non-violent if practical beneficence as well as internal benevolence required. But as Lisa Sowle Cahill has noted, "Although Augustine pre-serve[d] a motive of love in the violent restraint of injustice, he [did] not specify the circumstances in which the 'readiness' for nonviolence is acted upon."[14]

Second, logic, exegesis, and pastoral concerns nonetheless pre-vented Augustine from turning evangelical self-denial into a wholly hidden matter of the heart, and instead prompted him to keep many of his ethical teachings concrete. (2a) Logically, a Christian could hardly practice interior love of neighbor without attention to the con-crete, temporal sufferings of others; if an interior disposition toward cruelty or enmity was the "real evil" in war, for example,[15] that evil was real only because it also afflicted real suffering in time and flesh. (2b) Exegetically, scripture itself required attention to the concrete.[16] When he wrote *On Christian Doctrine*, Augustine had noted that a Christian teacher must not only remember the danger of interpreting the Bible too literally, but must also beware of figurative and allegorical inter-pretations of biblical passages that required a literal reading.[17] At a deeper theological level, no one could know rightly without embrac-ing the truth of Christ's incarnation, which had itself embraced our lowly "clay."[18] Augustine might therefore insist on the priority of a right interior disposition, yet add (concerning humility, for example) that "it is far better, and beyond all dispute more accordant with the truth, that it should also be done with the hands."[19] Even when Augustine favored allegorical interpretations, their lessons might move the hearer toward concrete love of neighbor rather than mystical contemplation or metaphysical speculation.[20] (2c) Pastorally, a bishop who had found in love for God and for neighbor the key to all Christian truth, and who for years had exposed himself to the scripture, simply could not be callous to the conflicts, the marginalized, and the hungry within his own community—especially a bishop who was first of all so passion-ate a human being as Augustine, and who had begun his pilgrimage pained over the problem of evil.

Third, however, the complex of social forces to which some now refer as "Constantinianism" was impinging in angular, contradictory ways on the community Augustine pastored and on his thought. (3a) Where first tolerance and then the establishment of Christianity seemed to result in soldiers as devout, conscientious, and chaste as Marcellinus (whom Augustine addressed affectionately as "my son dearly beloved and longed for"),[21] Augustine took for granted that they could be both

Christians and soldiers, and tended to limit the purview of evangelical self-denial to the formation of interior dispositions. (3b) Augustine's sermon 88 reveals a social dynamic, however, in which that same situation of tolerance had resulted in a church community where the many nominal Christians almost seemed to "persecute" the fewer fervent Christians intent on following Christ as disciples. In response, Augustine tended to uphold the concrete demands of the gospel and sustain them with his larger doctrine of love and continence. Meanwhile, Augustine's ecclesiology remained an unfinished project, as he both rationalized the presence of rude and merely nominal Christians in the church with his interpretation of Jesus' Parable of Wheat and Tares, yet insisted that Jesus' call to deny self, take up the cross, and follow him applied universally to all Christians and defined the true church.

Fourth, one way or another Augustine certainly did need to translate the meaning of evangelical self-denial for his own situation, yet that need did not relieve him of the danger of losing something of the New Testament's meaning in translation. (4a) Augustinian continence might be a helpful and defensible way to translate for later times the self-denial of which Jesus had spoken, but even if we accept and argue for that possibility, we should not see in his translation an exact equivalence. Augustine himself was aware that continence might be mistaken for mere delayed gratification, even as he used the likeness to explain why disciples might willingly suffer for the greater cause of the Christ they love. Thus he risked a false translation whereby self-denying Christian love might become one more self-interested natural love. Likewise, (4b) the meaning of *cross-bearing* might legitimately need to widen as overt persecution ebbed, yet when Augustine called Christians to bear patiently *any* troubles that resulted from their commitment to Christ's cause, some might miss his nuance and begin to equate "the cross" with any human suffering whatsoever that they bore. (4c) And again, the meaning of *the church* in its relationship to *the world* was also in flux.

To these four variables we must add an additional one. Augustinian love for neighbor, we may recall, involved "seizing and carrying others up to God." This involved the possible obligation of paternalism. Even if some moral situations do call for paternalism, Augustine's defense of it opened up a way to rationalize policies of violent coercion.

Fifth, then, the paternalism deep within the structure of Augustine's conception of *caritas* was like a fuel tank hidden within a vehicle—

potent and necessary, but explosive enough to destroy the whole construct. To repeat a point that previous chapters have recognized, love does argue both for intervention on behalf of what we judge to be others' true good, and for respect of their dignity as creatures of God who must appropriate that good for themselves. To love other creatures "in God" was, for Augustine, to wish and work for them to participate fully and rightly in their supreme good, through shared love for God. To love one's neighbor as oneself required that one first learn right self-love through love for God, but then "seize and carry them up to you [God]."[22] This formulation of neighbor-love could hardly have been any different within a doctrine of Christian love built upon the conviction that to love God was the highest good of any human being:

> First see if you know yet how to love yourself [by loving God]; and then I will commit to you the neighbor whom you are to love as yourself. But if you do not yet know how to love yourself, I fear lest you should deceive your neighbor as yourself. For if you love iniquity, you do not yet love yourself.[23]

While the principle might be defensible *qua* principle, it was fraught with dangers in practice. For as soon as human beings begin endeavoring to approximate now the ultimate good of communion with God and in God, their conceptions of how that good instantiates itself within history will differ in fallible ways. That alone need not be fatal for either Augustinian theology or the continued appropriation of his teaching on Christian love, so long as other dimensions of his thought supply checks against the dangers.

Augustine's *caritas* theology may remain both coherent and practicable so long as his eschatological sense of the incompleteness of the best human projects obtains, and so long as his "hermeneutic of humility"[24] constrains those who would love their neighbors from violently and arrogantly coercing (rather than simply persuading) neighbors to "enjoy" their ultimate good.[25] Further still, the principle of continence as we discerned it in chapter 3 would remind Christians that they cannot have higher goods through coercive and manipulative grasping even if they try. In supporting state sanctions of the Donatists, however, Augustine laid aside and undermined both his humility and his eschatology. Arguably, he was incontinent.

Grasping at the End

Sampling sermons by Augustine on Gospel texts that include some of Jesus' hard sayings has shown us both the potential and the problems of his theology for sustaining evangelical self-denial. The greatest and most tragic paradox of Augustine's doctrine of love is that some of his clearest and most eloquent teaching on the subject emerged amid the very controversy wherein he rationalized state sanctions against Donatist "schismatics." An additional sermon may underscore that paradox. It suggests the difficult and perhaps untenable path Augustine was trying to hew. He was encouraging the suppression of Donatism through nonevangelical means, even while discouraging recriminations against sometime Donatists through evangelical proclamation.

Love of Enemies

Scholars are not certain when Augustine preached the sermon on Matthew 22:1–14 that they list as number 90, but they are more certain about where he preached it. Dates range from 411 to 420—the years following a momentous summit meeting between Donatist and Catholic bishops, and a period that saw the apparent decline of Donatism. In 405 an imperial edict against the Donatists had mainly affected their clergy, but after 411 new measures extended sanctions against lay people who merely refused to become Catholic.[26] The figurative location of sermon 90 is clearly within the context of Donatist suppression. The actual location, in fact, seems to have been Carthage, where a disputed episcopal election in 312 had ensured a split in North African Christianity, and where the episcopal summit in 411 had failed in a final attempt to heal it.[27]

Though sermon 90 does not name the Donatists, it bears every mark of the controversy with them. Matthew 22:1–14 is the parable of a wedding banquet with too few guests, though unlike its parallel in Luke 14:16–24, which has the master telling his servants to "compel them to come in [*compelle intrare*]" and which provided Augustine with a prooftext for rationalizing coercion, the Matthean version speaks only of invitation—"*quoscumque inveneritis, vocate ad nuptias.*" In the Matthean parable and thus in Augustine's sermon, the pivotal issue is the nature of the wedding garment one must wear to be found fit for the wedding. This spoke to a most basic Donatist conviction, that Christ will only have as his bride a church that is "without spot or wrinkle or anything of the kind."[28] To be sure, Augustine drew out a lesson similar to the one he so famously found in the Parable of Wheat and Tares; he pointed out that only the master, not the servants, noticed and judged who was worthy to remain at the banquet.[29] In sermon 90 Augustine did not, however, directly contest claims that the church must be pure; rather, he insisted that charity, not ritual purity in the sacraments, constitutes the garment that makes God's people fit for the eschatological banquet.[30] Love must extend to the whole human race throughout the world and not only to Christians of one's own region,[31] a view he often charged to the Donatists. Charity must not be the false kind that co-conspirators seem to have, and it will not do to have faith without love.[32]

If Augustine had directed this sermon mainly against the Donatists themselves, however, he would almost certainly have mentioned that lack of mutual love by which he believed they had attacked the church's bond of unity so forcefully that their schism actually qualified them as "heretics."[33] Instead, the message that he drove home at the climax of sermon 90 was one aimed at the suspicions and recriminations that kept Catholics from fully embracing "returned" Donatists, much less loving their Donatist enemies with the gentle humility that might truly correct them in love. Like much of what he said about Christian love amid the thorny Donatist controversy, the sermon shows the potential Augustine's doctrine of Christian love still had for sustaining evangelical self-denial, even when his support for imperial sanctions against the Donatists undercut the kind of cruciform love that Jesus taught and practiced when he refused recourse to violence in defense of his own most just of causes. Theoretically, authentic love of enemy itself had some chance of surviving within Augustinian doctrine.

In sermon 90, the overall structure of Augustine's doctrine of Christian love is evident in now-familiar themes: the preeminence of love even over sacraments and right belief, the zero-sum opposition of *caritas* and *cupiditas,* the call to learn right self-love through love of God so that one's love of neighbor would then be trustworthy, and the insistence that love of neighbor extend to all members of the human race, including enemies. This last sort of love obviously seemed hardest, but Augustine exhorted that it not be so, promising that those who loved their enemies would gain far more than they lost.[34]

In clear contrast to those with a misguided zeal against Donatism, the biblical Stephen was Augustine's model of enemy love. In Acts 7 Stephen only *seemed* to rebuke his opponents out of "rage and resentment," according to Augustine. "You have heard therefore how Stephen was severe; now hear how he loved." He was in fact so severe in his rebuke that his listeners took offense and stoned him, yet he forgave them and his final prayer was for his enemies. In both disposition and action Stephen contrasted with those (in the listening congregation, perhaps) who approached the Lord's table praying that God would slay their enemies. Such a prayer was dangerous as well as wrong, for God had every reason to reply that the one praying deserved death first, having also derided and blasphemed God. God could surely ask, "'If I had slain you when you were My enemy, how could I have made you My friend? Why, by your wicked prayers do you teach Me to do what I did not [do] in your own case?'" Instead God offered: "Let me teach you to imitate Me. When I was hanging on the cross, I said, 'Forgive them, for they know not what they do.'" This is how God had recruited that "brave soldier" Stephen, and continued even now to recruit people to battle the devil. So "[i]n no other way will you fight at all unconquerably, unless you pray for your enemies."[35]

If his listeners wanted to ask permission to persecute their enemy, Augustine teased, they certainly should do so—with discernment. They should discern that their real enemy was the evil within the man, not the man himself. "What he has made himself is at enmity with you; in that he is evil, he is your enemy; not that he is a man." God seeks to heal the evil but preserve the created nature of the human being. By doing so, in fact, God *does* avenge evil truly and slay one's enemy: "'I take away that which makes him evil, I preserve that which constitutes him a man: now if I shall have made him a good man, have I not slain your enemy, and made him your friend?'" But "if you pray for this, that the man may die, it is the prayer of one wicked man against another; and when you say, 'Slay the wicked one,' God answers, 'Which of you?'"[36]

Of course a certain ambiguity resided in the "no other way" by which Augustine said one must fight to "fight unconquerably." The text of Augustine's sermon itself is unclear; could one properly pray for one's enemies in any kind of fight, or must such prayer form part of a nonviolent fight such as Jesus had waged on the cross and Stephen had waged through martyrdom? If allowing such ambiguity did not already violate the New Testament record, it certainly opened possibilities for later abuse. But of course the anti-Donatist context makes clear that Augustine was hardly a pacifist.

Already by 408, Augustine had begun to cite Luke 14:23's "compel them to come in" as a mandate for religiously directed imperial coercion. In 417 he developed this argument at length for Boniface, the imperial tribune and later count of North Africa, in the letter (no. 185) that sometimes comes to us as *On the Correction of Donatists*. As he countered Donatist claims that the true church is a persecuted church in that letter, Augustine insisted on both the hypocrisy of Donatists in making those claims, and on distinctions between righteous and unrighteous persecution according to goals and intentions. "The Church of Christ . . . persecutes in the spirit of love, they in the spirit of wrath; she that she may correct, they that they may overthrow: she that she may recall from error, they that they may drive headlong into error." Of course the church prefers to correct and convert through teaching and persuasion rather than through fear of punishment, "[b]ut while those are better who are guided aright by love, those are certainly more numerous who are corrected by fear." Like a loving mother with sons, and like a shepherd with sheep, the church keeps its charges from erring, sometimes through "tender words" and sometimes through "the pain of the whip." "For the wandering of the sheep is to be corrected in such wise that the mark of the Redeemer should not be destroyed on it."[37]

Even so, when Augustine appealed for restraint in the imposition of sanctions, the principles and examples to which he appealed were ones that could theoretically have moved Augustinian theology closer toward the renewal of an earlier Christian pacifism, rather than toward the rationalization of later medieval inquisition. According to sermon 90, for example, Stephen's paternalistic severity was decidedly persuasive, not coercive. Stephen had learned to imitate Christ not just through interior disposition but through concrete yet peaceable action. Augustine's listeners should see in their own status as reconciled former enemies of God the motivation to treat their own enemies as God had treated them, both by forgiving and by refusing to slay, thus keeping open prospects for a fuller reconciliation. Implied in the distinction between a man and one's enmity with that man was a somewhat eschatological (though also somewhat Platonic) vision of the redeemed human form even in one's enemy.[38] Above all, Augustine appealed for the kind of self-critical humility that he had embodied in his *Confessions* but was undermining with his later Donatist policy. For years Augustine's doctrine of original sin had been answering that question, "Which of you [is wicked]?" For if all are sinners, and if pride skews their judgment, all may need discipline and correction, but none may qualify to exercise irreversible judgment upon other sinners.[39]

Change of Mind and Policy

If Augustine's doctrine of love could just as well have prevented him from supporting imperial suppression of Donatism, it is all the more intriguing that he initially opposed such a policy, claimed he changed his mind reluctantly, and never approved of torture or capital punishment in such cases.[40] But of course he *did* change his mind. And love, he argued, was at work there, too.

Augustine claimed to have assented to state sanctions against Donatism later than many of his episcopal colleagues in North Africa, and then only reluctantly. Writing warmly to Vicentius, a bishop in a Donatist offshoot group who had objected to Augustine's support for coercive measures, Augustine explained how the gratitude of former Donatists had changed his mind, for although they first came to the Catholic Church out of fear of imperial laws, they now loved the unity of the Church ardently.

> I have therefore yielded to the evidence afforded by these instances which my colleagues have laid before me. For originally my opinion was, that no one should be coerced into the unity of Christ, that we must act only by words, fight only by arguments, and prevail by force of reason, lest we should have those whom we know as avowed heretics feigning themselves to be Catholic.[41]

In his work on Augustine's theology of history and society, Robert Markus noted the pastoral problems Augustine had earlier encountered when imperial laws forced still-quite-pagan semi-Christians to enter the church; Markus concluded therefore that "[t]here is every reason for accepting Augustine's explanation of his reluctance at face value."[42] On the other hand, W. H. C. Frend, author of a study on the

Donatist church that broke much new ground in 1952, was more skeptical than Markus. Frend believed that Augustine's reluctance was merely politic through most of the 390s; after all, imperial control of North Africa was too tenuous to offer the promise of support for Catholicism. Augustine might publicly appeal to Donatists as "brothers" yet in the same period refer to them privately as "heretics."[43] Though Frend's case is not convincing, the measure of truth behind his more sinister speculation is twofold. First, Augustine may have concurred with colleagues who supported the imperial suppression of paganism that began in 391 with a series of edicts by Emperor Theodosius.[44] Second, Augustine's earlier and later positions on the suppression of Donatism were in continuity at their most basic level, for both rested largely on pragmatic considerations. In other words, when he opposed coercion, he did so because an influx of false Catholics would prove a pastoral headache. When he favored coercion, he did so because he believed the policy was succeeding after all, and proving a pastoral advantage.[45]

This is not to say that Augustine took neither principles nor scruples to the Donatist question, however. Instead it means that his conscience is most evident not in his policy-making but rather in his attempts to restrain those who carried out that very policy. His fear was that civil authorities might abuse their mandate, act vindictively, and, in their official zeal to punish, fail in their Christian responsibility to "correct."[46] Here he hewed his difficult path. One one hand, the pattern follows Augustine's tendency to interiorize Jesus' calls for self-denial and nonresistance. On the other, once Augustine tapped into Jesus' call to love one's enemies, he was not only eloquent and forceful, but he also appealed to the very principles that could have sustained an even larger place for evangelical self-denial within his doctrine of love.

But why did he change his mind in the first place? There are the obvious but largely pragmatic reasons: Donatism had its violent side too, on the part of Circumcellion extremists whom at least some Donatist bishops tacitly supported. Repeated attempts at persuasion and negotiation had failed, in hindsight because Catholics and Donatists were talking past each other, but in Augustine's sight because of Donatist stubbornness or even hatred. And again, the coercive sanctions that Augustine at first had rejected *seemed* to be working.[47]

Some cite subtle reasons of mood that are therefore harder to document. Peter Brown has described the "profound and ominous changes [that] had taken place in Augustine's attitude to the church and society in his first ten years as a bishop," during which hard pastoral experience played upon his ideas of grace and predestination. Brown's view was that this produced an aging pessimism about the power of human free will, and thus, an acceptance of the need for forceful discipline.[48]

And there are other illuminating but imprecise reasons. For example, an Augustine writing to a Marcellinus or a Boniface about how to treat Donatists had obviously accepted and was now consolidating a new "Constantinian" alliance of ecclesiastical and imperial power. Yet when applied to Augustine, at least, the notion of Constantinianism may serve better as a heuristic device for prying at his assumptions than it does as an explanation of their source. As Markus has shown in *Saeculum: History and Society in the Theology of St Augustine,* Augustine's Donatist policy was in many ways out of synch with his developing critique of the Roman Empire, his growing distance from the kind of triumphalistically "Constantinian" celebration of the new order in which the church historian Eusebius had engaged, as well as his deepening sense that even the best human institutions could play only a limited role in God's ultimate purposes.[49]

Even if all of these explanations for Augustine's change of mind are valid, they remain incomplete. Scholars have overlooked an additional factor in the complex that shaped Augustine's Donatist policy. Though this is hardly the place to attempt a definitive ordering of the entire complex, we can and must insist that no such attempt will succeed without attention to one additional factor: Augustine passionately longed for the perfection of mutual love; ultimately, however, the joy he found in being loved and respected by others—a joy that he knew was empty unless oriented toward the love of God—seems to have tempted him to grasp at its fulfillment through his own proud domination, rather than to receive it from God as an eschatological gift. Augustine's Donatist policy, therefore, expressed a kind of realized eschatology that did not rest well with his larger theology or with the doctrine of love that structured it.

Donatist Policy as Realized Eschatology

Given its place both in Augustine's theology and in his experience, mutual love—among true friends first and within the Christian communion later—was by all accounts the good he longed for more than any other in this life. While the very highest good was eternal communion with God and with all other creatures "in God," the mutual love of the body of Christ *was* that communion as it had begun to realize itself and make itself tangible in time. We need hardly be surprised, then, when we find indications that Augustine's most abiding, poignant, yet subtle temptation was to grasp at the completion of this good within time, before its eschatological time. In the end, Augustine apparently succumbed to this temptation and grasped incontinently after the end of mutual love. Paradoxically, the greatest vindication of Augustinian continence as a coherent structural element in his doctrine of Christian love will prove to be the judgment that it exercises upon Augustine's own incontinence.

When Donatists spurned Augustine's overtures and declarations of love, he seems to have taken their rebuffs personally.[50] No intricate exercise in psychohistory is necessary to explain such a conclusion. Augustine has left us his own self-analysis and acknowledged his most abiding temptation. Augustine had recognized in book ten of the *Confessions* that an incontinent "passion for self-vindication" remained in him, even though God had begun to heal him of its more crass and worldly forms. The progress of his healing in this area was particularly difficult for him to assess, because morally neutral longings to be loved, respected, and recognized for his contributions to the good of others were virtually indistinguishable from his sinful drive to be loved, feared, and praised *simply* for the self-enclosed delights that love, fear, and praise might bring:

> Lord, you who alone dominate over others without pride, for you are the sole true God, you who have no lord, I ask you, has this third kind of temptation [cf. 1 John 2:16] ceased for me, or can it cease throughout all my life, this wish to be feared and to be loved by men, for no reason but that from it there may come a joy that is yet no joy? A miserable life is this, and a foul boast! Hence most of all it comes that I neither love you nor have a chaste fear of you. Therefore, you "resist the proud [*superbis*], but give grace to the humble," and you thunder down upon the ambitions of the world [*ambitiones saeculi*], and the foundations of the mountains tremble. But now, since by reason of certain official positions in human society, it is necessary for us to be both loved and feared by men, the

adversary of our true happiness keeps after us, and on every side amidst his snares he scatters the words, "Well done! Well done!"

Though Augustine had renounced worldly ambition, he had nonetheless been elevated first to the priesthood and more recently to the episcopacy. As with other "official positions in human society," a call to faithful service on behalf of his flock actually increased his need to influence others, both by inspiring them (thus evoking their love) and by disciplining them (thus evoking their fear). That meant, however, that "the adversary" could easily exploit his old "passion for self-vindication" and provoke again his love of praise for its own sake.[51]

The temptation might not be unique to bishops and other prominent figures, however. Could *anyone* get along "without any praise whatsoever," Augustine wondered? To live in isolation from the love and affirmation of others, and thus from mutual encouragement to live "a good life" and do "good deeds," would be to live "an evil life, so abandoned and inhuman a life." "What greater madness can be named or conceived than this?" Precisely because human beings are created for the good of mutual love and communion, Augustine implied, they are vulnerable to offers from an adversary who "in a perverse and tortured way imitates you [God]"—in this case by offering a reciprocal "comradeship in punishment [*consortium supplicii*]," in place of true "union in charity [*concordiam caritatis*]." When the true joy of mutual love did not come to Augustine soon enough, it would seem, "an excuse" readily "steals into my mind." That excuse was benevolence, the neighbor's good, the command to love not just God but one's neighbor also. If Augustine were praised, or loved, or feared because either his domination or his eloquence had helped a neighbor progress, it just might be "my neighbor's good" rather than "my praises on account of myself" that moved him. Yet in the end, Augustine could not be sure. "For other types of temptation I have some kind of ability for self-examination, but for this scarcely any."[52]

Yielding to the temptation to generate the love, fear, or praise of others, willfully and impatiently, thus led all too easily to a domination of others that disguised itself as paternalistic benevolence but in fact stemmed from pride. When we encounter dissonant chords within some of Augustine's most lyrical homilies on Christian love, they often betray these very personal sources—self-vindication, pride, and a craving to be loved or at least respected, all issuing in rationalizations for paternalistic coercion putatively aimed at restoring not just formal church unity but bonds of mutual love.

Augustine's *Homilies on 1 John* are the most important case in point. In previous chapters we have turned to them for key components in Augustine's conception of *caritas;* but the homilies also contain his arguments in favor of Christian paternalism. Augustine would trust such paternalism to discipline the erring with "harsh or savage" measures, so long as one had a properly benevolent intention: "Love and do what you will."[53] The theory *might* be defensible, except that Augustine himself had confessed his inability to sort benevolent intentions from proud ones.[54] In fact he failed to notice when he betrayed incontinent motivations amid these very homilies.

Augustine's self-vindication recurred in the *Homilies on 1 John* with a series of proofs, tests, and enquiries that he proposed for determining the true church where charity resides, thus showing that his own Catholic Church rather than the Donatist's was true.[55] The whole of homily six shows how tricky such efforts can be, and thus, the difficulty of self-examination. Augustine began the sixth homily insisting that all should examine their *own* consciences before God in search of authentic "love for the brother." Yet by the end of the homily he had subtly inverted the test into an examination of the Donatists, *not* himself. Of course they failed it because their schism from the global church allegedly proved their lack of love, or even their outright hatred, for other Christians: "See if [the Donatist vessel] sounds true and whole: see if charity is there. You are removing yourself from the world's unity, you are dividing the Church by schisms, you are rending the Body of Christ."[56]

Perhaps they were; our task is not to decide the old question of which ecclesiastical body bore a stronger claim to being the "true church." Nor is it to argue that one should never defend one's Christian credentials, examine those of others, or formalize the testing of credentials in church practice. We are simply suggesting that the "passion for self-vindication" which Augustine knew could disguise itself as benevolent pastoral guidance played havoc with the ethical judgment that led to his Donatist policy—just as it had inverted a call for examination of self into a self-vindication aimed at others. Only the greatest humility and patience could prevent such ethical havoc.

So how did Augustinian humility fare in the homilies? Ostensibly well. The prologue to the *Homilies on 1 John* stated, and the first homily argued, "Where there is charity there is peace: where there is humility, there is charity." Augustine insisted that Christians must know themselves as sinners, confess that they were not just sinners but liars, and never become self-satisfied. In practice, however, Augustine directed these very exhortations mainly to the other party, not to his own, in another self-satisfied twist. And in any case, he refused even to entertain the notion that *he* could be wrong: "Our text [1 John 2:18–19] gives us warning and requires us to confess the truth. Either they have gone out from us, or we from them. *But the latter is unthinkable. . . .*"[57]

It would be all too easy to conclude, however, that everything Augustine taught amid the Donatist conflict concerning Christian love was disingenuous—nothing but a ruse that yields will-to-power without remainder once we deconstruct his motives. Augustine's human condition was more subtle than that. His will-to-power, his dominating over others with pride, seems also to have responded, amid the mixed mystery of clay-impacted human motivation, to an even deeper longing.

We have much evidence of Augustine's longing for connection. In his youth Augustine had sought true friendship; in his conversion he had shared the burning flame of love for God with enkindling friends; in his mature theology he promised that when members of the body of Christ loved one another mutually, they were already participating in the very life of the Trinity.[58] Augustine longed for all of these because he longed for the eschatological fullness of all love for God and for neighbor—when "God would be all in all," and when all creatures in loving God as their *summum bonum* would also be bonded together in mutual love for one another "in God."

For a passionate, forceful personality such as he, the great temptation was then to rush the creation of an order of mutual love. His preconversion desire to be loved and esteemed had not gone away. According to his theology of love, in fact, it could not and need not go away, for such desire alone was not sinful. Yet such desire could and did become an incontinent desire as it goaded his impatient effort to create that order of mutual love through human power.

Augustine was begging for communion with the Donatists, but then attempted to enforce such communion. Against their charge that the Catholics simply wished to confiscate Donatist church property out of greed, Augustine protested that his wish was that they "become

Catholics, and possess in peace and love with us, not only what they call theirs but also what confessedly belongs to us." "What avaricious man ever wished for another to share his possessions?" he continued. "Who that was inflamed with the desire of empire, or elated by the pride of its possession, ever wished to have a partner?"[59] Perhaps blind to ways that Catholic bishops would have dominated any partnership they created through what we might now call a hostile takeover, Augustine was essentially honest here, nonetheless. After all, desire for possessions hardly motivated the austere bishop. If he sought power in more subtle ways than he sometimes recognized, that was because he was reaching for the mutual love that he believed to be the highest human good. Against his deepest insights into continence, however, this reaching for the proper end, before God gave it at the end, finally became a grasping.

Amid long reflection on Augustine's religious vision, John Burnaby left unexplored clues suggesting that a fault line runs through Augustine's eschatology at precisely the points where he grew impatient with the Donatists: "Augustine constantly appealed against them . . . to the scriptural promises of a world-wide extension of the Church, and he seems never to have considered the possibility that these promises may have to wait much longer for their fulfillment."[60] As both Oliver O'Donovan's study on Augustinian self-love and the present study on Augustinian self-denial have shown, however, eschatology was crucial for the coherence of Augustine's entire theological project.[61] Wherever else Augustine may have maintained an eschatological tension, his ecclesiology lost that tension when he tried to realize the order of mutual love through imperial coercion.[62]

"Has This Temptation Ceased?"

We have identified five variables in Augustine's attempt to sustain evangelical self-denial. Initially (1) he tended to *interiorize* Jesus' ethic by emphasizing the need for a loving disposition and readiness to suffer even when waging war or imposing sanctions. Though he never entirely abandoned that tendency, (2) he also confronted pastoral situations that required him to re-*concretize* evangelical self-denial. (3) One way or another he did in fact have to *translate* Jesus' call to deny oneself and take up one's cross within a situation in which the prospect of persecution and martyrdom had receded. But he faced problems both from outside and inside his thought. (4) As Christianity had first gained toleration and then become the official religion of the Roman Empire, what some now call *Constantinianism* presented contradictory pressures, both to interiorize Jesus' teachings so that they would retain a hold on Christians with worldly power, and to keep those teachings concrete in order to stem the tide of worldliness eroding his congregations' Christian fervor and moral resolve. (5) Within his doctrine of love, however, the obligation of *paternalistic intervention* to "seize and carry" one's neighbor up to God was in tension with the nonviolent respect that continence requires.

In hindsight, we can sort through some of the pressures that followed upon Constantinian settlement and Theodosian establishment. However, the contradictory directions of those pressures made them the most difficult for Augustine to understand and to manage. Like all Christians, he needed to translate the gospel into his own historical situation, adapting Jesus' imperatives precisely in order to adopt them. A situation of growing religious toleration is not in itself "Constantinian" in the pejorative sense by which some interpreters label the changing polity of the era. Even if Augustine had avoided alliances with Roman officials in pursuit of churchly goals, the need to adapt Jesus' teachings would have remained as strong as the need to adopt them for this new situation. Though any Christian runs the danger of losing something of Jesus' meaning in translation, continence can be a legitimate, helpful, and cogent way to appropriate evangelical self-denial within a situation where overt persecution has ebbed.[63]

Already within a situation of possible persecution, the Matthean author had recorded Jesus' insistence on interior as well as exterior righteousness. Now that external forces seemed no longer to frame the Christian's moral choices quite so starkly, a prior interior continence was *all the more important* if Christian lives were going to issue in concrete action. Augustine did show a slight and, in hindsight, worrisome tendency to broaden the meaning of cross-bearing to the point of diffusing its meaning. But some translation could be helpful even here, and Augustinian continence could in fact yield new insights into cross-bearing that were appropriate to a new situation, yet in continuity with New Testament eschatology. Continence, after all, was what should enable the Christian to resist present evil while patiently awaiting the gift wherein God will perfect all things.[64] In fact, to bear with the tension of living in the world as an exile, in continence and patience, would itself seem to be a kind of cross-bearing.[65]

Yet that possibility actually stands in judgment of Augustine's own policies to the extent that he collapsed the eschatological tension, lost patience, neglected humility, and began to force the tarrying promise of an order of mutual love, in the name of Christian love. Insofar as he succumbed to this temptation, Augustine undermined rather than sustained evangelical self-denial in practice. Even so, we need not conclude that Augustine thereby undermined his entire doctrine of Christian love or his theory of continence, thus rendering it altogether suspect and without promise for later theological ethics, down to our day.

For Augustinian continence itself diagnoses and stands in judgment of Augustine's policy. In the face of schism, Augustine attempted to have the great good of mutual love in the body of Christ by grasping at it through domination, rather than through continent trust in the power of God's gracious gift. That gift was already incarnate in the servant-hood of Jesus Christ in whom we see "the Godhead at our feet," beginning to be realized in the present church, yet still to be reached in the fullness of mutual love wherein "God will be all in all."[66]

Augustine's theory of continence should have yielded a prediction that grasping at the good prematurely would be his great temptation and failure. And in a way it did. For as we have seen, in *Confessions* 10.36 and the following chapters Augustine confessed that even as a bishop he still had great difficulty knowing when he was loving his neighbors rightly and when he was succumbing to temptations of pride, passion for self-vindication, and love of praise.[67] For Augustine, the problematics of friendship always provide a window into the problematics of society—for these are simply different levels of *societas*.[68] Thus, "since by reason of certain official positions in human society, it is necessary for us to be both loved and feared by men," Augustine's temptations in friendship became his temptations as a bishop whose official position in the newly established church had import far beyond the domain of strictly ecclesiastical affairs. Had "this third kind of temptation" ceased for him, this temptation to dominate with pride, in order to be loved and feared for its own sake?

By Augustine's own standard, the answer must be no; temptations of pride and power did not cease for him. The requirements of Augustinian continence make all dominance or forceful grasping at the good problematic and sinful. To attempt to dominate out of churchly "necessity" must then invite subtle yet severe temptations. Temptation itself is not sin, of course, and some might see the willingness to risk temptation for the sake of one's community or even for Christ as a kind of heroic virtue. But if only God can dominate without pride, the very effort to dominate righteously must itself involve the first of Augustinian sins, arrogation of God's place.[69]

Certainly the mature Augustine never expected any Christian to reach perfection in this life. Yet by his own standard of realism, continence did in fact remain a reasonable earthly goal for him; it was the highest possible earthly perfection for those who knew they would be struggling against sin and temptation all their lives.[70] We must allow any theologian or church leader a certain gap between their theory and their own practice. What is at stake is finally not just an assessment of Augustine's historical record, but the question of whether and how we may appropriate his thought. For Augustine to contradict his deepest insights, and then to rationalize them besides, struck a fissure near the very core of his theology. Thus, to be consistent, coherent, and cogent, any "Augustinianism" that appropriates his theology must in turn either suffer great internal stress or be self-consciously and self-critically selective.

CHAPTER SIX

Sustaining Self-Denial

What good would it do me, if [Christ] were born a thousand times
and if this were sung to me every day with the loveliest airs,
if I should not hear that there was something in it for me
and that it should be my own?

Martin Luther, "Wartburg Postil"

How can women continue to affirm the delicious self-abandonment
that can come in self-forgetfulness when they are dedicated to a
larger purpose than self alone?

Brita Gill-Austern, "Love Understood
as Self-Sacrifice and Self-Denial"

We began by arguing in chapter 1 that Christian ethics needs a unified account of right self-love and proper self-denial. The tendency in Protestant ethics to portray self-sacrifice as the most telling mark of authentically Christian love has drawn legitimate critique, especially from feminists. Yet feminism and other liberation struggles themselves require some account of the proper place of self-denial, as must any ethic that has normative "bite." The intervening chapters have attempted to recover at least the structure of Augustine's doctrine of Christian love. For in spite of the fact that later centuries of Christians have found a wide range of reasons to be uneasy about Augustine's legacy, the very range of contrasting criticisms suggests that he may have understood the unity of right self-love and proper self-denial in a way that his critics have not. This does not mean that critics who have appropriated only one fragment or another of Augustine's thought were necessarily wrong to be selective. In the last chapter, I too argued for a principle of selection that allows us and even requires us to appropriate the overarching structure of Augustine's doctrine of Christian love without committing ourselves to all of his ethical judgments and ecclesial policies. The difference between the fissure in Augustine's own thought as I have identified it and the fragmentation of his thought that we have attempted to repair is this: By recognizing this fissure we can respect what are arguably Augustine's deepest insights into Christian love, while rejecting certain other elements of his legacy on the very basis of what we thereby appropriate.

Now it is time to illustrate and test what it might mean for contemporary Christian ethics to reappropriate the structure of Augustinian love or *caritas,* by means of seven theses that Augustine would recognize but that also mediate his insights for contemporary Christian ethics. At several points these theses will also enter into conversation with specific issues requiring ethical discernment in Christian communities. In chapter 1 we imagined a Christian woman committed to "an ethic of love whose ultimate standard is the sacrificial love of Jesus Christ." That commitment has led her into a vocation of social activism; that in turn has led her to the edge of "burnout" and to the realization that in order to sustain her ethic and her vocation she must act from self-concern. We also suggested that the life of whole Christian communities that attempt to follow Jesus' ethic and example of love will follow the same pattern; in order to sustain self-denial over time, they must reintroduce considerations of self-concern into their ethic. This is not necessarily because they reject or fall short of that ethic, but precisely to the degree that they are faithful to it. The problem of self-denial as it presents itself in "ordinary time"—not in the face of martyrdom or abuse, nor because powerful Christians have used their teachings to rationalize domination of others—demonstrates our need for a unified account of right self-love and proper self-denial.

Still, we cannot ignore the ethical challenge that outright abuse presents to any ethic which holds Jesus' cross and teachings of enemy love to be normative. If we have regularly spoken of *proper* self-denial, the very purpose of the adjective has been to remind ourselves that Jesus' call to deny ourselves and take up his cross surely does not justify *every* form of self-denial. Even if we say we are committed to "nonresistance" or nonretaliation according to Jesus' teaching of enemy love in Matthew 5:39 and elsewhere, we must ask what *qualifies* as biblical nonretaliation. In other words, we must adjudicate the problem of self-denial in both ordinary time and in cases that require us to discern the difference between proper self-denial and gratuitous victimization

Theses and Tests

Thesis 1:   *Augustine held together a unified account of self-love and self-denial that contemporary Christian ethics has tended to fracture, and needs to recover.*

Twentieth-century debates over the nature of Christian love that emphasize one dimension of love over another, or stress one kind of love at the expense of another, represent in certain ways an Augustinian problem. For one thing, Augustine long ago noted the tendency of human beings to fragment their loves. For another, many of those in the debate have in some way grappled with Augustine's legacy. Though Augustine himself puzzled long over how to account for the unity he intuited in all love, few Christians have thought more deeply about the problem or achieved a more coherent account of the unity of all love in the love of God.

If some Christians continue to doubt the wisdom of unifying our account of Christian love to include both right self-love and proper self-denial, one large reason is the ongoing influence of Anders Nygren and his 1930s book *Agape and Eros.* Nygren drew a sharp antithesis between self-giving Christian love or "agape" as expressed supremely through Jesus Christ in God's own forgiving, self-sacrificing love, and acquisitive, egocentric human love or "eros" expressed even in the noblest efforts of Hellenistic religion to achieve unity with the divine. Because "agape" is preeminently God's own uncoerced, unmerited love for sinners, argued Nygren, it is Christianity's most fundamental idea or "motif." The greatest threat to the sovereignty of agape as Nygren understood it, however, was not eros itself but any effort to synthesize agape with eros. Hence Nygren dedicated more pages to Augustine than to any other single figure in Christian history, for he held what to Nygren was a dubious honor: Augustine had attempted the most impressive synthesis of Christian and Greek conceptions of love. According to this "*caritas* synthesis," loving and clinging to God as one's highest good is the highest and truest way to love oneself. Nygren was certain that Augustinian *caritas* remained egocentric and acquisitive, and that it thus betrayed the sovereignty of God's own agape, both at work in Christ and channeled through a Christian's love of neighbor.

By recognizing his greatest rival in Augustine, Nygren inadvertently argued that anyone who would rejoin what Nygren has put asunder should consider Augustine's synthesis a resource. There are different ways to appropriate Augustine's thought, of course. The influential Christian ethicist Reinhold Niebuhr, for example, appropriated Augustine's doctrine of sin and his critique of proud self-love but did so in a way that shares the tendency of Nygren and other Protestant thinkers to make self-sacrificial love the whole of Christian love.

Positions such as Nygren's and Niebuhr's are open to critique from contemporary feminists who have underscored the conceptual as well as the pastoral problems that ensue when self-sacrifice becomes the test of authentically Christian love. The most characteristic sin of women—according to arguments by Valerie Saiving, Judith Plaskow, and Susan Nelson Dunfee—is too little rather than too much self-concern. When someone like Niebuhr conceives of salvation as beginning with the "shattering" of the self, and goes on to speak of sanctification as a life of self-sacrificial love, this may exacerbate the sin of women and contribute to their victimization.

Still, a feminist ethic must also identify points at which an agent will refrain from acting in a way that presents itself as advantageous. With its large place for the cross and its continuing call to discipleship, Christian ethics must surely indicate the place of self-denial; but so must any liberation ethic that calls for potentially costly struggle. And the intriguing case of "ecofeminism" suggests that as feminism moves from critical to constructive projects, it will need to find an integrated way to conceive of right self-love while denying the collective human self-interest that environmentalists refer to as "anthropocentrism."

Thesis 2:   *Not all self-love is of a piece; at least one kind of self-love has a legitimate place in Christian ethics, for true self-love is consistent with a theocentric (not egocentric) desire for all creatures to participate in the common good of the universe according to God's will.*

John Burnaby and Oliver O'Donovan have countered Nygren's claim that Augustinian *caritas* is, at bottom, egocentric. The obvious test case is love of self. Augustine had claimed that one only loves one-self truly by loving God as one's highest good; Burnaby argued that if one loves God, God will not allow one's will and desires to go un-changed. Loving God must therefore transform the very self one loves, so that one increasingly desires what God wills for one's self in relation to the common good, not a private good of one's choosing. O'Dono-van went on to note four different notions of love as Augustine em-ployed them; of these, the most satisfactory was "benevolent love," which rationally recognizes an objective order of created good, but in addition, freely affirms this order and seeks to help realize it. To love any creature then, including oneself, is to seek the good of that creature not according to a teleological order that one imposes but according to God's will for that creature within the teleologically ordered good of the whole. Not even Augustinian self-love is egocentric, therefore. Rather, it is theocentric.

Building on the work of Burnaby and O'Donovan, chapter 2 pre-sented the overarching structure of Augustine's doctrine of love. In criticizing Augustine for allowing self-love into Christian doctrine, Ny-gren failed to engage Augustine's most cogent explanation of how self-love could be right: love for any creature whatsoever, including one-self, is right when it is "in God." The love of God orients all possible human loves—not only for God, but for neighbor, temporal goods, as well as one's self—in a gestalt vision of love-as-a-whole-in-coordina-tion-with-its-parts. This was Augustine's abiding intuition from early in his theological career, but because the content of love for the tran-scendent God is elusive, Augustine generally traced its meaning by negation and "from below." To love temporal goods as anything other than temporal and useful for higher loves would ultimately be futile as well as sinful. For love of neighbor to involve more than the merely temporal good of mortal friendship, one must love friends and neigh-bors not for their value as tools of one's self-interest, but for their value as God's creatures. In other words, one should enjoy neighbors, but do so "in God," recognizing and praising God as the source of all their good, for they only have life and goodness as gifts of God, who is the supreme good of all creation. Love of self follows this exact same pat-tern, proceeding indirectly (or "by refraction") through the love of God. As stated in chapter 2: In the gestalt unity of love as a whole, insofar as I participate in it, I cannot help but desire for myself exactly what I desire for my neighbor and for every creature, namely, that each one together fulfill its part within the whole common good of the universe, of which the Supreme Good or *Summum Bonum* is none other than God.

Thesis 3:   *Not all self-denial is of a piece; evangelical self-denial must in some way be "for the joy set before us"—oriented by and contributing to that fullness of communion with God and other creatures which Christian scriptures and theology have known by various names and announced as the good news of God's Reign.*

Perhaps the point should be obvious—not all self-denial is of a piece—yet it is one that both Augustine and contemporary Christian feminists have needed to clarify. Christian feminists who seek to retain a clear place for self-sacrificial love or redemptive suffering in their ethic consistently insist that any such self-denial must be freely chosen and in teleological relationship with a larger good, such as liberation, the Reign of God, or the "project of God."[1] Augustine was no doubt more prepared than they to re-narrate all suffering as potentially meaningful for the Christian who trusts God,[2] but in his treatise *On Patience* he insisted that one should not consider just any endurance of suffering to be virtuous without first examining its cause and purpose.[3] For him, of course, the love and enjoyment of God is the ultimate purpose of any loving action, but as we have seen, such love must yearn for and encompass the good of other creatures in right relation to God and each other, thus including a yearning for the fullness of God's Reign. Whatever the differences in these accounts, they coincide in their assumption that proper self-denial will somehow be "evangelical"—that the kind of self-denial to which Jesus called his disciples in the Gospels is one that is only meaningful in light of his invitation to participate in a good that even Christians who "deny themselves" may identify as their own. In going to the cross, after all, Christ himself looked "for the joy set before him" and thus endured.

Precisely by keeping sight of the joy set before us will Christian ethics identify the resources it needs to respond pastorally to the "burned-out" social activist whose case we considered toward the end of chapter 1. She must exercise self-concern precisely so as *not* to become self-centered. As Brita L. Gill-Austern and Jeanne Stevenson Moessner have suggested in their exploration of pastoral care for women, care for those who excel as caregivers to their own neglect or self-abnegation must encourage them to attend to their own needs— but without simply falling back upon the ethical egoism of American individualism or abdicating "public responsibility to use [one's] God-given gifts on behalf of the greater community and for the common good."[4] For these Christian feminists the response to pernicious notions of self-sacrificial Christian love is not to jettison every conception of Christ-like self-giving but to locate individual self-giving in a larger communal setting that will both give it meaning and sustain it.[5] "Self-development within the context of faithfulness to God is not to be equated with anxious straining to obtain the goods of this world whatever they be: wealth, prestige, knowledge, or power," Gill-Austern has insisted. We must continue to "affirm the delicious self-abandonment that can come in self-forgetfulness when they are dedicated to a larger purpose than self alone," but the way to do this is to "begin with the premise that Jesus' central and deepest desire was that in following him we might have life and have it in all its abundance." Thus, "self-giving in whatever form it takes must ultimately be for the sake of helping to create, redeem, and sustain love that furthers abundant life."[6]

By rejecting any possible motive for love, Nygren's theory of divine, unmotivated agape would seem in contrast to leave both him and our burned-out activist without resources for self-regarding nurture. Later agapeists such as Paul Ramsey and Gene Outka have paid more attention than Nygren to the actual psychological conditions of one who loves the neighbor.[7] Nonetheless, agapeist discussions of right self-love tend to treat it as a kind of pastoral concession, or necessary adjustment to the psychological realities of human life. With no more of a basis than this, the high calling of pastoral care easily devolves into pop psychology's advice to split the difference between one's own needs and those of others. In an Augustinian teleology of love, however, one does more than make a concession when one insists that we may rightly desire to participate in a community of mutual love, which in turn will be necessary to sustain the discipleship of the individual Christian. For as it begins to participate in the fullness of communion in God, such community enjoys its full dignity in relation to both the trinitarian ground and the eschatological *telos* of self-giving love.

The first resources for sustaining the properly evangelical self-denial of the burned-out activist should be the liturgy, prayer, mutual support, and feasting at the table of Eucharist by which the Christian community sustains its own inner life. In their preoccupation with principles, criteria, and decision making, Christian ethicists should not take for granted core practices that shape the Christian life itself. In a way, Gill-Austern turned to just such resources as she sought to replace destructive images of self-sacrifice and self-denial with "healing images of self-giving" drawn from the New Testament itself. First among these was a reading of the Good Samaritan story which notices that it does not present a model of heroic, individual extraordinary self-giving at all, but rather a model of love based on interdependence. The Samaritan, after all, relied on communal resources (the innkeeper) in order to care for the victim, and then did *not* cancel his own plans entirely but resumed his journey. Second was the story of Mary and Martha, which honors both active doing, and taking the time to sit and find nurture in the presence of Christ and those gathering around him; one must receive love in order to continue giving love. Third was the John 15 account of Jesus telling his disciples that he would not longer call them servants but friends, for he was sharing with them all that the Father had shared with him.[8]

To sustain evangelical self-denial through participation in the life of the Christian community is to do more than split the difference between the needs of self and neighbor. Rather, it changes the shape of our problem. The real problem is what to do when a Christian community that should be a sustaining one is dysfunctional or absent. To this we will shortly turn. Where sustaining Christian community is in fact present, its members do not merely split the difference between their needs and those of others because the whole is greater than the sum of the parts. To use classical trinitarian language, when the Father and the Son love one another in pure self-giving, a third subsistent proceeds—the bond of mutual love between them which is the Holy Spirit. Reinhold Niebuhr would be right to point out, of course, that for creatures living in time, pure self-giving is no simple possibility. Because we live in time, however, it is not only true that self-sacrificial love without guarantee of reciprocity is paradoxically necessary for mutual love (much as Niebuhr insisted), but also that mutual love is necessary to nurture self-sacrificial love. Pure self-giving and mutual love are eternally simultaneous in the Godhead, but in time and among creatures either one may lead to the other, or have chronological priority. In other words, in some lives and in some times of life, self-sacrifice will help realize mutual love, while in other lives and times mutual love will create the condition of the possibility for sacrificial love.

None of this need taint the sovereignty of divine agape, properly understood. In his concern to acknowledge that sovereignty, Nygren posited a "conduit" theory of love that entirely eliminates human agency from the very working of neighbor love: "In relation to God and his neighbour, the Christian can be likened to a tube, which by faith is open upwards, and by love downwards. . . . He has nothing of his own to give. He is merely the tube, the channel, through which God's love flows."[9] Nygren was surely right that all truly Christian love begins through the self-giving initiative of God. What he did not recognize, however, is that agape may leave traces in history. As Oliver O'Donovan has argued, God's agape is *not* always without presuppositions—it does not always create something *ex nihilo* and unprecedented in the object of love—"for God presupposes that which he himself has already given in agape."[10] As it creates good in the sinners God loves, divine agape does not always start over from scratch but draws upon the traces that God's love has already effected in history. To participate in the life of the Christian community through liturgy, mutual aid, pastoral exhortation and encouragement, prayer, and sacrament is to retrace these traces back to God, celebrating and confessing as Augustine often did (in quoting 1 Corinthians 4:7) that we have nothing we have not received as a gift, and thus are giving only as we have been given. For the burned-out social activist to seek nurture through participation in Christian community and celebration of God's love is not egocentric self-concern but theocentric.

Thesis 4:   *Whether self-love is right or self-denial is properly evangelical depends in both cases on the larger good toward which they aim, and thus, requires a teleological framework to give them meaning. Theological descriptions of that larger good should converge around some ecology of mutual love, ordered according to God's will and realized through the love of God.*

To love any creature rightly was, for Augustine, to recognize and act on the fact that all creatures have their being, goodness, and very life from God, and thus to love God above all else. The love of God in turn unites all other loves "in God." Even temporal goods and their love could regain a certain dignity within this gestalt vision. Augustine eventually concluded that one could begin with any right love and grow into the others. To be perfect or complete, that growth must ultimately extend love of neighbor to love of enemy. But whether Christians love themselves out of motives that included a desire to be happy and blessed, or love their enemies at cost to temporal happiness, the goal was one—that each creature participate in that communion "in God" whereby each fulfills its part within the common good of the universe. Right self-love did not seek the thriving of one's sinful self, which egocentrically defines and seeks some private good, but only the thriving of oneself "in God," a self for whom God alone has determined the good in coordination with the whole. Likewise, love of enemy finally could not be content to desire for enemies any good other than the shared communion by which God transforms them into brothers and sisters. Only when self-denial or continence or patient forbearance had that good as its ultimate object were such virtues "true."

Christians, of course, have spoken in different ways of the ordered ecology of mutual love toward which their ethical lives move. Christians have used various names, reflecting various cosmologies, to speak of this order: the Reign or Kingdom of God, the beatific vision, the body of Christ, that state when God will be all in all,[11] the restoration of the image of God, participation in the trinitarian life of God. The differences here are not unimportant; there is certainly room to debate which conception of the good most adequately reflects the biblical proclamation of good news. What we have most wanted to demonstrate, however, is the common structure that unifies self-love and self-denial, insofar as the good that makes self-denial meaningful must in some way be a good even for the moral agent who suffers on behalf of others. For the Christian that good no doubt must ultimately be transhistorical—rooted in the eternal promise of God—but it cannot be unknown to time and history, for Christians confess that we only know of this promise because God has come near to us in Jesus Christ.

So learned Augustine. In one sense, Augustinian "love of God" must remain ever elusive. Augustine would not have taken this as a fatal criticism, for his *Confessions* contend at every point with the impossibility of grasping or knowing God as God knows us, and leave us with no other hope than that the God who sent a Mediator will grasp us instead. The content of love for the transcendent God must remain open-ended and ever ready to learn to love what God loves. Yet because this very God has become incarnate in the person of Jesus Christ, the content of love both for God and for all that God loves has also become ever more concrete. Human beings obviously cannot know thoroughly the good of the whole or the details of each creature's good. But in Jesus Christ they can see "the face of God," and thus, the character and the intention of the creator who is the Supreme Good of the whole. Preeminently in Jesus Christ, the content of all love begins to find its concrete specification. Further still, the love by which God sent Jesus Christ has begun to bear fruit in a new creation that anticipates the time when "God will be all in all." Thus, the mutual love by which Jesus said that "I and the Father are one" becomes concrete and specific in the community of mutual love that is bound together in the Holy Spirit. Augustine's gestalt vision of love is more precisely a trinitarian vision of love.[12]

Thesis 5:   *The love of God is preeminently God's love for us, but because God's own love draws us into a responsive relationship of love according to the trinitarian principle of God's own life, the incarnation of Jesus Christ and the mutuality of community in the Holy Spirit provide concrete criteria for judging when self-denial is proper.*

Here then is the real problem: Although mutual love in the body of Christ should sustain truly evangelical self-denial, such love is certainly not a completed task. Precisely as a goal or *telos* it remains unfinished, an eschatological reality at best. Its partial fulfillment may certainly anticipate and witness to the final *telos* or *summum bonum* of the universe, that state wherein God will be all in all through mutual love. Because the "already" of eschatological reality does not preclude the "not yet" of incompletion, however, tough ethical challenges and apparent dilemmas remain. Even so, to recognize a field of eschatological tension between the "already" and the "not yet" of life in the body of Christ turns out to be a resource. For the role that continence plays in Augustine's conception of Christian love teaches us to suspect that attempts to grasp prematurely at the end will lead to abuse. Such suspicion need not stifle all human agency that seeks the good of others. But it does insist that to be charitable indeed, all such agency must work continently, by clinging to God in trust and respecting the dignity of others. For in the underlying grammar of Augustine's teaching on Christian love, continence is the operative mode of charity.

Insisting that love of the transcendent God must always be open-ended and ready to learn to love what God loves does not prelude the naming of criteria to guide the outworking of mutual love in time. Because of God's incarnation in Jesus Christ, faithful son of Israel and founder of the Church, the first great commandment is not altogether elusive and the second is not simply a vague general principle. If Augustine's thought offers a coherent structure for responding to Jesus' teachings in other historical situations, then we ought to be able to test our conclusions in the face of concrete ethical challenges. We thus return to the case of the burned-out activist, and will then address the challenge of domestic abuse, which has prompted many Christians to ask whether New Testament language of self-denial and sacrifice is even serviceable.

What if our burned-out social activist does not have mutual love in the body of Christ as a readily accessible font for sustaining evangelical self-denial? What if the practices of prayer, liturgy, pastoral care, and mutual aid that ought to express and sustain such love have instead become suspect for her? What if that is because unloving members and leaders have betrayed those very practices and now eat the bread and drink the cup of the Lord unworthily?[13]

In one way, there is no fully adequate answer, precisely because this is not the will of God and represents a breakdown of the order of love. The point here is not to give up immediately on ethical deliberation, for the discipline of ethics exists precisely to deal with life in a fallen world. The point is rather to underscore the argument that Christian faithfulness, witness, and self-denying love are *not* intelligible simply as heroic individual action, and in so doing to set priorities. When the social witness of the Church falls short, many Christian activists are tempted to abandon the Church and work for social change entirely through other venues. No doubt, such an option may sometimes be the only way for them to survive as sane human beings and to husband their activist energies. But survival decisions are inherently tragic and costly. In this case, the cost includes loss of connection to specifically Christian witness, thus beginning to give up on the possibility that the Church may yet fulfill its calling to be the archetypically alternative community that offers a new social reality to the world—or, in the language of the Second Vatican Council, is the sacrament of the world's salvation. One lesson for our burned-out activist and her pastors, therefore, may be to place a high priority on keeping social action integrated within the collective witness of the Christian people. If doing so is itself a source of frustration, we should recognize that the very way that agents of change work within the Church for its greater faithfulness—urgently yet patiently, prophetically yet lovingly, dissenting yet loyally so—can already witness to a qualitatively new social reality in the world.

For all that, we cannot discount the temptation to despair or the virtual impossibility of sustaining the struggle alone. The martyr in solitary confinement or the torture chamber is not really alone who knows the communion of saints and could not now be enduring faithfully if it were not for prior nurture in the Church. But those who struggle with betrayal by the Church itself, in the person of domineering leaders or parents or mentors-turned-abusers, may actually sense themselves more alone than any martyr.

Thus, the challenge of sustaining evangelical self-denial may still fall back upon Christians who, in one way or another, are struggling in a more solitary fashion than either they or God would desire. Even here, Christian ethicists, in their attention to criteria for making decisions in tough cases, should not overlook basic elements of Christian practice as though they were "merely" pious. Decisions are momentary without practices to give them longevity. If the personal prayer of Christians must sometimes be all-too-solitary, their very groaning and wrestling with God over the Church's failure, or their sighing over a dearth of sustenance, may itself prove to be sustaining. After all, a prayer prayed in anguish with the Psalmist—"How long, oh Lord?"—is the beginning of its own fulfillment, for it sustains hope and longing even when that for which it longs seems far distant.

Finally, though, we must recognize those victims of abuse whose very victimization has deprived them of direct existential access to the faith, hope, and love they need even to pray with holy anger, "How long, oh Lord?" Instead of faith they may doubt that the God of whom Christians speak has anything to offer them. Instead of hope they may despair even of their own self-worth. Instead of authentic Christian love they may only know destructive accounts of self-sacrifice and self-denial that have locked them into abusive relationships too long, telling them they dare not leave. If we are to sustain a properly evangelical account of Christ-like self-denial we must be able to distinguish it from gratuitous victimization, not just in principle but by developing explicit criteria for dealing with cases of domestic and sexual abuse. Among such criteria, I would propose the following:

(1) *Self-denial is proper when it contributes to an order of mutual love that in turn witnesses to God's Reign and God's love.* As Gill-Austern has put it, "Self-denial is not first and foremost about meeting another's need before our own but rather aligning oneself and one's will to God so that every part of one's life might be governed by God" through a love of God and neighbor that contributes to the common good and that risks the displeasure of those (especially men) who would have a woman contribute only to limited groups (including the family).[14] A teleology of self-denial that is rightly oriented in witness to the ecology of mutual love that God lovingly desires for heaven and earth, clearly rules *out* putative "orders of mutual love" that are fundamentally exclusionary, collectively egocentric, or in servitude to some human ideology. It rules *in* orders of mutual love that invite others to participate with a message of good news. Violence, abuse, or silence within the Christian community simply cannot be justified as "for the common good," because the particularity of this community's vision of the good is itself ordered "teleologically" to a further good, according to its call to witness to God's Reign and God's love, realized through the nonviolent love of Jesus Christ.

(2) *Self-denial is also proper and redemptive when it comes as a consequence of faithfulness to God's Reign and God's love.* Suffering should not be glorified or welcomed for its own sake. The cross should not come before its time, before other ways of working for justice have been exhausted. Mary Schertz has made this point as a Mennonite feminist committed both to a Christian nonviolence that sees redemptive possibilities in a willingness to absorb violence rather than inflict counterviolence, and to making that pacifist argument in such a way that its claims do not inflict new injustices against the victims of abuse. "The event of the cross took place only when the options were limited to either absorbing violence or returning it in kind," Schertz has argued. We thus misconstrue the cross when we separate it from the ministry that led to it. Jesus did not seek to die, but rather to announce good news for the poor and a transformation of human relationships. To this end, the cross "was a means, not an end in itself, and it was a means of last resort. It was the course chosen only when the alternative was abandonment of the project, only when the choice really was

between absorbing the violence or perpetuating it through acquiescence or retaliation."[15]

The self-sacrifice of the woman who remains in an abusive relationship—blaming herself if she begins to consider her own needs, or
never even naming honestly the abuse she suffers—is not the self-
denial of which the Gospels speak at all. Whatever other personal suffering she might someday have the strength to incur voluntarily, it will
only be evangelical self-denial if it comes as consequence of confronting this very evil for the sake of God's Reign. Whatever reconciliation might someday become possible, it will only be authentic if the
abuser has been confronted, the abused has been honest, and the fruit
of repentance has been tested. None of this will be possible for a victim of abuse without long nurture in a supportive community. And
that will not be possible unless one of the community's first acts of
support has been to help her leave the abusive relationship—for a
time, probably a long time, maybe for a lifetime.

(3) *In both of the above two cases, the self-sacrificial dimension of God's
own love in Christ expresses itself in a willingness to go first, to take the initiative in living according to God's Reign even without guarantee of success
or reciprocity.* Citing Martin Luther King Jr. and Daniel Day Williams,
Stephen Post has insisted that while radical self-denial should not be
conflated with Christian love, bearing the cross may still be necessary
to restore broken community; for while communion is the core of love
and was Jesus' own goal even as the cross loomed, it is in the very character of God to take unilateral and sacrificial action to restore communion.[16] Lest we confuse taking *initiative* with taking up the cross
prematurely, Schertz's warning to that effect came with a suggestion:
Perhaps "taking up one's cross, which is a daily necessity according to
the gospel, means not so much setting one's course by the star of suffering love as setting a course which involves announcing good news
to the oppressed and living a new relationality." Doing so, she noted,
will involve many creative actions that all may risk but do not immediately resort to the cross—"all the confrontation, healing, strategiz-
ing, persuasion, denunciation, parables and demonstrations of which
we are capable."[17]

Though deeply suspicious of Christianity and classical theism,
Sharon Welch in her *Feminist Ethic of Risk* has helped clarify what it
means to act without guarantee of success. Her critique of standard
"ethics of control" deals with a different set of issues, but coincides in

surprising ways with critiques that our retrieval of Augustinian continence has opened up. Welch has noticed how consistently both policymakers and the public in the United States assume "that it is possible
to guarantee the efficacy of one's actions"; thus they equate responsible
action with an absolute control that will eliminate all risks.[18] Welch
has drawn her alternative from the writings of African-American
women, who tell of those who must act responsibly without any assumption of control and must sustain their struggle without promise
of any victory, much less total victory. In an ethic of risk, "responsible
action does not mean the certain achievement of desired ends but the
creation of a matrix in which further actions are possible, the creation
of the conditions of possibility for desired changes." Such a matrix is
decidedly communal: "Responsible action does not mean one individual resolving the problems of others," for that would revert to an
ethics of control. "It is, rather, participation in a communal work, laying the groundwork for the creative response of people in the present
and in the future." Such an ethic does not encourage martyrdom, and
in fact recognizes when *not* to take risks that might endanger others,
but it does recognize that to risk harm and even death may sometimes
be necessary. The measure of an action's worth is not in its risk to life
per se, but in its contribution to the courage and imagination of the
community of resistance and dignity in the face of injustice.[19]

(4) *Suffering that would have been gratuitous victimization may yet be
transformed into a redemptive witness if it too comes as the last resort in a
nonviolent effort to confront the unjust situation—but "transformation" here
will almost certainly require "transference" of at least some suffering to those
who accept it voluntarily.* Emphasizing only the transformative possibilities of risks and suffering that one knowingly chooses for the sake
of God's Reign might suggest that some situations of injustice are beyond possibility of transformation, and some abusive relationships are
beyond hope of reconciliation. Does all this mean, therefore, that some
circumstances are beyond redemption, and that Christian nonviolence
might not be called for in those cases? In practice, many—including
Augustine—have said yes to the latter part of the question without recognizing that they are implicitly affirming the former. And that must
mean that there is some area of human life that is outside the reach of
its very Creator, impervious to the Lordship of Jesus Christ, and stronger
than the Holy Spirit. Before we contemplate such awful possibilities,

we should consider a different question. What would it take to transform even the suffering of one who has suffered gratuitous victimization into a redemptive witness?

Though the issues here have had a long and contentious history of debate that Augustine in fact helped shape, they are brutally concrete for the battered wife and for any shelter or support group coming to her aid. How should she go about extracting herself from an abusive relationship? How may she defend herself? If it is a church-related shelter or support group coming to her aid, should they turn to the police for help in doing so? Lest I seem to be evading tough questions by posing alternate ones, let me make clear: The Christian community (pacifist or otherwise) has little if any moral basis for condemning the battered wife who reaches for a kitchen knife to defend herself, or the woman's shelter who calls upon armed police force for help in extracting and protecting her, if it does not have committed leaders and members prepared to risk their own suffering in order to accompany her. But precisely to the degree that Christian communities are prepared to risk suffering together in solidarity with their most vulnerable members will they be in a better position to develop their own forms of nonviolent civil defense and nonlethal policing.[20] That very pattern deserves closer study.

When we talk about transforming passive suffering into redemptive suffering, we are continuing to talk about members of the Christian community engaging in an active witness to Christ's way of inaugurating qualitatively new relationships even at risk to themselves. Such suffering continues to qualify as the last resort in a nonviolent effort to confront an unjust situation. But we must continue to pay attention to the conditions that make such witness possible. Those most victimized will rarely be the ones able to take the lead in such witness, and if after much nurture they are able to participate publicly at all, it will never be alone. Again, because we are creatures who live in time, and who need a matrix of mutual love in order to develop the capacity for self-denying love, little of this is possible for victims themselves without time—often much time—away from the abusive relationship. In order for forgiveness and reconciliation with the abuser to be a goal at all, the Church may sometimes have to recognize it as an eschatological one. In the worst cases, a lifetime may simply not be long enough to allow adequate healing and rebuilding. Where reconciliation does become thinkable, it will only come with long and unrushed nurture in the self-worth and self-confidence needed for confronting past wrongs truthfully and for insisting on a thoroughgoing repentance that will make reconciliation something other than new acquiescence or forgetfulness.[21] Even then, the only reconciliation for which the community should hope may sometimes be one that stops short of the renewal of the original remarriage.[22]

By now, however, the burden of suffering that we are contemplating has begun to shift. It has begun to rest more heavily upon a larger community whose members are capable of solidarity with the battered wife. Of course, the community's suffering may never have the searing, destructive intensity that once threatened to shrivel the victim's psychological capacity for self-direction. But there may still be real, life-threatening dangers for those who help her escape and go into hiding. There will certainly be long and tiring conversations for those who patiently help her rebuild a sense of dignity. There can often be economic costs for those who help her make the transition to financial independence. If these forms of self-denying love are not what Christians are talking about when they say that suffering can be redemptive, then the Church's critics have every right to say bluntly, "Put up or shut up."

(5) *The self-sacrifices of individual Christians derive from the church's mutual, collective vocation to witness through both sacrificial and mutual love to God's purposes and character.* As Gill-Austern has said, "The work of compassion often begins with the act of joining with, accompaniment, solidarity, rather than self-sacrifice."[23]

If the whole life of a Christian community is to be a witness to God's larger redemptive purposes for creation, that may in turn suggest further criteria: (a) Individuals ought not to bear the brunt of self-sacrifice alone. The injustice of such self-sacrifice would in fact undermine the witness of the community's mutual love and aid. (b) Thus, violation and abuse within the community itself ought not to go unchecked in the name of "self-denying love" or "nonresistance," nor should the community avoid internal conflict or protect the outward reputation of the community as a whole by suppressing the fact of such violations. The message such suppression in fact communicates both to members and to society is the confusion of Christ-like love with victimization. (c) Forgiveness for abusers is only possible when the community first names abuses truthfully, and when forgiveness is an action primarily of the gathered community, not of individual victims suffering in silence.[24]

The community must still deal with its own internal injustices redemptively and nonviolently, in ways that are in keeping with its witness to God's Reign. But to put the matter differently, in its internal life the self-sacrifice that the Christian community asks of its members is the pain of sharing the burdens of its most vulnerable members, not the pain of those vulnerable members' silence and acquiescence. In risking its own cohesion by dealing truthfully with abuses rather than avoiding conflict, the community *as a whole* will also be practicing Christlike self-denial, risking its very survival or "laying down its life." The community may certainly hope to gain its true life of mutual love thereby, but not without a real risk that defies neat and confident calculation. Communal self-denial is not possible, of course, unless specific individuals take personal risks on the frontlines of confrontation and accompaniment. But that role is for the strongest in the community, not the weakest—with "strongest" meaning those most fully nurtured and trained in the virtues that the community seeks to embody.

All of this suggests the sense in which we need to aim at creating communities of mutual love precisely in order to sustain a witness of self-sacrificial love. Thus, even while recognizing that "Christian love does assume the posture of radical self-denial when the circular flow of give and take is interrupted," Post insisted that "participation in the mutual good is the irreplaceable basis of moral growth."[25] This is the matrix for further moral action of which Welch has spoken. These are the communal resources that Moessner and Gill-Austern have noticed the Good Samaritan drawing upon. If the Samaritan transported the wounded person to an inn, noted Moessner, today the inn might be a church, battered women's shelter, rape crisis center, eating disorders clinic, or some other support group, but "always, when the teamwork between the Samaritan and the innkeeper becomes obvious, there is great relief."[26]

Against Niebuhr's paradoxically simplistic rendering of the relation between sacrificial and mutual love we note, then, that to aim at mutual love and equity not only does not undermine sacrificial love, *but actually makes it possible on a wider communal scale.* In Niebuhrian ethics, Jesus' self-denying love is allegedly impracticable in all but the very smallest units of human social life. Niebuhr argued consistently that any Christians who would allow Jesus' ethic to shape their lives must withdraw from the social order and renounce social responsibility. Yet if Niebuhr was suggesting that a life being regenerated within history will contribute less and less to history precisely to the degree that it is regenerated, the claim so stated seems counterintuitive at the very least. Such a claim only makes sense if the "tangent toward eternity"[27] which lives of Christ-like love begin to follow fails to thread together a community of mutual love that makes a distinct contribution to history and society on its way to eternity, and does so precisely insofar as the community longs for and anticipates the mutual love that can be perfect only in eternity.

Mutual love is as much a precondition for sacrificial love as vice versa. The suggestion here is that it is the Christian community together and as a whole that is called to bear the cross in witness to God's Reign; the self-sacrifices of individual Christians derive from that mutual vocation, as acts of integrity in keeping with God's Reign and the church's vocation. Mutual love, solidarity, and mutual care release the creativity, hope, and character that make self-sacrifice possible both for groups and individuals. Again contrary to Niebuhr, there is a sense in which even outright nonresistance—the refusal of persons and community to defend themselves through lethal force—is *more* rather than *less* feasible for social groups than for individuals, at least groups that enjoy a common vision of God's purposes and calling.

Note that once again the trinitarian shape of Christian love has emerged and corrected both Nygren's allegation that agape must lack motive and Niebuhr's account of the relationship between self-sacrificial and mutual love. To use classical trinitarian language, the "procession" and "mission" of the Son reveal God's love in the willingness to act first, not without motive but without *guarantee* of reciprocal love. In turn, the "procession" and "mission" of the Holy Spirit are revealed to be at work as communities of mutual love are not only created through sacrificial love (unintentionally, said Niebuhr) but also create the conditions that make sacrificial love possible (intentionally, contra Niebuhr).

Thesis 6:   *In the actual operation of Christian love, continence plays a critical but often unnoticed role, for because all that is truly good is God's gift, the good cannot be had through manipulative and coercive human grasping; Augustinian continence is not*

merely negative self-restraint, then, for it makes authentic love
effective through benevolent respect of others and trusting faith
in God.

None of this is consequentialist; decision making here does not
depend solely on a calculation of short-term efficacy. Even while there
is a logical separation of means from ends so as not to confuse self-
sacrifice with the end, that end or *telos* continues to shape those means
employed and to delegitimize some means altogether. Yet here most
of all, in his choice of means toward ends, Augustine would seem a
dubious ally to many.

Augustine's gestalt vision of love, as noted in chapter 3, is nothing
more than a vision if sinful human beings can only behold it from afar
and not practice it. But Augustine's own practice of mutual love was
problematic at best, insofar as he attempted to effect an order of mutual love through state-enforced church unity. Augustine did recognize
that God alone could dominate others without pride.[28] But a writer
such as Welch may be forgiven for neglecting the implications of this
distinction and concluding that doctrines of divine omnipotence such
as Augustine's have directly led Christians to glorify domination. After
all, Augustine himself seems to have neglected these implications and
left later Christian traditions vulnerable to all kinds of confusions.[29]

There is, however, a principle that is fundamental to the operation
of Augustinian *caritas,* that argues from deep within orthodox Christianity against domineering power itself rather than against mere misuse of power for wrongful ends, and that also provides a reasoned basis
for reading Augustine against himself—thus rejecting some of his ethical judgments and ecclesial policies on the basis of his core theological
insights. Chapter 3 recovered this principle from Augustine's writings,
and chapter 5 used it to assess Augustine's arguments for imperial
sanctions against his Donatist rivals. It is the principle of continence,
which insists that we can only acquire the good through respect for
others and trust in God.

Chapter 3 began by proposing to test the intelligibility of Augustine's claim that through continence we reintegrate all loves within the
one love of God. In book ten of the *Confessions* Augustine's claim to
this effect is forthright, yet the prominence of specifically sexual continence both in his own narrative and in his later controversies has probably distracted scholars from what he once called "higher continence,"

the continence involved in *all* right loving and acting. In Augustine's phenomenology of continent love, one only acquires the good if one does so in a way that is not acquisitive in Nygren's sense. One "has" by not having—by trusting God, respecting the other, and receiving all goods as God's gifts, not by domineering power and manipulation. Not even Augustinian right self-love is acquisitive, for the only self worth loving is a gift of God's grace. Nor is salvation to be had through human striving, but through trusting faith. If stable relationships of love for God (and for all that God loves) are salvation itself, according to Augustine, and if that love solidifies through continence, one must in fact have continence itself in a continent way, as a gift of God's grace. Thus, Augustine portrayed the interior movement of his very conversion with a vision of a "virtuously alluring" woman named Continence. He could only have such a woman through an "embrace" that respected her "chaste dignity." To violate and to dominate her would be to destroy the very continence that made her beautiful, thus stealing but not really acquiring her name. Only by respecting her could he enjoy her beauty and share in the good of a right relationship. In turn, her message for him was that he could not be healed through his own quest for God, but only through the gift of God.

Continence shapes the deep grammar of all Augustine wrote about Christian love. Like any grammar, it often went unnoticed, even by him. Yet evidence for its pervasive role emerged when we traced the Latin verbs he used to describe how human beings relate to the objects of their love. Love is "the hand of the soul," Augustine once said. "If it is holding anything, it cannot hold anything else. But that it may be able to hold what is given to it, it must leave go what it holds already."[30] Linguistic analysis in chapter 3 confirmed the pattern: For false and problematic loves, Augustine consistently used verbs whereby people acquire the objects of their love through operations of *grasping*, which close in upon and control those objects. In contrast, loves that are right and true open wide the "hand of the soul" in an act of *clinging* to God, to Christ, to the truth, and to wisdom, none of which one can control or manipulate. Love for friends and neighbors also is properly a love that clings rather than grasps, for human beings love one another most truly when all cling to God and thus to one another "in God."

It is by insisting upon continence in our love for other human beings that we prevent a necessary tension within all love from serving to rationalize coercive policies. As we noted in chapter 2, love argues both for intervention on behalf of what we judge to be others' true good, and for respect of their dignity as creatures of God who must appropriate that good for themselves. It is precisely because love must have content—because benevolence wishes some good for "your neighbor as yourself"—that love always runs the risk of paternalistic intervention. But because love necessarily runs that risk, it must check that risk with continent respect for the other and a self-restraint grounded in trust of God, the ultimate giver of all good.

For Augustine, mutual love among Christians was the greatest of all goods short of the supreme good that it anticipates, which is eternal participation in the trinitarian life of God. The mutual love that binds people together in the love of God is the Holy Spirit; that love is the mutual love whereby Father and Son love each other; Christ loves himself in his "body" the church when member loves member. Christian mutual love anticipates and reaches toward the eschatological end wherein all will love all, and the whole of the universe will love the whole, not because of some inevitable cosmic principle of unity but because God's own self-giving love longs that "God shall be all in all." Precisely because this love was such a great good, grasping at that end *before* the end—God's eschatological end—became Augustine's greatest, most abiding, and most subtle temptation.

Augustine's own policies and ethical judgments offered the first test case of whether his doctrine of Christian love or *caritas* is able to sustain evangelical self-denial, and whether Augustinian continence translates that self-denial into postcanonical settings with a reasonable degree of faithfulness. Augustine certainly believed that when he renounced "wife [and] ambition in this world" he was in a direct line of continuity with the first disciples who responded to Jesus' hard sayings. In the episcopacy, however, power and prominence eventually caught up with him again.

Augustine's rationalization of religious repression raises serious doubts about whether his doctrine of love offers a helpful framework for contemporary Christian moral discernment. Chapter 5 nonetheless argued that selective appropriation of Augustine's thought is possible and defensible even for Christians who differ with some of his specific and most famous ethical judgments, precisely because Augustinian theology is self-correcting. Augustinian continence provides a principle of selectivity: *If the core of Augustine's theology is his doctrine of love for God and for all creatures "in God," then one may only participate consistently in such love insofar as one does so in a way that is also consistently continent.*

Augustine's theology and ethic could cohere only if they retained their eschatological tension—the sense that all human projects are tenuous, the insistence that Christians grow toward but do not realize perfection in this life, and a corresponding humility. Augustine's policy toward the "schismatic" Donatist Church of North Africa, however, amounted to a kind of realized eschatology at odds with his deepest theological convictions. By consenting to imperial sanctions that would "compel them to come" back into the established Catholic Church, Augustine attempted to force the realization of that greatest of all earthly goods, an order of mutual love. Arguably, the effort was an act of incontinence, of grasping domineeringly for a good that Christians must rather receive as a gift.

Augustinian continence diagnoses Augustine's own incontinence. In *Confessions* 10 Augustine had in fact predicted that of all the temptations against which he must pray that God would give him continence, the most difficult one for him to overcome or even assess was the temptation to pride and self-vindication in his relationships with others. In the mutual give-and-take of Christian *societas,* he could not imagine how to live without some praise and approval from others, but neither could he be sure when his pride was disguising itself as apparently benevolent words and deeds aiming at the good of others. Augustine later rationalized imperial sanctions against the Donatists by appealing precisely to principles of benevolence. But only God can dominate others without pride, he had recognized in *Confessions* 10.36.58. The mutual love that he sought to restore among Catholics and Donatists would have been a true good for all parties. Yet if loving neighbors and all other creatures "in God" requires that one acquire the great good of mutual love itself in a consistently continent way, then Augustine fell short. In his passionate longing for that good, he grasped through a subtle but still-prideful domination when, according to his own theology, he should have clung to God in trust.

The diagnosis of Augustine's incontinence according to his own principle of continence, then, is what vindicates the overall structure of his teaching, even as it provides a reasoned basis for appropriating

Augustine's thought only selectively. In doing so according to the principle of continence, however, we are not simply insisting on negative restraint. For if continence is the only way to enter into relationship with the good, it is in fact *the* way that *caritas* becomes effective. If continence is a "chaste embrace," the accent finally falls on *embrace*. Through a trust in God, which knows that grasping control of others will inevitably destroy the ecology of mutual love that God graciously gives, we may share with hope in the first fruits of that love already in time, and do so fully beyond time.

Thesis 7:   *What ultimately sustains evangelical self-denial is what sustains trusting faith in God and frees us to respect rather than manipulate others—the gracious love of God who ever initiates that communion which is our salvation, and who is always the power that enables us to respond in kind.*

Recovering the role of continence within Augustine's doctrine of Christian love or *caritas* suggests ways to sustain self-denial in both of the senses that the opening chapter called for. (1) Christian ethics can show how the self-denying love of Christian disciples is sustained over time. And (2) Christian ethics can sustain a proper account of self-denial in the face of critiques that question the foundational role that symbols of cross, self-sacrifice, and martyrdom have played in Christianity. In both cases an Augustinian answer emerges from the following summary thesis: Self-denial, self-sacrifice, and costly "suffering service" are not ends in themselves but rather are only meaningful within the teleological framework of love for God and for all creatures "in God," through the trusting hope that God our Highest Good wills all creation to enjoy together the common good of participation in the trinitarian life of God.

On one hand, if continence is the operative mode of *caritas,* then desire and duty, self-love and self-denial, are so inextricably integrated that neither loses out to the other; Augustinian *caritas*-working-through-continence sustains self-denying love without subverting the New Testament's call to Christ-like "agapeic" love. What makes joy in the mutual love that is "set before us" something more than mere reciprocity is what Jesus Christ shows us about the way God creates and restores relations of mutual love: God has loved and suffered first.

Thus, all who seek mutual love in Christ-like ways will likewise be prepared to risk and to act first—not without hope nor without thought of receiving love in return (as Niebuhr and Nygren believed), but without *guarantee* of receiving love in return.

On the other hand, self-denial within this *caritas* framework is not degrading. The good of the human agent remains a proper end within the ecological order of right relationship between all creatures, which God our Creator has always willed for us in love. Self-denial is possible and sustainable for the Christian because the Creator's intended end has already come near; God is now restoring the mutual love of creation through the suffering love of Jesus Christ, and through the love of God that "has been poured into our hearts through the Holy Spirit that has been given to us."[31]

"In the Manner of Pilgrims"

In its broadest dimension, the challenge of holding together a unified account of right self-love and proper self-denial while still on our pilgrimage amid the earthly city is the problem any Christian or Christian community has in negotiating its life there, its life in time. Just what is "the manner of pilgrims"?[32] How are we to participate in the good of mutual love now, in time, with respectful gratitude for all the gifts of God that make it possible, yet sustain the disposition of disciples and martyrs to leave all this behind if necessary? The vulnerable and imperfect mutual love by which the Christian community witnesses to God's purposes in history is not *quite* yet the end, after all. It is not itself the fullness of God's purpose, nor yet the mutual love that has drawn all enemies into the communion of love "in God." No Christian community or tradition can claim to have resolved this problem definitively.

For one thing, even though we have argued that Reinhold Niebuhr's warnings about aiming to realize orders of mutual love were overwrought, they are not altogether unwarranted and should serve as salutary reminders: Every order of mutual love carries within it the seeds of new and subtle forms of collective egotism, enemy construction, and rigid exclusion. As a people blessed to be a blessing to all peoples, as the followers of a Lord who loved and died for his enemies, the Church's very identity is tied up in the call to break with this social pattern. But the temptations are subtle, for in fact they grow rather than diminish when Christians are faithful in building qualitatively new forms of community, and then enjoy a good that is all the more worth protecting.

For another thing, no Christians can definitively resolve the problem of living in time, because to God alone are all times present.[33] God alone will resolve the problem at God's final resolution of time and history. To recognize ourselves as a pilgrim people is to recognize the inexorable dynamics of eschatological tension and of life in exile, which render every resolution tentative, partial, and situational in the best sense of the word.[34]

Crucial to our opening argument that Christians need a unified account of right self-love and proper self-denial was the observation that to recognize the problem of sustaining self-denying love through time is to re-admit considerations of self-concern, and thus self-love, into our account of Christian love. If we, as Christian human beings, cannot resolve how to sustain self-denying love through time, is that an admission that this entire project has failed? Yes and no.

At its very best, Augustine's writing was a glorious failure. As James O'Donnell has noted, "Augustine's experience of God has shaped our world" and "that power of one man's literary output is striking," yet it is all "the more so because it is built on failure; the failure of language in the presence of God is the center of Augustine's thought."[35] For writers who have entered into Augustine's world, the highest success to which we may aspire must be to fail in the same way that he did—to reach the limit of words, and thus to write words that do not themselves claim to grasp God or faithfulness, but only to cling to God by opening outward in a confession that it is God who grasps us and sustains whatever faithfulness we live. In this sense, no book and no community can expect to resolve once and for all the problem of how to sustain self-denying love. Yet that very confession may nonetheless open us to trust in the God who does sustain.

To think otherwise would be to grasp in one more presumptuous way at God's end, before the end. Faithfulness to God's ways and purposes is finally sustained through neither intellect nor will—through neither a systematic theology nor our own resolve to follow Christ as disciples. We do not need Augustine so much as we need God. But

Augustine is a fellow pilgrim. Augustine is an eloquent witness to God's love. And that witness is a gift we should neither confuse with the Giver, nor disdain.

The supreme Gift, however, is Jesus Christ.

Our study has sought to retrieve the structure of Augustine's doctrine of Christian love and has identified the grammar of continence within that structure. But if this task has been fruitful it has also been limited. A theological or ethical thought structure alone is just a formal consideration. The form must still be filled up with specific material content. While the lessons of Augustinian continence have yielded some such content, it too would remain merely formal without concrete specification by Jesus Christ. Augustine pointed to this reality but may not have stressed it enough when he paused once to exclaim with the Psalmist, "'Convert us and show us your face,' O God of hosts, 'and we shall be saved.'"[36] For as he was suggesting when he paused, love for God must long for the right relation of all parts in the whole of creation—but we cannot see enough of that whole to be sure of what God's love asks of us in relation to each part. What we can see is the face of God, and thus the character of God's loving will, in Jesus of Nazareth, the Christ, through the entirety of his life, ministry, death, resurrection.

As Augustine himself would expect, here is where we must move beyond him, as we must always move beyond every doctor of the Church. Here is where we both continue to appropriate Augustine's aid and expect at times to appropriate his thought precisely by critiquing it. In his own critique of the Platonists, Augustine faulted them for claiming to seek God while rejecting the Mediator between God and humanity who had come so completely in the flesh that his blood had been shed.[37] Yet the very reality to which Augustine pointed as he pointed to Christ the Mediator should remind us that it is not the *concept* of a Mediator that saves us. *Qua* concept alone it remains too weak and Platonic. So too with "the Incarnation," for though the doctrine is a guide to speaking rightly of the reality to which it points, it is not the doctrine or even its structure that saves and transforms us. Again, like Augustine's, my words can succeed only through a failure that points beyond words: what saves is the very Godhead at our feet, in our clay, Jesus of Nazareth entering the life of Israel and struggles of Galilee, Jesus Christ forming a new people out of the alienated peoples of Jew and Gentile.[38] It is this Jesus who in his humanity is very

God, revealing in his flesh the character of the God. It is this Jesus whose loving relationship with his heavenly Father draws even us who once were God's enemies into reconciliation with God and one another through the bond of the Holy Spirit.[39] Can there be any face of God other than that revealed in the life, ministry, and death of this Jesus? Can there be any way of establishing that order of mutual love which is God's will, except through the nonviolent love by which this Jesus endured the cross for the joy set before him? I do not know how one can be adequately trinitarian without also being Christocentric.

In other words, the very concreteness of Jesus' life must finally tell us what it means to cling to God as our *Summum Bonum*, to love one another "in God," to love as God loves, and to live patiently through the inevitable incompleteness of our apprehension. Of course, all this is possible only as the Holy Spirit draws us into the mutual love of the first two persons of the Trinity, transforming our incompleteness into living trust. But that trust is first of all in the efficacy of the whole trajectory of that life, ministry, death, and resurrection which the Gospels narrate. The early Christian hymn that Paul recorded in Philippians 2 affirms that Christ lived this trajectory by refraining from grasping even at that which was his own by right. Augustine has helped us understand that all grasping closes "the hand of the soul," thus precluding trustful clinging to God, while eventually choking off the very good that we hope to hold. Mere imitation of Jesus' way of giving his life for others is not a *sufficient* cause of clinging to God and loving neighbor "in God," since imitation alone can be another covert form of grasping through our own power. But such imitation as adopts the Jesus narrative for our own context, through a discipleship made creative through the loving power of the Holy Spirit, is still a *necessary* cause. The content of love for God, neighbor, and self can take no other shape than the one we already see in Jesus.

We bless the Lord our God, who gathered us together to spiritual joy. Let us be ever in humility of heart, and let our joy be with God. Let us not be elated with any prosperity of this world, but know that our happiness is not until these things shall have passed away. Now, . . . let our joy be in hope: let none find the fullness of joy in a present thing, lest that person stick fast on the journey. Let joy derive wholly from hope to come, let desire derive wholly from eternal life. Let all sighings breathe after Christ. Let that fairest one alone, who loved the foul to make them fair, be all our desire; after Christ alone let us run, for Christ alone let us pant and sigh; "and let them say always, The Lord be magnified, who wishes the peace of God's servant."

Augustine
Homilies on the Gospel of John
closing prayer, 10.13

Notes

INTRODUCTION

1. Stanley Hauerwas, *The Peaceable Kingdom: A Primer in Christian Ethics* (Notre Dame, Ind.: University of Notre Dame Press, 1983), 4, 122–25, 129–30.

2. Hauerwas, *The Peaceable Kingdom,* 30–34, 72–95.

3. These three clauses allude to three of the most formative Mennonite thinkers of recent generations—Harold S. Bender, Guy F. Hershberger, and John H. Yoder. See Harold S. Bender, "The Anabaptist Vision," *Church History* 13 (March 1944): 3–24; Guy Franklin Hershberger, *The Way of the Cross in Human Relations* (Scottdale, Pa.: Herald Press, 1958); John Howard Yoder, *The Politics of Jesus,* 2d ed., reprint, 1972 (Grand Rapids, Mich.: William B. Eerdmans, 1994), 246.

4. Cf. Gerald Schlabach, "More Than One Task: North American Nonviolence and Latin American Liberation Struggle," epilogue in *Relentless Persistence: Nonviolent Action in Latin America,* ed. Philip McManus and Gerald Schlabach, with a foreword by Leonardo Boff (Philadelphia: New Society Publishers, 1991), 252–65.

5. Nadine Pence Frantz, "Women: Bearing the Cross of Discipleship," *Women's Concerns Report of the Mennonite Central Committee on Women's Concerns* (March–April 1990): 2. Pence Frantz was herself a member of the Church of the Brethren, another "historic peace church" with some common roots in the Anabaptist movement of the sixteenth century. Also see two collections of essays: Elizabeth G. Yoder, ed., *Peace Theology and Violence against Women,* Occasional Papers 16 (Elkhart, Ind.: Institute of Mennonite Studies, 1992); and *Mennonite Quarterly Review* 68, no. 2 (April 1994).

6. In addition to the feminist thinkers with whom I interact in my first chapter, see many of the articles collected in Carol J. Adams and Marie M. Fortune, eds., *Violence against Women and Children* (New York: Continuum, 1995).

7. Genesis 12:1–4. See Gerald W. Schlabach, "Beyond Two-Versus One-Kingdom Theology: Abrahamic Community as a Mennonite Paradigm for Engagement in Society," *Conrad Grebel Review* 11, no. 3 (Fall 1993): 187–210; *To Bless All Peoples: Serving with Abraham and Jesus*, Peace and Justice Series, no. 12 (Scottdale, Pa.: Herald Press, 1991); "The Blessing of Abraham's Children: A Theology of Service," *Mission Focus* 19, no. 4 (December 1991): 52–55.

8. *Confessiones* 6.8.13.

9. *Conf.* 7.8.12.

10. Thomas Aquinas, *Summa theologiae* I 60.3–5.

11. Aquinas, *Summa theologiae* I–II 1–21.

12. Anders Nygren, *Agape and Eros: The Christian Idea of Love*, trans. Philip S. Watson (New York: Harper and Row, 1969).

13. The comparison between Kant and Nygren is not simply methodological. There are deep affinities between Kant's conception of a good will and Nygren's conception of agape. A perfectly good will, which wills with perfect rationality to do its duty for duty's sake according to the categorical imperative, is not really possible in Kant's "sensible world," but only in the "intelligible world." Likewise, pure agape, which is entirely other-directed and self-giving, is not really possible for human beings in history, but is only possible for God. All the same, both Kantian duty and Nygren's agape serve in their respective systems as the final standard and guide for concrete human actions. Each obtains independently of and prior to every sensible or historical consideration of the agent's own interests.

14. Augustine's refusal to condone personal self-defense, which Aquinas justified, is but one sign of the greater tug that evangelical self-denial continued to exercise on Augustine's thought, however inconsistently. Of as much interest to Nygren is the fact that Augustine (eventually) took greater stock of the dangers of perverse self-love (cf. *Agape and Eros*, 532–38) than Aquinas seems to have done. Further, Nygren may have considered Augustine's doctrines of the incarnation, of grace, and of predestination (cf. 468–70) to have affirmed the priority and sovereignty of God's love more strongly than those of Aquinas—although Nygren's discussion of Aquinas (642–45) is too short for one to be sure, and in any case, Thomists would undoubtedly debate the point. Nygren actually read Aquinas as staying "in closest agreement with Augustine" (643), but this is probably because he read Aquinas back into Augustine, as Oliver O'Donovan argued in *The Problem of Self-Love in St. Augustine* (New Haven: Yale University Press, 1980), 145.

15. John Howard Yoder, *The Christian Witness to the State*, Institute of Mennonite Studies Series, no. 3 (Newton, Kan.: Faith and Life Press, 1964).

16. R. A. Markus, *Saeculum: History and Society in the Theology of St. Augustine*, 2d ed., reprint, 1970 (Cambridge, England: Cambridge University Press, 1988).

17. Many of these scholars have articles in the July 1995 issue of *Mennonite Quarterly Review* (69, no. 3), and have also been reprinted in John D. Roth, ed., *Refocusing a Vision: Shaping Anabaptist Character in the 21st Century* (Goshen, Ind.: Mennonite Historical Society, 1995).

18. Frederick W. Norris, "Black Marks on the Communities' Manuscripts," 1994 NAPS Presidential Address, *Journal of Early Christian Studies* 2, no. 3 (Winter 1994): 465.

CHAPTER ONE   The Problem of Self-Denial

1. Cf. *Confessiones* 2.1.1., 10.29.40.

2. Barbara Hilkert Andolsen has noted that nineteenth-century feminists had already "recognized the destructive effects of an overemphasis on self-sacrifice as the quintessential Christian virtue." Andolsen, "Agape in Feminist Ethics," *Journal of Religious Ethics* 9 (Spring 1981): 75.

3. Anders Nygren, "Intellectual Autobiography," trans. Peter W. Russell, in *The Philosophy and Theology of Anders Nygren,* ed. Charles W. Kegley (Carbondale: Southern Illinois University Press, 1970) 6.

4. Nygren, *Agape and Eros,* 6.

5. Thor Hall, *Anders Nygren,* Makers of the Modern Theological Mind (Waco, Tex.: Word Books, 1978), 167. Though the point concerning Nygren's influence stands, the point concerning the difference between Greek words for love is actually less intact than Hall thought. See James Barr's careful refutation of the whole attempt to make sharp distinctions between them, in "Words for Love in Biblical Greek," in *The Glory of Christ in the New Testament* (Oxford: Clarendon Press, 1987).

6. See Paul Ramsey, *Basic Christian Ethics* (New York: Scribner's, 1950); Joseph Sittler, *The Structure of Christian Ethics* (Baton Rouge: Louisiana State University Press, 1958); Gene Outka, *Agape: An Ethical Analysis* (New Haven and London: Yale University Press, 1972). Reinhold Niebuhr, *An Interpretation of Christian Ethics* (New York and London: Harper and Brothers, 1935), stands (as we will learn to expect) in a paradoxical relationship to Agapeism insofar as Niebuhr saw agape as normative for Christian ethics in some ways but not others. Joseph Fletcher, *Situation Ethics: The New Morality* (Philadelphia: Westminster Press, 1966), must be included as a kind of Agapeist, however much other Agapeists contested his popularization. In fact, his book and the controversy surrounding it may have simply brought to the harsh light of publicity the tensions within Agapeism over what principles (deontological, consequentialist, etc.) it needs *besides* the norm of agape for agape actually to be operative. In this regard, note Ramsey's harsh criticism of Sittler in *War and the*

Christian Conscience; How Shall Modern War Be Conducted Justly? (Durham, N.C.: Duke University Press, 1961), 50 n. 13.

7. Nygren, *Agape and Eros,* 67, 75–77. On the notion that agape creates rather than discovers value in its objects, cf. Martin Luther, thesis 28 of the *Heidelberg Disputation,* which appears in *Luther's Works* 31, pp. 35–70. Nygren placed Luther's thesis at the beginning of the second part (originally the second volume) of *Agape and Eros,* 233.

8. Hall, *Anders Nygren,* 46, 151; cf. Nygren, *Agape and Eros,* 105.

9. Nygren, *Agape and Eros,* 110 [emphasis *sic*]; 115, quoting 1 Corinthians 2:2; 117, citing Romans 5:6–10; cf. 117–23.

10. Many in the nineteenth century had cited Jesus' double love commandment as the starting point for identifying what is "distinctive and original" about Christianity, but, insisted Nygren, "if we start with the commandment, with Agape as something demanded, we bar our own way to the understanding of the idea of Agape." Both parts of that commandment, love for God and love for neighbor, were already in the Old Testament and so could hardly suggest the distinctive key to Christianity. Nygren went on to argue, in fact, that "There is scarcely a more insidious way of emptying the Christian idea of love and Christian fellowship with God of their vital content than to treat God's love for sinners—that clearest of all expressions of the *new* way of fellowship with God—as merely a special case of the old legalistic religious relationship" characterized by command, which was for Nygren the *nomos* motif (Nygren, *Agape and Eros,* 61, 75).

11. The Parable of Laborers in the Vineyard (Matthew 20:1–16; see Nygren, *Agape and Eros,* 86–90); the Parables of the Prodigal Son, of the Sower, and of the Lost Sheep (Luke 15:11–32; Matthew 13:3–8, Mark 4:3–8, Luke 8:5–8; Matthew 18:12–14, Luke 15:3–7; see Nygren, *Agape and Eros,* 90–91); as well as the Parable of the Unmerciful Steward (Matthew 18:23–35; see Nygren, *Agape and Eros,* 91).

12. Nygren, *Agape and Eros,* 86, 89–90. Just like the all-day laborers who grumbled, those who want the justice that requires reason-giving or "motivated" action alone will take offense at God's generous agape and refuse to accept it.

13. For Nygren's oft-reproduced tabulation of the contrasts between the two love motifs, see *Agape and Eros,* 210.

14. Nygren, *Agape and Eros,* 216–17.

15. Nygren, *Agape and Eros,* 451–52.

16. Nygren, *Agape and Eros,* 272, 451, 464–73.

17. Cf. *Conf.* 10.29.40, 10.31.45, 10.37.60. Nygren found this to be Augustine's way of using his *caritas* synthesis to provide an explanation for the unity between Old and New Testaments. The character of fellowship with God does not change across the testaments; rather, in the New, God adds or

infuses the grace of love for God which humans need as a help in fulfilling the righteousness of the Old, so as to merit fellowship with God. Nygren, *Agape and Eros,* 454.

18. Nygren, *Agape and Eros,* 452–55.

19. Nygren, *Agape and Eros,* 453, 476, 495, 499–503, 509, 524–32, 538, 549–55.

20. "It was in [1930] that Anders Nygren first distinguished what he took to be two radically different kinds of love. He so effectively posed issues about love that they have had a prominence in theology and ethics they never had before. His critics have been legion, but few have ignored or been unaffected by his thesis." Outka, *Agape,* 1.

21. Of course, it is possible that Augustine and Nygren were *both* wrong, in asymmetrical ways. In other words, Nygren may have been wrong to reject Augustine's understanding of Christian love simply because it integrated the self-referential and self-denying dimensions of love, but Augustine may nonetheless have synthesized these in ways that introduced other problems into Christian theology and ethics. Feminist critics of Nygren have their own reservations about Augustine's apparent reliance on Neoplatonism, since he allegedly passed on its negative attitudes toward the body to Western Christianity. This commonplace of current scholarship is more often repeated than defended, however. Neoplatonism offered Augustine a route out of Manichaeism, which evaluated bodies and material reality far more negatively. Neoplatonism in fact allowed Augustine to affirm that all creation is essentially good, for evil is not a substance itself as the Manichaeans believed, but is the privation of good. Cf. *Conf.* 7.12.18–7.16.22.

22. John Burnaby, *Amor Dei: A Study of the Religion of St. Augustine,* The Hulsean Lectures for 1938 (London: Hodder and Stoughton, 1938), 177–78; O'Donovan, *The Problem of Self-Love,* 152–59, especially 157. Also cf. William Riordan O'Connor, "The 'Uti/Frui' Distinction in Augustine's Ethics," *Augustinian Studies* 14 (1983): 45–50.

23. See Margaret A. Farley, "New Patterns of Relationship: Beginnings of a Moral Revolution," *Theological Studies* 36, no. 4 (1975); Judith Plaskow, *Sex, Sin, and Grace: Women's Experience and the Theologies of Reinhold Niebuhr and Paul Tillich* (Washington, D.C.: University Press of America, 1980), 89. Also see Susan Nelson Dunfee, *Beyond Servanthood: Christianity and the Liberation of Women* (Lanham, Md.: University Press of America, 1989), 80; Andolsen, "Agape in Feminist Ethics," 77–80. Mary Daly has a tenuous but influential relationship to Christian feminist ethics, and has made a very explicit place for desire in her project; see Daly, *Pure Lust: Elemental Feminist Philosophy* (Boston: Beacon Press, 1984).

24. See note 22. Of the many critics who have entered into debate with Nygren over the adequacy of his reading of Augustine, John Burnaby stands

out due to the span of his engagement with Nygren, and Oliver O'Donovan thanks to his thoroughness. In addition to Burnaby and O'Donovan see Gunnar Hultgren, *Le commandement d'amour chez Augustin; Interprétation philosophique et théologique d'après les écrits de la période 386–400* (Paris: Vrin, 1939), and Ragnar Holte, *Béatitude et sagesse; Saint Augustin et le problème de la fin de l'homme dans la philosophie ancienne* (Paris and Worcester, Mass.: Etudes Augustiniennnes; Augustinian Studies, Assumption College, 1962). For a thorough bibliographic survey see Dany Dideberg, "Caritas: Prolegomenes à une étude de la théologie augustinienne de la charité," *Signum pietatis: Festgabe für Cornelius Petrus Mayer zum 60. Geburtstag,* ed. Adolar Zumkeller, Cassiciacum, vol. 40 (Wurzburg: Augustinus-Verlag, 1989), 369–81.

25. Burnaby, *Amor Dei,* 127.

26. Burnaby, *Amor Dei,* 18.

27. Burnaby himself considered the mutual love in John 17:11, where Jesus prays that the disciples may be one as he and his Father are one, to be "the Holy of Holies of the New Testament," but "Nygren, with a candour which we may admire, owns that he can make nothing of it" (*Amor Dei,* 18). Burnaby apparently was referring to Nygren's inability to fit Johannine notions of agape into either the pure concept of agape he believed Paul to have held, or into the alien concepts of eros that he believed were able to enter into later Christian thought by way of the Johannine "metaphysic of Agape." See Nygren, *Agape and Eros,* 151–59. In Burnaby's 1970 essay "Amor in St. Augustine" (in *The Philosophy and Theology of Anders Nygren,* ed. Kegley, 184), he added the suggestion that Nygren could not have presented Augustine's doctrine of *caritas* as so crudely individualistic if he had paid more attention to Augustine's doctrine of the church. Having isolated the agape motif, he had to see the motif as watered down in Johannine writings that emphasize Christian love as love for fellow Christians. Yet that, noted Burnaby, is also one of Paul's primary ethical teachings, which Augustine endeavored to develop.

28. Burnaby, *Amor Dei,* 121.

29. Burnaby, *Amor Dei,* 119, with notation particularly to Augustine, *Sermones* 96.2 and *Epistulae* 118.15.

30. Augustine, *De civitate Dei* 14.28.

31. Burnaby, *Amor Dei,* 121. Augustine knew quite well, argued Burnaby, that it is impossible to love God *in order* to satisfy love of self, thus objectifying and using God to satisfy goals and desires one has determined independently of God. Those who love God do not desire God as a private good. "The self-denial for which Christ calls is a denial of the individual, personal, 'private' will, in so far as it falls short of the will of God. I must will to belong to God rather than to myself." If none other than God is the object of and reward for our love, worship, or even our "ascent," then the very nature

of human desire changes. We do not love God for the sake of reward apart from God, for "*Deus ipse praemium* understood as Augustine meant it to be understood, does not encourage but forbid self-centredness." After all, "God will not reward our service by becoming the servant of our desires. . . . The 'possession' of God is the knowledge of Him and the love of Him as He is, not as we in our sinfulness might wish Him to be." Burnaby, *Amor Dei,* 122–23, 251–52. Also cf. 243–44, with quotation from Augustine, *Enarrationes in Psalmos* 55.17.

32. O'Donovan, *The Problem of Self-Love,* 14.

33. O'Donovan, *The Problem of Self-Love,* 19–36. The first of these four aspects of love was the one Augustine found most useful in the apologetic setting. O'Donovan called this *cosmic love,* the love that is a natural law of the universe. All things *do* move toward their goal, or final cause, he sometimes argued, therefore humans *ought* to do so. Yet human love can seek improper objects, which means cosmic love "proves too much" (19–24; quotation is from p. 21). Second, the need to define an order that related love of neighbor to love of God led Augustine to take the "false step of which his critics accuse him" (24, cf. 29). This, O'Donovan claimed, was an "experiment" (26), using a second possible aspect of love, *positive love,* wherein subjects posit the value of what they love according to an order of means and ends. Since the love that enjoys (*frui*) is proper only to God, all love of created things ought to be a love that uses (*uti*) such goods for the enjoyment of God (Augustine, *De doctrina christiana* 1.3.3–5.5). When this turned out to mean "using" our neighbors, according to O'Donovan, Augustine found he could not excise the crassly instrumental implications of the formula. Already by the end of that book (*De doctrina christiana* 1.32.35), he discarded it once and for all in favor of the notion of enjoying one another in God (24–29; cf. 137). [Against O'Donovan's dismissal of *uti*-love for neighbor, see Helmut David Baer, "The Fruit of Charity: Using the Neighbor in *De doctrina christiana,*" *Journal of Religious Ethics* 24, no. 1 (Spring 1996): 47–64.] Third and more promising was *rational love,* wherein the subject has an admiring appreciation of the good of the object. Such love recognizes that the object of love has a purpose or *telos,* but it is one that she did not impose. Rational love provides a more flexible, coherent statement of the order of love than does positive love. Still, while rational love may involve an observer's disinterestedness, it may also encourage an observer's detachment (29–32). Finally then, *benevolent love* adds something more to rational love. Each object has a destiny to fulfill in the order of things. The loving subject recognizes this order, affirms it, and though she did not devise it, adds the weight of her agency toward its full realization. Thus the objective order of God's creation evokes more than delight, it implies obligation as well. Things demand assent to their fulfillment, or *benevolentia.* Love has a goal for the beloved and the lover must promote this goal if

possible. Nonetheless the subject has not imposed that goal for some ulterior purpose. Love can be either because (*quia*) others are righteous, or in order that (*ut*) they may become righteous (32–36).

34. Augustine's critics, O'Donovan argued, cannot "have it both ways." If they complain about the metaphysic by which Augustine insisted that there is an objective, final good for human beings, they cannot use their complaints to contest the place he made for right self-love. Such self-love would admit the kind of perverse self-interest they claim it conceals only if Augustine had held that the final good of a person is whatever a person makes it. To summarize O'Donovan's case, if critics reject Augustine's teaching because he used a teleological ordering to relate the claims of both self and neighbor to love of God, they must recognize that neither his teleology nor his notion of right self-love could have been egocentric. Rather, for Augustine both end and motive were theocentric. O'Donovan, *The Problem of Self-Love,* 144, 155–56.

35. If this suggested a conflict between reason and authority, Augustine resolved it by suggesting that we do not need to be taught to love ourselves, but we do need to be taught how to do it properly. O'Donovan, *The Problem of Self-Love,* 56.

36. O'Donovan, *The Problem of Self-Love,* 40; Augustine, *De civitate Dei* 10.3.2, *Serm.* 128.3.5. In the Kantian tradition that shaped Nygren, the worry is of course precisely the opposite: a person's motives (whether Kantian goodwill or Christian love of neighbor) are untrustworthy so long as self-interest plays a role, for the agent might at any time turn upon the beneficiary if costs to the agent rise too high. Augustine's point finds *prima facie* evidence in cases of well-intentioned benefactors who make matters worse or impose alien and paternalistic solutions upon others; their good will, whether from duty or agape, is by itself a purely formal category, leaving a vacuum as to what the good of the neighbor actually is. That both cases are plausible suggests that the requirements for love of neighbor are actually double; the only way to offset both legitimate distrusts (of the benefactor's self-interest *and* the benefactor's naivete) are with reference to a good that is larger than both benefactor and beneficiary, both self and neighbor. If there is disagreement in a society or a community about what that good is, that is a large but nonetheless separate problem, the one that Alasdair MacIntyre has been debating since his publication of *After Virtue: A Study in Moral Theory,* 2d ed. (1980; Notre Dame, Ind.: University of Notre Dame Press, 1984). His thesis is that moral debates in the post-Enlightenment West are so often intractable and incoherent precisely because of a principled refusal even to debate and work toward consensus on the nature of the human good.

37. Augustine's influence upon his thought, Niebuhr once insisted, was greater even than that of the Reformers. Of course Niebuhr's Detroit pastorate

during the twentieth century's second decade was his first great theological influence. "In my parish duties," he wrote four decades later, "I found that the simple idealism into which the classical faith had evaporated was as irrelevant to the crises of personal life as it was to the complex social issues of an industrial city." Not until he had already begun to emerge as a leading voice in American Protestantism, to formulate one version of what would later carry the name of Neo-orthodoxy, and to occupy a chair in Christian ethics at Union Theological Seminary in New York in 1928, did Niebuhr have occasion to read Augustine closely. In retrospect, Niebuhr expressed surprise that his careful study of the great Latin theologian of Christianity's fourth century came so late. "The matter is surprising," he noted in 1956, "because the thought of this theologian was to answer so many of my unanswered questions and to emancipate me finally from the notion that the Christian faith was in some way identical with the moral idealism of the past century." Reinhold Niebuhr, "Intellectual Autobiography," and "Reply to Interpretation and Criticism," in *Reinhold Niebuhr: His Religious, Social, and Political Thought,* ed. Charles W. Kegley and Robert W. Bretall, The Library of Living Theology, vol. 11 (New York: Macmillan, 1956), 6, 9, 436.

38. Reinhold Niebuhr, *Moral Man and Immoral Society,* reprint ed., The Scribner Lyceum Editions Library (1932; New York: Scribner's, 1960); *An Interpretation of Christian Ethics* (New York and London: Harper and Brothers, 1935).

39. The classical definition of sin in the New Testament was Paul's, Niebuhr argued, and Augustine had understood it far better than other Church Fathers. Reinhold Niebuhr, *Human Nature,* vol. 1 of *The Nature and Destiny of Man,* The Scribner Lyceum Editions Library (1941; New York: Scribner's, 1964), 140, 230.

40. Niebuhr, *Human Nature,* 1–4, 150, 163–70; *Human Destiny,* vol. 2 of *The Nature and Destiny of Man,* The Scribner Lyceum Editions Library (1943; New York: Scribner's, 1964), 1–2, 113.

41. Niebuhr, *Human Nature,* 137–40, 189–202, 228.

42. Niebuhr, *Human Destiny,* 107–26, especially 108–10 and 114.

43. Niebuhr, *Human Destiny,* 68, 76, 96, 244. Though Niebuhr's theological anthropology drew on a wide-ranging reading of Western history, contemporary world events, and major Christian thinkers through the centuries, he always insisted that its most important source was the biblical witness to both the human condition and the possibilities for redemption.

44. Reinhold Niebuhr, *Love and Justice,* ed. D. B. Robertson (Cleveland: World Publishing, Meridian, 1967), 37; Niebuhr, *Human Destiny,* 71.

45. Niebuhr, *An Interpretation of Christian Ethics,* 39.

46. Niebuhr, *An Interpretation of Christian Ethics,* 39.

47. Niebuhr, *Human Destiny,* 68; see also 81.

48. Niebuhr, *Human Destiny,* 70, 81–82.

49. Niebuhr, *Moral Man and Immoral Society,* 265–66. He also noted here that "This is how the madness of religious morality, with its trans-social ideal, becomes the wisdom which achieves wholesome social consequences."

50. Niebuhr, *An Interpretation of Christian Ethics,* 53.

51. Niebuhr, *Human Destiny,* 95.

52. Niebuhr argued that the Christian doctrine of incarnation opposes all dualistic promises of escape from history as rigorously as it does every expectation that history will find fulfillment too easily. Likewise, Christian revelation shows God engaged in the world, and thus does not present human perfection as "a unity of being from which all natural and historical vitalities have been subtracted." (Reinhold Niebuhr, *Human Destiny,* 92, 94–95.)

53. Augustine, *De doctrina christiana* 1.6.

54. Of course, in Niebuhr's ethic, sacrificial love is appropriate for one level of social organization and not for another, while mutuality might be a legitimate goal where sacrificial love is inappropriate. Niebuhr's paradoxical tendencies thus work at different institutional levels and in different lives. This may only mean, however, that Niebuhr has either refused or decided it is impossible to order various goods according to a unified account of the human good. Feminists sense the difficulties here when they seek to show why the severe split in Niebuhr's ethic between private and public spheres is untenable; Andolsen, "Agape in Feminist Ethics," 75–76. Likewise, Mennonite pacifists have sensed the problem when they have pointed to his neglect of ecclesiology and argued that to live out Jesus' ethic through alternative communities that seek to anticipate God's final Reign, may be a more rather than less responsible way to contribute to social justice. A thoroughgoing critique of Niebuhr would need to fill out these lines of argument. On Niebuhr's neglect of ecclesiology and eschatology, see John Howard Yoder, *Reinhold Niebuhr and Christian Pacifism,* A Concern Reprint (Scottdale, Pa.: Concern, n.d.), 17 (also printed in the *Mennonite Quarterly Review* 29 [April 1955]); cf. Yoder, "Peace Without Eschatology," *The Royal Priesthood: Essays Ecclesiological and Ecumenical,* ed. Michael G. Cartwright (Grand Rapids, Mich.: William B. Eerdmans, 1994), 143–67.

55. John 10:11–15, Philippians 1:15–18 and 2:21, and 2 Timothy 3:2ff. See chapter 3, in the section "Seeking Not One's Own," 85–88.

56. Hebrews 12:2.

57. Mary Daly has insisted that if a symbol has lent itself to abuse throughout a tradition, we must ask whether the symbol itself is problematic; she has argued that the virtues Christianity idealizes are those of a victim, and that the "scapegoat syndrome" whose epitome is the Jesus "who dies for our

sins" only reinforces the "scapegoat syndrome" of women in sexist society (Daly, *Beyond God the Father: Toward a Philosophy of Women's Liberation* [Boston: Beacon Press, 1973], 71–77). Rosemary Radford Ruether, also recognizing ways that the symbol of Christ is problematic for feminist theology, has nonetheless been prepared to search for and recover positive models in Jesus of Nazareth; she has distinguished Jesus' call to servanthood from insistence on servitude to human masters, suggesting that Jesus' own self-denying servanthood in fact manifests the putting off or the *"kenosis of patriarchy, the announcement of the new humanity through a lifestyle that discards hierarchical caste and privilege and speaks on behalf of the lowly"* (Ruether, *Sexism and God-Talk: Toward a Feminist Theology* [Boston: Beacon Press, 1983], 121–37; quotation is from p. 137). Of feminists still seeking to work within the Christian tradition, Joanne Carlson Brown and Rebecca Parker have perhaps gone farthest in insisting that if women are to find in the church a haven from cycles of abuse, the church must "condemn as anathema the glorification of suffering" that is intrinsic to the very doctrine of atonement; they have argued that traditional Christian theology is itself abusive, for its most prominent image is that of "'divine child abuse'—God the Father demanding and carrying out the suffering and death of his own son" (Brown and Parker, "For God So Loved the World?" in *Christianity, Patriarchy, and Abuse: A Feminist Critique,* ed. Joanne Carlson Brown and Carole R. Bohn [New York: Pilgrim Press, 1989], 4, 26).

58. Valerie Saiving, "The Human Situation: A Feminine View," reprinted in *Womanspirit Rising: A Feminist Reader in Religion,* ed. Carol P. Christ and Judith Plaskow, A Harper Forum Book (San Francisco: Harper and Row, 1979), 25–26, 37. Saiving used the work of cultural anthropologist Margaret Mead to identify what she considered fundamentally distinct about the experiences of men and women across all cultures. It is the maturation process of the infant and child; while girls need only to await the process to become fully feminine in a way that identifies them with their mothers, boys must differentiate themselves from their mothers in a way both more complex and more heavily laden with anxiety. These distinct processes have implications for theology, according to Saiving: "A mother who rejoices in her maternal role . . . knows the profound experience of self-transcending love. But she knows, too, that it is not the whole meaning of life. . . . She learns, too, that a woman can give too much of herself. . . ." Saiving was careful to suggest that biology does not entirely determine either the experiences or the temptations of women and men. Saiving described as feminine the specific temptations of women "not because they are confined to women or because women are incapable of sinning in other ways but because they are outgrowths of the basic feminine character structure." But though women too might experience "pride" and

"will-to-power," these sins certainly did not seem to be at the root of those traditional characteristics of women in traditional roles, traits that Saiving considered "specifically feminine forms of sin." These were "triviality, distractibility, and diffuseness; lack of an organizing center or focus; dependence on others for one's own self-definition; tolerance at the expense of standards of excellence; inability to respect the boundaries of privacy; sentimentality, gossipy sociability, and mistrust of reason."

59. Niebuhr, *Human Nature*, 179, 185; cf. 228–40.

60. Plaskow, *Sex, Sin, and Grace*, 62.

61. Men could just as easily "'lose themselves in some aspect of the world's vitalities,'" except that society's expectations leave women "more liable to 'become lost in the detailed processes, activities and interests of existence.'" Plaskow, *Sex, Sin, and Grace*, 63. Quotations are from Niebuhr, *Human Nature*, 179, 185.

62. Plaskow, *Sex, Sin, and Grace*, 51, 73, 84–85.

63. Plaskow, *Sex, Sin, and Grace*, 85, 87, cf. 156. Plaskow took Niebuhr to task for taking issue with the suggestion by psychologist Erich Fromm that love is a "phenomenon of abundance"—or as Plaskow explained, "a by-product of the overflow of vitality from the secure and self-accepting self" (89). Plaskow noted that self-reconstitution did not mean that the self can become "abundant" by itself, apart from its relationships with others; but without replenishment of personal resources in solitude, self-sacrifice will be meaningless because there is no self to sacrifice (90). Thus, "making abundant is an ongoing process which involves both giving and taking" (90).

64. Susan Nelson Dunfee, "The Sin of Hiding: A Feminist Critique of Reinhold Niebuhr's Account of the Sin of Pride," *Soundings* 65 (Fall 1982): 317–24. Also see Dunfee, *Beyond Servanthood*.

65. Dunfee, "The Sin of Hiding," 320.

66. Dunfee, "The Sin of Hiding," 320–21.

67. Dunfee, "The Sin of Hiding," 322–24.

68. Wanda W. Berry, "Images of Sin and Salvation in Feminist Theology," *Anglican Theological Review* 60, no. 1 (January 1978): 25, 47, 51–54.

69. The critique of more radical feminists thus may be more to the point, since it targets not just a given Christian theology such as Niebuhr's, but the whole Christian tradition, which they find grounded in the untenable but inextricable symbol of self-sacrifice.

70. Dennis McCann, *Christian Realism and Liberation Theology: Practical Theologies in Creative Conflict* (Maryknoll, N.Y.: Orbis Books, 1981), 83.

71. James Davison Hunter, *Culture Wars: The Struggle to Define America* (New York: Basic Books, 1991).

72. Julia Esquivel, "Christian Women and the Struggle for Justice in Central America," *Speaking of Faith: Global Perspectives on Women, Religion, and*

Social Change, ed. Diana L. Eck and Devaki Jain (Philadelphia: New Society Publishers, 1987), 9–10.

73. Plaskow, *Sex, Sin, and Grace,* 70. The immediate context here was Niebuhr's criticisms of contemporary exploitation of nature, which Plaskow found inadequate.

74. Lynn White, Jr., "The Historical Roots of Our Ecological Crisis," *Science* 155 (March 1967): 1203–7. For a more explicit critique of Augustine, see Matthew Fox, *Original Blessing* (Santa Fe, N.M.: Bear, 1983), 9–14, cf. 42–56.

75. Karen J. Warren, "The Power and the Promise of Ecological Feminism," *Environmental Studies* 12 (1990): 125–46. Cf. Ruether, *Sexism and God-Talk,* 72–92.

76. A basis for constructing this case study appears in essays by Brita L. Gill-Austern ("Love Understood as Self-Sacrifice and Self-Denial: What Does It Do to Women?") and Jeanne Stevenson Moessner ("From Samaritan to Samaritan: Journey Mercies") in Moessner, ed., *Through the Eyes of Women: Insights for Pastoral Care* (Minneapolis: Fortress Press, 1996). On one hand, anecdotes drawn from counseling experience often recount women who are deeply involved in some kind of caregiving yet fail so profoundly to care for themselves that they barely know how to say who they are or what they need (304, 305, 309, 310). Moessner sums up the pastoral challenge by noting that "professional and paid caregivers must confront the paradoxical question, What is a useful ministry with women who have so often excelled as caregivers themselves?" (199). On the other hand, Gill-Austern and Moessner are keen to distinguish proper self-concern from the ethical egoism of American individualism and to identify the proper place for Christ-like self-giving (205, 315–18). Thus, Gill-Austern lists among the negative effects of traditional notions of self-sacrificial love their tendency to encourage women to abdicate "public responsibility to use their God-given gifts on behalf of the greater community and for the common good"—such that real caring (as opposed to manipulative caring) actually disappears (313–14).

77. Carol Gilligan, *In a Different Voice: Psychological Theory and Women's Development* (Cambridge, Mass.: Harvard University Press, 1982). In analyzing interviews with girls and young women who had responded both to hypothetical case studies and actual moral decisions they were facing, Gilligan had found them emphasizing different issues than the standard studies of moral development by Jean Piaget and Laurence Kohlberg had noted. Articles such as the following have developed the implications of Gilligan's work for moral theory that is normative for men as well as women: Seyla Benhabib, "The Generalized and the Concrete Other: The Kohlberg-Gilligan Controversy and Feminist Theory," *Praxis International* 5 (1986): 402–24; Owen Flanagan and Kathryn Jackson, "Justice, Care, and Gender: The Kohlberg-Gilligan Debate Revisited," *Ethics* 97 (1987): 622–37; Phyllis Rooney, "A Dif-

ferent Different Voice: On the Feminist Challenge in Moral Theory," *The Philosophical Forum* 22, no. 4 (Summer 1991): 335–61.

78. Gilligan, *In a Different Voice*, 82.

79. There is, of course, an eminent philosophical tradition that resists tracing sources that determine the human will in the world of natural causation, and then looks somewhere else for the determination of will. This is the tradition stemming from Immanuel Kant, and Anders Nygren stood firmly within it. In his *Groundwork of the Metaphysic of Morals* (trans. and analyzed by H. J. Paton, 3d ed., The Academy Library [1948; New York: Harper and Row, 1964]), Kant recognized that he had come to the extreme limit of moral inquiry when he admitted that even though a pure and undetermined will could have no cause except in the "empty . . . space of transcendent concepts known as the 'intelligible world'" (130 [126]), the very purity of moral law grounded in reason alone produces a "kind of causality" by "infusing a feeling of pleasure or satisfaction in the fulfilment of duty" (128 [122]).

CHAPTER TWO   The Structure of Augustinian *Caritas*

1. *De doctrina christiana* 1.23.22: ". . . there are four kinds of things which may be loved—first the kind which is above us [God]; second, the kind which constitutes ourselves [self]; third, the kind which is equal to us [neighbor]; and fourth, the kind which is below us [temporal goods, including one's body]. . . ."

2. Both quotations in this paragraph are from the *Tractatus in epistolam Joannis* 10.3. Cf. also Augustine's prologue to this collection of ten homilies, in which he spoke of "one single charity," and 5.7, where he noted that in 1 John, all roads lead to charity. Also see *De trinitate* 8.8.12: "So with one and the same charity we love God and neighbor; but God on God's account, ourselves and neighbor also on God's account."

3. *De moribus ecclesiae catholicae* 3.4–8.13.

4. Psalm 73(72):27–28.

5. Matthew 22:37–39.

6. *De moribus ecclesiae catholicae* 26.51. 26.48–49 suggests that love of self initially had a more secure place in his thought. Thus, at least for the early Augustine, Anders Nygren was surely right to insist that love of neighbor seemed to intrude on a system built around the poles of love for God and love for self (see Nygren, *Agape and Eros*, 453, 500–501, 549–53). Even when Augustine began to write *On Christian Doctrine*, as a new bishop a decade later, he spoke of the problem of defining love of neighbor as the *"magna questio,"* the great and profound question (*De doctrina christiana* 1.22.20).

7. *Conf.* 3.4.7–8.

8. Scholars of Augustine who agree that he was an eminently systematic thinker still debate whether he actually produced a system. James J. O'Donnell has likened his writings to jazz improvisation ("The Authority of Augustine," *Augustinian Studies* 22 [1991]: 13). Recurring riffs rather than an architechonic, Mozart-like system structure Augustine's thought.

9. Oliver O'Donovan has noted that earlier church fathers of both East and West said surprisingly little about Jesus' love commands, at least as a "summary of the law" and of the Christian life. "Until more detailed research proves otherwise, we must take the supposition that Augustine is responsible not only for the currency of 'self-love' in the theology of the West but also for the predominance of the 'summary' in Western Christian ethics." *The Problem of Self-Love*, 4. Cf. Anders Nygren, *Agape and Eros*, 450.

10. *De doctrina christiana* 3.10.16.

11. *De doctrina christiana* 1.35.39, 1.36.40, 2.7.10, 3.10.14, 3.16.24.

12. Augustine regularly quoted not only Jesus' reiteration of the two great love commands in Matthew 22:37–39 and parallels, but also texts such as Romans 13:8, Galatians 5:14, and James 2:8, which called love (of neighbor) the fulfillment of the Law. (Also see Matthew 5:17, John 13:34, and 1 Timothy 1:5.) In sermons in the context of the Donatist schism (*Tractatus in epistolam Joannis* 9.8; *Tractatus in Joannis evangelium* 65.3, 83.3; *Serm.* 125.10, 145.4), as well as in the *Enchiridion* (117) of the early 420s, he sometimes stressed with Paul in 1 Corinthians 13 that every Christian message, work, or virtue was no more than a "tinkle" without love, "the greatest of these." If such New Testament texts sometimes dealt exclusively with love of neighbor, Augustine increasingly found a basis for conflating them not only in the second love command's likeness to the first and greatest one, but in the merging of believers' mutual love with the mutual love of Father and Son, as John 14–17 portrays it; Augustine's tenth homily on 1 John summarizes this merging of loves quite succinctly (*Tractatus in epistolam Joannis* 10.3).

13. Augustine developed this approach early. See *De moribus ecclesiae catholicae* 2.3.

14. *De doctrina christiana* 1.3.3. Augustine had already (1.2.2) presented the *a priori* categories of signs (*signa*) and things (*res*), but neither set of categories is more basic than the other. "Signs and things" suggest the basic grammar of meaningfulness; every*thing* has meaning in relation to something else. "Enjoyment and use" suggest the basic direction of this signification; to actually be meaningful rather than arbitrary, a thing or sign must be purposive, but some purposes are means to an end while other purposes are ends in themselves. Anticipating that human beings will prove both to serve and derive meaning from a higher end, yet somehow remain ends in themselves,

Augustine at once left open the possibility of a category of things both used and enjoyed.

15. *De doctrina christiana* 1.4.4; cf. 1.10.10.

16. *De doctrina christiana* 1.3.3; 1.7.7–1.10.10; 1.22.20. For quotation see 1.5.5, and cf. 1.33.37.

17. *De moribus ecclesiae catholicae* 3.4–8.13.

18. *De civitate Dei* 10.3. Meanwhile, on another front, Augustine had begun to debate with the Pelagians, who, he believed, were trusting in their works and willpower for salvation, rather than in God's grace. In an anti-Pelagian tract such as *On Patience*, Augustine might insist that "a will which loves God and [one's] neighbor for God's sake" was in fact a gift of God—but the teleological structure of his thought remained. *De patientia* 22; also see 3–4 and 26.

19. My decision not to eradicate this ambiguity from my presentation of Augustine's doctrine of love is deliberate. Nygren made much of Augustine's alleged confusion as indicating Augustine's departure from the New Testament's emphasis on God's love (cf. *Agape and Eros,* 452–55, 532 ff.). The issue does not rest simply on proper interpretation of the Latin or even the Greek genitive. Adjudication of the question depends on whether Augustine was right to see in New Testament notions of love an inevitable mutuality that Nygren could not or would not recognize. John Burnaby acknowledged long ago that when Augustine exegeted texts such as Romans 5:5 (". . . God's love is poured into our hearts . . .") or Romans 8:35 (". . . who will separate us from the love of Christ?") as though these referred primarily to human love for God, he was clearly mistaken on narrowly exegetical terms. Burnaby insisted, however, that the mistake tellingly reflects Augustine's deep theological insight that love for God is ours only through the gift of God's own love (Burnaby, *Amor Dei,* 99). If Augustine had coherent, defensible reasons to consider New Testament love mutual, and if the foundation of that love was God's own love as a free gift of human acquisition, then Augustine's ambiguity of usage will prove to have been an insight rather than a confusion.

20. *Conf.* 1.1.1; cf. Psalms 144(143):3 and 146(145):5. On God's immensity, see *Conf.* 1.2.2–1.3.3; on God's inscrutability and God's mysterious love, see 1.4.4; on the apparent impossibility of a finite human being loving God in return, see 1.5.5–6 and ff. On learning to see God, cf. *Tractatus in epistolam Joannis* 5.7–8, 9.10–11; *Tractatus in Joannis evangelium* 17.8; cf. *De moribus ecclesiae catholicae* 7.11.

21. Nygren, *Agape and Eros,* 464. See *Conf.* 7.10–7.18, 9.10, 10.6–10.27. Cf. Plotinus, *Enneads* 1.6.

22. On the failure of most ascents in the *Confessions,* see James J. O'Donnell, *Augustine: Confessions,* Latin text with English commentary, vol. 2 (Oxford and New York: Oxford University Press, 1992), 261. Augustine recorded the Ostia vision at *Conf.* 9.10.25. I have outlined the failure of all

other ascents at greater length elsewhere. See Gerald W. Schlabach, "Augustine's Hermeneutic of Humility: An Alternative to Moral Imperialism and Moral Relativism," *Journal of Religious Ethics* 22, no. 2 (Fall 1994): 315–20. For similar arguments concerning other of Augustine's texts, see John Cavadini, "The Structure and Intention of Augustine's *De trinitate*," *Augustinian Studies* 23 (1992): 103–23; Cavadini, "Time and Ascent in *Confessions* XI," *Augustine: Presbyter Factus Sum,* ed. Joseph T. Lienhard, Earl C. Muller, and Roland J. Teske, Collectanea Augustiniana (New York: Peter Lang Publishing, 1993), 171–85; Cavadini, "Voice and Vision in the *Confessions*: The Place of Bk. XIII," unpublished paper (Notre Dame, Ind., 1995).

23. Cf. *Tractatus in Joannis evangelium* 102.5: "'For the Father Himself,' He says [in John 16:27], 'loves you, because you have loved me.' Is it the case, then, that He loves, because we love; or rather, that we love because He loves?" The same evangelist, noted Augustine, reminded us in 1 John 4:19 that we love because God loved us first. "This then, was the efficient cause of our loving, that we were loved. And certainly to love God is the gift of God. He it was that gave the grace to love Him, who loved while still unloved. Even when displeasing Him we were loved, that there might be that in us whereby we should become pleasing in His sight. . . . God, therefore, it was that wrought this religious love of ours whereby we worship God; and He saw that it is good, and on that account He Himself loved that which He had made. But He would not have wrought in us something He could love, were it not that He loved ourselves before He wrought it."

24. Compare *Conf.* 3.5.9 with 7.20.26–7.21.27.

25. Psalm 73(72):27–28; *Conf.* 1.13.21.

26. Matthew 6:19 ff. For a highly effective homily underscoring the biblical lesson, see *Serm.* 60.1–6.

27. *Tractatus in epistolam Joannis* 2.10.

28. *Conf.* 6.11.18–20, 6.14.24, 8.7.16–18, 9.2.4, 10.34.51–10.35.57. James O'Donnell has suggested that of the three categories of sin and temptation listed in 1 John 2:16, *ambitio saeculi* (according to the Latin version Augustine cited in *Conf.* 10.30.41, in contrast to the Vulgate's "*superbia vitae*") was the temptation over which Augustine first gained some control, according to *Conf.* 6. O'Donnell, *Augustine: Confessions,* 1:xxxvi, 2:329, 2:356, 3:228.

29. *Conf.* 6.15.25, 8.1.2, 8.5.12, 8.7.17, 10.30.41–10.33.50. *Conf.* 10.31.47 summarizes: "Set in the midst of such temptations, I struggle each day against concupiscence in eating and drinking. It is not something that I can resolve to cut off once and for all and touch no more, as I could concubinage." Also see *De continentia* 2.5, 8.19, 8.20, 13.29; *Tractatus in Joannis evangelium* 41.12.

30. Note that Augustine's Old Latin text differed from the Vulgate on the third temptation, which it translated "*superbia vitae.*" Augustine did however

connect *ambitiones saeculi* and the *superbis* whom God resists (1 Peter 5:5 et al.) in *Conf.* 10.36.59.

31. The NRSV translates the Greek *"hē alazoneia tou biou"* of 1 John 2:16 as "pride in riches." While parallel usages justify the NRSV translation, Augustine's Latin gave him no reason to treat issues of wealth in this category. As noted two paragraphs prior, wealth and luxury fell back into the category of curiosity, according to *concupiscentia oculorum,* for Augustine.

32. This is the situation Augustine was analyzing in *Conf.* 10.36. 58–10.37.62. Of course, that situation has another level of complexity because Augustine's circle of friends is now a circle of fellow priests and bishops. In the episcopacy, Augustine regained the worldly influence he thought he had renounced upon conversion, and all for a good cause. O'Donnell comments: "Here we reach central issues behind the writing of *Conf. c.* 397: A[ugustine]'s perplexity and fear . . . at the role he must now play as bishop. He loves praise, loves to be the centre of attention: now he has a captive audience much larger, and much more likely to heed his words, than ever he had when he was in the business of merchandising his words. How is he to respond?" (O'Donnell, *Augustine: Confessions,* 3:229).

33. *Conf.* 10.36.58, 10.37.61–62. Biographer Peter Brown's comment is eloquent: "[T]he most characteristic anxiety of Augustine, was the manner in which he still felt deeply involved with other people. . . . Having read the life of this extremely inward-looking man, we suddenly realize, to our surprise, that he has hardly ever been alone. . . . Augustine [had] hardly changed in this: in middle age he remain[ed] delightfully and tragically exposed to that 'most unfathomable of all involvements of the soul'—friendship." *Augustine of Hippo: A Biography* (Berkeley: University of California Press, 1969), 180, quoting *Conf.* 2.9.17.

34. *Conf.* 2.6.14, 4.8.13. I have argued at greater length elsewhere that books 4 to 6 of the *Confessions* show that before Augustine struggled to account for the alleged role of sexuality in the transmission of original sin, "sexuality was first of all a metaphor for understanding social reality at its most basic link, friend to friend." See Schlabach, "Friendship as Adultery: Social Reality and Sexual Metaphor in Augustine's Doctrine of Original Sin," *Augustinian Studies* 23 (1992): 125–47; quotation is from p. 127.

35. *Conf.* 4.4.7–8.

36. *Conf.* 4.4.9, my own translation; 4.6.11.

37. *Conf.* 4.6.11. Augustine did not name this reciprocal instrumentality in quite so many words, but many things in book four conspire to produce this conclusion. In an intriguing parallel, Augustine had first described the relationship with the mother of his son as a similar kind of *"pactam libidinosi amoris"* (4.2.2). Later, he portrayed a new circle of friends in Carthage that rejuvenated him as an adulterous reciprocity in which they reinforced

one another's illusions (4.8.13). Above all, when his now-baptized friend seemed to recover, Augustine was more concerned to restore the joviality they had once had with each other, than he was for his friend's true and eternal good (4.4.8). See Schlabach, "Friendship as Adultery," 127–29.

38. *Conf.* 4.6.11, 4.7.12, 4.8.13. See Schlabach, "Friendship as Adultery" 128–29, 135–36.

39. O'Donnell has suggested that *ambitio saeculi* is the characteristic sin of *Conf.* 4 (*Augustine: Confessions,* 2:217).

40. *Conf.* 10.36.59: ". . . *domine, qui solus sine typho dominaris, quia solus verus dominus est, qui non habes dominum. . . .*"

41. *Conf.* 4.7.12; my translation of "O dementiam nescientem diligere homines humaniter!"

42. *Conf.* 4.7.12.

43. *Conf.* 4.9.14; translation altered.

44. *De moribus ecclesiae catholicae* 26.48, 50–51. As Augustine continued, he expressed his uncertainty one more time: "However that may be [*Quoquo modo autem*]. . . ."

45. Nygren, *Agape and Eros,* 552. For a close analysis of these and other images of ascent with which Augustine attempted to coordinate these two loves, see Raymond Canning, *The Unity of Love for God and Neighbour in St. Augustine* (Heverlee, Belgium: Augustinian Historical Institute, 1993), 37–69.

46. O'Donovan, *The Problem of Self-Love,* 25–29, 98, 114; O'Donovan, "*Usus* and *Fruitio* in Augustine, *De doctrina christiana I,*" *Journal of Theological Studies,* n.s. 33, no. 2 (October 1982): 361–97. For treatments that suggest how Augustine's positive notion of "use of neighbor" is intelligible and defensible, see O'Connor, "The 'Uti/Frui' Distinction in Augustine's Ethics," 45–62; Canning, *The Unity of Love for God and Neighbour,* 79–115; Baer, "The Fruit of Charity"; and John Cavadini, "The Sweetness of the Word: Salvation and Rhetoric in Augustine's *De doctrina christiana,*" *De doctrina christiana: A Classic of Western Culture,* ed. Duane W. H. Arnold and Pamela Bright (Notre Dame, Ind.: University of Notre Dame Press, 1995), 169–70. My own reading is that the notion of *uti*-love in book one of *De doctrina christiana* was not so much "experimental" (O'Donovan) as "transitional"—one phase in an argument intended all along to show that neighbor-love combines both "use" and "enjoyment," as Augustine had already signaled in 1.3.3.

47. *De doctrina christiana* 1.22.20–21 (cf. 1.4.4, 1.31.34); 1.32.35; 3.10.16. 1.33.37 also suggests that when we enjoy one another in God, we are enjoying God in our neighbor rather more [*potius*] than we are enjoying even the neighbor.

48. *Conf.* 4.9.14: "*Beatus qui amat te, et amicum in te, et inimicum propter te.*"

49. *Conf.* 4.10.15–4.11.17.

50. All quotations in this paragraph are from *Conf.* 4.10.15. The final sentence quoted reads in Latin: "*Aut quis ea comprehendit, vel cum praesto sunt?*"

51. *Conf.* 4.11.16–17. Biblical allusions are to Psalm 103(102):3–4, Matthew 4:23, and 1 Peter 1:23. In *De civitate Dei* 12.4 Augustine would later observe that we cannot see or take delight in the beauty of what we might now call the ecological pattern of constant succession throughout the temporal universe, because "under our condition of mortality," the smaller parts (frogs in plague-like proportions, wildfires, etc.) are a threat to our own individual lives. This more somber assessment of our difficulty in comprehending the good of the whole only underscores further Augustine's overall point in the present section of the *Confessions*.

52. *Conf.* 4.12.18.

53. *Conf.* 4.12.18. *De doctrina christiana* 1.28.29–30; cf. also 2.7.11.

54. See for example *Epistulae ad Romanos inchoata expositio* 18; *Tractatus in epistolam Joannis* 1.9, 8.10; *Ep.* 130.6.13; *Ep.* 140.26. For a thorough treatment of Augustine's definition of the neighbor as extending to all human beings, and including enemies, see chapter 5 of Canning, *The Unity of Love for God and Neighbour,* 167–248.

55. *Serm.* 317.2, citing Matthew 5:44–45 and Romans 5:8; cf. *Serm.* 5.2 and *Serm.* 314.2. The occasion for sermons 314 and 317 was the feast of St. Stephen; Augustine stressed that the martyr's exemplary forgiveness of his enemies according to Acts 7:59–60 removed any excuse that Jesus might have loved his enemies but such love is impossible for ordinary human beings.

56. *De sermone domini* 1.21.70; *Tractatus in epistolam Joannis* 8.10, 9.3; *Serm.* 56.14; *Enchiridion* 73. Cf. O'Donovan, *The Problem of Self-Love,* 121; Canning, *The Unity of Love for God and Neighbour,* 54, 198–215.

57. *Enchiridion* 73. Augustine's main point in this and the paragraphs that followed was that if a person has not yet attained to the perfection of loving those who are actively seeking their harm, they must at least forgive from the heart those who are moving away from enmity by asking forgiveness. To forgive one's enemies was the greatest of alms.

58. *De sermone Domini in monte* 1.21.69–1.21.70. But also see *De civitate Dei* 18.51, where Augustine wrote much later in his career of heretics serving to train the church in goodness, patience, and love of enemy. Cf. Canning, *The Unity of Love for God and Neighbour,* 201–5.

59. *De civitate Dei* 1.35: "Such is the reply (which could have been amplified and extended) which the redeemed household of servants of the Lord Christ—the pilgrim City of Christ the King—may return to its enemies. She must bear in mind that among these very enemies are hidden her future citizens; and when confronted with them she must not think it a fruitless task to bear with their hostility until she finds them confessing the faith." Augustine's definition of "God's enemies" in *De civitate Dei* 12.3 is that they are those who

continue to resist God, but they cannot of course harm God, he noted; nor in the end will they be able to thwart God's redemptive purposes. Also cf. *Tractatus in epistolam Joannis* 8.10, quoted later in this paragraph, and at the end of this chapter.

60. *Serm.* 56.14. *Tractatus in epistolam Joannis* 8.10. Cf. also Augustine's discussion in *De trinitate* 8.6 of what it is we have loved in someone we thought was just, but who has disappointed us.

61. *Conf.* 4.12.18–19.

62. *Conf.* 4.12.19.

63. The accusation is of course a methodological, not a moral, one.

64. Shaker folk song, "'Tis a Gift to Be Simple."

65. *Tractatus in epistolam Joannis* 10.3. That Nygren believed Augustine's chief difficulty in formulating his *caritas* synthesis came when he attempted to make a place for neighbor love in the God/self polarity, is a sign of Nygren's apparent inability to work his way from either Augustinian self-love or neighbor love to this theocentric, gestalt vision of love. Whether one begins with self or with neighbor, the status and operation of both loves turn out to be quite equivalent once we recognize what it means to love *any* creature "in God."

66. *De moribus ecclesiae catholicae* 26.48.

67. *De civitate Dei* 14.28.

68. *De civitate Dei* 19.14 (emphasis added).

69. Cf. *De trinitate* 8.6.9: "Whoever therefore loves men should love them either because [*quia*] they are just or in order that [*ut*] they might be just. [N.B.:] This is how he ought to love himself, either because he is just or in order to be just; in this way he can love *his neighbor as himself* (Mk. 12:33) without any danger. Anyone who loves himself any other way loves himself unjustly, because he loves himself in order to be unjust, in order therefore to be bad, and thus in fact he no longer really loves himself; for *the man who loves iniquity hates his own soul* (Ps. 11:5)." On the *ut* and *quia* of benevolent love, cf. O'Donovan, *The Problem of Self-Love,* 36.

70. *De trinitate* 8.8.12.

71. For two of Augustine's clearest statements to this effect, see *Tractatus in Joannis evangelium* 87.4 and *De trinitate* 14.14.18.

72. *Tractatus in Joannis evangelium* 123.5; emphasis added. Augustine continued: "For he who cannot live by himself will certainly die by loving himself; he therefore loves not himself who loves himself to his own loss of life. But . . . a man, by not loving himself, only loves the more, when it is for this reason that he loves not himself, [namely] that he may love Him by whom he lives."

73. Or again, self-love was paradoxical but only from the side of human agency, when one attempted to outline the lexical order of motivation, epis-

temology, or development. It was not paradoxical from the perspective of the gestalt vision of love-as-a-whole-in-coordination-with-its-parts.

74. *De libero arbitrio* 3.25.76; cf. O'Donovan, *The Problem of Self-Love,* 96.

75. *De doctrina christiana* 1.23.23. The dating of these texts a full fifteen years prior to the beginning of the Pelagian controversy belies Nygren's implicit claim that Augustine only began to sense fully the difficulties in self-love after Pelagianism forced him to do so. See Nygren, *Agape and Eros,* 519, 530, 561; cf. 468–70.

76. *De trinitate* 12.9.14. Though this passage echoes Neoplatonic thought by suggesting that pride once provoked the soul's prehistorical fall into the body, there are also strong hints to the contrary. For Augustine's claim was that "all that [the soul] tries to do on its own against the laws that govern the universe *it does by its own body [per corpus proprium]* . . ." (*De trinitate* 12.9.14; emphasis added).

77. Cf. *De trinitate* 12.10.15, the paragraph that follows.

78. *De trinitate* 12.9.14.

79. *De trinitate* 12.9.14. Note that Augustine has again followed the threefold categorization of temptations and sins in 1 John 2:16, but has altered the order of presentation according to an order of increasing degradation: The alienated soul first responds to mere curiosity about the possible uses of its own power according to the "desire of the eyes." It then becomes increasingly alienated from other people through the "pride of life." Finally it descends into what Augustine would call a merely bestial existence in pursuit of the "desires of the flesh."

80. *De trinitate* 12.11.16.

81. *De trinitate* 12.11.16.

82. *De trinitate* 8.8.12.

83. Just because all creatures have their being in God does not mean they themselves are *yet* united in the love of God, of course. The proud, for example, refuse to recognize God as their source and thus refuse God's unifying love as well. Nonetheless, God's love at work within us yearns for the fullness of love as it orients all other loves. In loving the proud who do not yet love God, we love them *because* they are still God's creatures, and that they too may join the final unity of all creatures in God. Hence, no account of Augustine's conception of Christian love can be complete without an eschatological dimension.

84. *De trinitate* 8.8.12.

85. *Tractatus in Joannis evangelium* 9.8; cf. 14.9, 14.11, 17.6, 39.5, 102.5. Also see *Tractatus in epistolam Joannis* 6.9–10, 7.6; *De trinitate* 6.5.7; *De patientia* 15; *Enchiridion* 37. Thus, Burnaby summarized his differences with Nygren this way: "The concept of *amor Dei* in Augustine is a psychological and theological complex, in which there is, as Nygren rightly observes, a synthe-

sis of religious ideas distinct in origin"; nonetheless, "[n]either Eros, nor Agape, nor the two together, will account for *caritas* without remainder: Augustine is not a compound of Plotinus and Luther, but a Father of the Catholic Church. In the Body of Christ, *caritas* is what it is in the mystery of the divine Being—as the Holy Spirit of unity" (*Amor Dei,* 21).

86. McKenna translation.

87. O'Donovan, *The Problem of Self-Love,* 128. The paragraph, incidentally, makes no direct mention of self-love.

88. All quotations from Augustine in this paragraph are from *De trinitate* 6.5.7.

89. O'Donovan, *The Problem of Self-Love,* 134–35.

90. Cf. *Tractatus in epistolam Joannis* 8.14: "'God is love, and he that abides in love, abides in God and God abides in him' [1 John 4:16]. There is a mutual indwelling of the holder and the held: your dwelling in God means that you are held by him, God's dwelling in you means that he holds you, lest you fall."

91. O'Donovan, *The Problem of Self-Love,* 135, 130.

92. *De moribus ecclesiae catholicae* 20.37. Cf. *De civitate Dei* 10.14 with Augustine's more moderate and considered notion of despising temporal goods *in comparison* with eternal ones. For classic statements on the use of temporal goods, see *De doctrina christiana* 1.35.39 and *De civitate Dei* 19.26.

93. *Tractatus in epistolam Joannis* 2.8, 2.10.

94. On the various uses of "the world" as Augustine discerned them in the Johannine literature, see *Tractatus in epistolam Joannis* 4.4, 5.9.

95. *Tractatus in epistolam Joannis* 2.11. Augustine's attitude toward temporal goods here is quite other than the indifference or exploitation of the natural world that some environmentalists allege Augustine to have legitimated. The faithful and loving fiancée will not worship the engagement ring—but neither will she trash it. Rather, she will care for it respectfully and gratefully in a way that honors her beloved.

96. Cf. *Tractatus in epistolam Joannis* 7.7, 9.9.

97. Cf. *Conf.* 7.18.24–7.21.27, 10.42.67–10.43.70, 11.2.4; *De civitate Dei* 10.20, 11.2, 13.23; *De trinitate* 13.10.13. In relation to Neoplatonic eudaemonism, O'Donovan (*The Problem of Self-Love,* 86–87) called book thirteen of *De trinitate* "the most important 'retractation' Augustine ever wrote." Cf. Cavadini, "The Structure and Intention of Augustine's *De trinitate,*" *Augustinian Studies* 23 (1992): 103–23.

98. *Conf.* 11.2.4.

99. Cf. *De doctrina christiana* 1.35.39–1.36.40.

100. *Conf.* 4.10.15, quoting Psalm 80:3(79:4).

101. *Tractatus in epistolam Joannis* 9.11; *Tractatus in Joannis evangelium* 55.2; cf. 17.6. Cf. *De doctrina christiana* 1.35.39.

102. *Tractatus in epistolam Joannis* 8.10 and 9.3 (cf. 1.11 and 8.4); 10.3–4. As 10.4 notes, to bear one another's burdens (Galatians 6:2) "is the consummation of all our works—love. There is the end, for which and unto which we run our course: when we reach it we shall have rest."

103. *Conf.* 12.16.23.

104. In fact, much of the following paragraphs were in the first instance a response to questions from that most eminent of critics, the late and leading spokesperson for Christian pacifism, John Howard Yoder.

105. *Tractatus in epistolam Joannis* 8.4; *Serm.* 90.6; *De civitate Dei* 19.12.

106. *De civitate Dei* 1.35, quoted in note 59 above.

107. *Tractatus in epistolam Joannis* 8.10.

108. *De bono conjugali* begins with this as a premise: "Forasmuch as each man is a part of the human race, and human nature is something social, and has for a great and natural good, the power also of friendship; on this account God willed to create all men out of one, in order that they might be held in their society not only by likeness of kind, but also by bond of kindred." Cf. *Ep.* 130 6.13 to Proba: "There is . . . no one in the whole human family to whom kindly affection is not due by reason of the bond of a common humanity." On the relationship between the good of human solidarity and original sin see *De civitate Dei* 12.11, where Augustine suggested that "Adam refused to be separated from his only companion, even if it involved sharing her sin."

109. According to *De civitate Dei* 19.26, citing Jeremiah 29:7.

110. *Ep.* 138 2.14 to Marcellinus: Though Jesus' precepts against returning evil for evil always apply to the Christian, Augustine wrote, "many things must be done in correcting with a certain benevolent severity, even against their own wishes, men whose welfare rather than their wishes it is our duty to consult; and the Christian scriptures have most unambiguously commended this virtue in a magistrate." Even in war, any commonwealth that observed Christian principles would immediately seek "provision . . . for enjoying in peace the mutual bond of piety and justice" with the vanquished. "For the person from whom is taken away the freedom which he abuses in doing wrong is vanquished with benefit to himself; since nothing is more truly a misfortune than that good fortune of offenders. . . ." Cf. John Langan, "The Elements of St. Augustine's Just War Theory," *Journal of Religious Ethics* 12 (1984): 24–25.

111. Paul Ramsey, *War and the Christian Conscience,* 15–18, 31–37.

112. *Ep.* 47.5 to Publicola: "As to killing others in order to defend one's own life, I do not approve of this, unless one happen to be a soldier or public functionary action, not for himself, but in defense of others or of the city in which he resides, if he acted according to the commission lawfully given him and in the manner becoming his office." Also see *De libero arbitrio* 1.5.

113. *Ep.* 134.2–4.

114. *Ep.* 134.4. In *Saeculum* Markus presented this text as a prime example of Augustine's tendency to think of Christian rulers not as "parts of a governmental machinery, of the 'state'," but rather as Church members (148). Augustine almost always spoke "of emperors rather than of empire, of kings and magistrates rather than of state or government. Thus he could continue to speak without inhibition of Christian emperors long after he had abandoned all talk about a Christian empire" (149). Thus the "perpetual liability of his conception of state to dissolve into a kind of atomistic personalism" (149).

115. All quotations in this paragraph are from *Tractatus in epistolam Joannis* 8.10, emphasis mine. Cf. *Tractatus in Joannis evangelium* 87.4, where Augustine argued that we are forbidden to love the world in the way that the world loves itself.

CHAPTER THREE   The Grammar of Augustinian Continence

An abridged version of this chapter, entitled "'Love is the Hand of the Soul': The Grammar of Continence in Augustine's Doctrine of Christian Love," appeared in the *Journal of Early Christian Studies* 6, no. 1 (Spring 1998): 59–92. Used with permission of the Johns Hopkins University Press.

1. *Conf.* 3.4.8.

2. *Conf.* 7.17.23; cf. 8.1.2 ("But I had now found the good pearl, and this I must buy, after selling all that I had. Yet still I hesitated.") and 8.5.10–12. *Conf.* 10.27.38–10.29.40.

3. Nygren, *Agape and Eros*, 548. One of the most bewildering aspects of Nygren's analysis of Augustinian *amor sui* is that he abruptly broke off that analysis immediately after admitting love for oneself "in God" into the discussion. He had just discussed two other forms of *amor sui* at length. "Amor sui 1" according to nature was morally neutral, the seeking of one's own *bonum*. "Amor sui 2" according to object was perverse, at least when it meant seeking one's own *bonum* in oneself. But there was a complication. Since the right objects of love were for Augustine threefold—God, neighbor, self—a further love of self, "amor sui 3," needed listing. Yet all Nygren did was list this possibility, without even a word of further exposition. Thus, in spite of all Nygren's attention to Augustine, he never quite engaged Augustine on the main point.

4. Nygren, *Agape and Eros*, 476, 495, 499–500, 509, 532, 538; final quotation is from p. 210.

5. *Conf.* 10.29.40.

6. *Conf.* 8.11.27. In chapter 1, I faulted Reinhold Niebuhr for insisting on the "unintended intentionality" whereby people can only achieve

mutual love within history if they do not intend to achieve it. The difference between Niebuhr's paradox and the one that I am drawing out of Augustine's thought is this: Niebuhr would teach his readers to recognize the paradoxical relationship between sacrificial and mutual love, only to tell them that their love is impure because they now know that their sacrifices may contribute to mutuality. As I read Augustine, however, knowledge of paradoxes—for instance, you love yourself truly by not loving yourself but rather loving God; you gain your life by losing it; you can only truly have the good by not grasping at it—may consciously serve to guide human action. Augustine will still lead his readers to the impasse whereby they recognize that like he, they cannot have the continence they need for this right action except in a continent way, through trust in God's gift. But where Niebuhr only frustrates, Augustine moves the reader toward hope.

7. In *Conf.* 12.15.19, for example, Augustine portrayed the "heaven of heavens" as the archetypically faithful creature who clings to God in chaste and unceasing love. In *De civitate Dei* 10.3 Augustine even wrote, with only slight embarrassment, of the highest human good as clinging to God in an embrace that impregnates the soul with virtue. Of course, Augustine seems to have taken a biblical warrant for such sexual imagery in the contrast that Psalm 73(72):27–28 makes between fornicating against God and clinging to God.

8. Brown, *Augustine of Hippo,* 388–90.

9. Gerald I. Bonner expressed the latter opinion in "*Libido* and *Concupiscentia* in St. Augustine," *Studia Patristica* 6 (1962): 303.

10. In the twentieth century, Freudian psychology and Nietzschian philosophy have suggested further rationales to dismiss Augustine's teaching. For if modern readers hold that psychosocial factors so determine a given thinker's position that the position itself is uninteresting, Augustine has obliged them with ample evidence to trace the genealogy of his thought back to sexual experiences and patriarchal assumptions. Christians may counter that they have long admitted themselves to hold the truths of their faith in earthen vessels (2 Corinthians 4:7). Thus, new ways of charting the earthy influences on a thinker such as Augustine fail to challenge either his arguments themselves or his conviction that God was at work at every moment of his life; deterministic readings that claim psychosocial forces alone were at work rest on articles of faith as surely as do Christian convictions. Matters then stand at a draw—but they also stand as a warning lest we allow any long-unresolved (and perhaps unresolvable) controversy that relates in some way to Augustinian continence to distract us, before we first attend to its pervasive role and, perhaps, its persuasive logic. The Christian confidence that "we have this treasure in earthen vessels" depends more on evidence that the human vessel really does contain some treasure, than it does on the all-too-obvious evidence of clay.

11. Bonner, "*Libido* and *Concupiscentia* in St. Augustine," 313. Peter Brown, *The Body and Society: Men, Women, and Sexual Renunciation in Early Christianity,* Lectures on the History of Religions 13 (New York: Columbia University Press, 1988), 418. Brown's book as a whole makes clear that a juxtaposition of sexual issues with issues of power and ambition, which we will further explore in this chapter, was hardly unique to Augustine. Also see George Lawless, "*Auaritia, Luxuria, Ambitio, Lib. Arb.* 1.11.22: A Greco-Roman Literary Topos and Augustine's Asceticism," *Studia Ephemeridis Augustinianum* 62 (1998): 317–31; and Nello Cipriani, "Lo schema dei tri vitia (voluptas, superbia, curiositas) nel De vera religione: Antropologia soggiacente e fonti," *Augustinianum* 38 (1998): 157–95.

12. The notion of a grammar is helpful precisely because it allows for both continuity and development in Augustine's thought. James O'Donnell and James Wetzel have suggested other ways to negotiate the question of continuity and change. As noted earlier, O'Donnell has compared Augustine's writing to jazz improvisation, with its variations on recurring riffs ("The Authority of Augustine," 13). Wetzel has sought to identify abiding questions that preoccupied Augustine through both his early philosophical inquiry and his later theological doctrine (Wetzel, *Augustine and the Limits of Virtue* [Cambridge, England: Cambridge University Press, 1992], 1–16). While I have benefited enormously from both of these suggestions, O'Donnell's approach seems to me to portray Augustine's continuities in slightly too weak a fashion, as merely stylistic, while Wetzel's approach seems to portray Augustine's continuities in slightly too strong a fashion, as a self-conscious program of inquiry. The notion of a grammar seems to strike a better balance. For this notion I undoubtedly owe a certain debt to George Lindbeck's *The Nature of Doctrine: Religion and Theology in a Postliberal Age* (Philadelphia: Westminster Press, 1984), but I do not mean to commit myself to all of Lindbeck's project or conclusions. I use "grammar" in a less philosophically freighted way, intending simply to identify structuring patterns in the background of Augustine's thought.

13. *Conf.* 10.30.41, quoting 1 John 2:16.

14. Robert A. Markus, *Conversion and Disenchantment in Augustine's Spiritual Career,* Saint Augustine Lecture 1984 (Villanova, Pa.: Villanova University Press, 1989), 5.

15. *Conf.* 10.29.40; cf. 2.1.1.

16. O'Donnell's suggestion is this: In recounting his dissolution in books 2–4, Augustine's narrative proceeds in the Johannine order; in recounting the beginnings of his moral reconstitution in books 6–8, Augustine reverses the order. See O'Donnell, *Augustine: Confessions,* 1:xxxv–xxxxvi; 2:65, 2:136; 3:44; 3:202–8. In his review of O'Donnell's commentary, John Cavadini points out ways that O'Donnell may have pressed a bit too hard for

rhetorical patterns that follow 1 John 2:16 in books 2–8 (Cavadini, "Making Truth: A New Commentary on Augustine's *Confessions*," *Religious Studies Review* 21, no. 4 [October 1995]: 297), but that does not change the thrust of my own point—that for Augustine, continence is necessary in the face of *all* human temptations, concupiscences, and sins.

17.   Though the third desire listed in 1 John 2:16 does not go by the name of *concupiscentia*, note that in *Conf.* 10.41.66 Augustine summarizes the previous chapters by writing, "Thus, therefore, I have considered the sicknesses of my sins in that threefold concupiscence [*in cupiditate triplici*]." Augustine sometimes used *concupiscentia* and *cupiditas* interchangeably. See note 24 below.

18.   Scholars once dated *De continentia* from around 395 or 396, but recent work has argued persuasively that Augustine wrote the treatise somewhere between 418 and 420. Cf. David G. Hunter, "The Date and Purpose of Augustine's *De continentia*," *Augustinian Studies* 26, no. 2 (1995): 7–24; Michael R. Rackett, "Anti-Pelagian Polemic in Augustine's *De continentia*," *Augustinian Studies* 26, no. 2 (1995): 25–50. For *De patientia*, a dating at 417 or 418 has long been standard.

19.   The heart of Augustine's controversy with the Pelagians actually became clearer when he moved away from protracted debates over sexuality and original sin. The argument in both treatises is that no one in themselves could produce a strong enough love of the good to resist all temptation or to patiently suffer for the good; to claim otherwise betrayed a pride that was incontinent in its very claim to have continently resisted evil. See *De continentia* 4.10–5.13, 7.17, 13.28–29; *De patientia* 12.15–20.23.

20.   Cf. *De continentia* 2.5: "*Ac per hoc illa quae genitalibus membris pudicitia refrenatis, solet maxime ac proprie continentia nominari, nulla transgressione violatur, si superior continentia, de qua jamdiu loquimur, in corde servetur.*"

21.   *De continentia* 1.2–2.4, 3.8–9, 8.20, 13.28.

22.   See Ray Kearney's translation of *De continentia* 2.5 in *Marriage and Virginity*, vol. I/9 of *The Works of Saint Augustine: A Translation for the 21st Century*, ed. David G. Hunter, John E. Rotelle, O.S.A., gen. ed., trans. Ray Kearney, Augustinian Heritage Institute (Hyde Park, N.Y.: New City Press, 1999).

23.   As I employ the English words "cling" and "grasp," they stand for two sets of words that Augustine freely interchanged. Behind "cling" (or in older translations, "cleave") stand various Latin verbs with *haereo* at their root—*inhaereo, adhaereo, cohaereo,* and *haereo* itself. Behind "grasp" stand various Latin verbs—*appetere, rapere, adipisci, capere, possidere,* as well as various words with *prehendeo* at their root (*comprehendeo, adprehendeo,* and *prehendeo* itself), at least in their noncognative senses.

24.   Augustine's linguistic flexibility is famous. Distinctions between *caritas, amor,* and *dilectio* are soft, for example. And on any given occasion his

choice of *libido, concupiscentia,* or *cupiditas* probably had more to do with the meter of his sentence, or with the need to retain parallels with other sentences, or with the scriptural allusion or Latin version of the Bible that he had in mind, than with any other factor.

25. In personal correspondence, James O'Donnell pointed out to me a possible objection against pairing off *continentia* and *concupiscentia* as opposites: continence is something one *does,* while concupiscence is more of an *attitude.* My reply is that continence and concupiscence pertain to different points in the process of disintegration or reintegration of the human will, but that this helps show the very sense in which they *are* opposite. Concupiscence characterizes that state in which previous actions have taken the will and its habits captive. Thus we associate concupiscence with the rebellious will—an interior state. Continence, however, characterizes the state in which actions are beginning to heal the will and its habits. So we associate continence with faithful actions. Concupiscence tends to characterize interior states only because it has yet to take full control of action; continence tends to characterize exterior action only because it has yet to regain full control of the will.

26. "The more the reign of cupidity is destroyed, the more charity is increased." See also *Confessions* 13.7.8, cited further in the next section.

27. The single most important example is *Conf.* 10.41.66, where "*in cupiditate triplici*" obviously alludes to 1 John 2:16, which Augustine had cited in 10.30.41 using the word *concupiscentia.*

28. Colloquially, we might think of *concupiscentia* as *cupiditas* with a jagged hook on it. Evidence is also present in *Serm.* 306B.5 that *concupiscentia* is desire gone into action: "Let [the adulterer] be afraid of losing the body, because he lives from the body; everything, you see that he desires [*totum enim, quod concupiscit*], he achieves through the body [*per corpus operatur*]. That's why pleasure never satisfies him; he's burnt up with desire [*inardescit cupiditate*]. . . ." Concupiscence is here in the doing, while cupidity is here in the burning. Also cf. *De patientia* 14.17: "The greater then is the love of God in saints [*in sanctis caritas dei*], the more do they endure all things for Him whom they love [*diligitur*], and the greater the lust of the world in sinners [*in peccatoribus cupiditas mundi*], the more do they endure all things for that which they lust after [*quod concupiscitur*]."

29. Cf. *Serm.* 75.5, where Augustine expounds upon Matthew 14:24 and the distress of Christ's disciples in the storm-tossed boat, by suggesting that a person who submits to desire (*cupiditate*) for wealth by bearing false witness for its sake, will feel that Christ is absent and find waves of their own avarice and lusts (*concupiscentiarum*). On the other hand, *De continentia* 3.6 suggests that when continence begins to regain control of wrongful desires, the proper word for those desires insofar as they are being restrained is

cupiditas, while the proper word for those desires insofar as they continue to tempt and agitate is *concupiscentiae:* "Continence would not labor in curbing lusts [*cupiditatibus frenandis*], if we had no wishes contrary to what is proper, if there were no opposition to our good will on the part of evil lusts [*ex mala concupiscentia*]."

30. "*Intendite amorem hominis: sic putate quasi manum animae.*"

31. *Serm.* 125.7; the date of this sermon has not been determined.

32. Nygren, *Agape and Eros,* 464–67.

33. E.g. *Conf.* 7.10.16, 7.17.23, 9.10.23–26, 10.7.11–10.29.40, 11.3.5–11.9.11.

34. See Cavadini, "Time and Ascent in *Confessions* XI," 174–78; and Cavadini, "Voice and Vision in the *Confessions*," 7–13. See note 22, chapter 2.

35. Cf. O'Donnell, *Augustine: Confessions,* 2:261.

36. Cf. Augustine's exposition of the Parable of the Ten Virgins (Matthew 25:1–13) in *Ep.* 140.31–37. In 140.37 Augustine summarized the difference between the two sets of virgins. Even though both sets seemed continent by virtue of their virginity, and seemed to have let their lamps shine through good works [Matthew 5:16], "the distinction is that [the wise virgins] took oil in their vessels, that is, they carry in their hearts an understanding of the grace of God, knowing that no one can be continent except God gives it, thinking that this also is a point of wisdom to know whose gift it is [Wisdom 8:21]; whereas those [foolish virgins] did not give thanks to the giver of all good things, but 'became vain in their thoughts, and their foolish heart was darkened, and professing themselves to be wise' [Romans 1:21–22], they became foolish."

37. *Serm.* 125.7.

38. Perhaps *Conf.* 8.3.5 implies something of the same image where it describes how the Christian community grasped hold of a newly converted Victorinus with the hands of love and joy: "*et rapiebant amando et gaudendo: hae rapientium manus erant.*" The term "*manum animae*" does appear in one other place, but in a context so different that it underscores the uniqueness of Augustine's analogical reference to love in sermon 125. In *De natura et origine animae* 4.18.28 Augustine was arguing that the soul is coterminous with the body, and speculated about what happens to a "hand of the soul" if an accident severs a hand from the body.

39. See *Tractatus in epistolam Joannis* 2.14.

40. We gain a side benefit by tracing the logic or grammar of Augustinian continence through the metaphor of the hand. Literally or figuratively, the hand is androgynous. However we interpret the role that Augustine's male sexual experiences initially played in shaping his teaching on love and continence, his insights into the soul's operations of grasping and clinging become intelligible, defensible, and applicable irrespective of gender.

41. *Conf.* 10.37.61.

42. *Conf.* 13.7.8. Of the "weight of lust [*pondere cupiditatis*]," of "charity lifting up [*sublevatione caritatis*]," and the places their affections and loves led, respectively, Augustine asked, "What is more like them, and yet what is more unlike them?".

43. Cf. *Conf.* 4.12.18–19, discussed in the previous chapter, and *De trinitate* 12.9.14–12.11.16, discussed further in the present chapter. To ascend in love to God, however, one must cling to Christ, according to *Serm.* 91.7.

44. *Tractatus in epistolam Joannis* 8.8.

45. The confluence of metaphors of clinging/grasping with metaphors of rising/falling should warn us against dismissing Augustine's doctrine of love simply because it employed the hierarchical language of Neoplatonism, which rings in many modern ears as patriarchal.

46. The following two sections present findings from comparative word studies I have done on the results of electronic searches of Augustine's writings, using the *Cetedoc Library of Christian Latin Texts* (CLCLT) textbase on CD-ROM (Turnhout: Brepols, Universitas Catholica Lovaniensis, Lovanii Novi, 1994). Augustine's writings are so numerous, however, that some selectivity has been necessary. First, anyone who uses the CLCLT tool exercises selectivity already in the construction of a word search. Further, I have paid most attention to works that I already knew to be pivotal in the development of Augustine's doctrine of love and thought on continence—*De doctrina christiana, Confessiones,* books 1, 11–14, and 19 of *De civitate Dei,* books 6, 8, 9, and 12–14 of *De trinitate, De continentia, De patientia,* the tractates on the Gospel and on the First Epistle of John, and other selected sermons on the Gospels. Finally, even within this more limited group of texts, I have not attempted to quantify and tabulate Augustine's usages of a given word in order to "prove" *definitively* that the patterns I report below are Augustine's own patterns of usage rather than patterns that my own interests and selectivity have imposed. (I have, however, attempted to note enough counterexamples and routine usages that readers will be able to begin weighing the linguistic evidence for themselves.) I do not, therefore, expect the evidence in the following sections to stand independently of my larger reading of Augustine's works. Rather, I present this evidence in the same spirit as I sought it out—as an attempt to test intuitions that have emerged from long reading of Augustine, in order to complement but also qualify my presentation of larger themes, such as the love of dominance and the role of continence. My suggestion that the phenomenology of clinging and grasping forms part of the deep grammar of Augustine's thought had already emerged slowly, from no single text, and at first from English translations alone. My study of Augustine's use of key Latin words has helped me pay more attention to routine and nonsinful ways of grasping, but it has done nothing to dissuade me from the basic thesis

concerning the deep grammar of Augustine's thought. Beyond that, more accomplished readers of Augustine's Latin should read the following sections as an invitation to do further research.

47. *Conf.* 2.5.11, my own translation.

48. In *Tractatus in Joannis evangelium* 6.12 Augustine distinguished the actions of doves (i.e., charitable Christians who participate in the life of the Holy Spirit who is a dove) from hawks and other more violent birds (i.e., false Christians, schismatics, and evildoers generally), precisely according to their nongrasping, nonrapacious nature.

49. In *De civitate Dei* 14.10 Augustine spoke of the existence of human beings in paradise, prior to the fall, as one in which "there was nothing lacking that a good will would seek to obtain [*adipisceretur*]." Obviously to acquire certain objects would be necessary even in a sinless human state, but some objects were proper.

50. The high drama of Augustine's conversion as it climaxed in the garden of Milan could hardly do without the more mundane action of seizing and picking up a book of the apostle Paul: "*Arripui, aperui et legi . . .*" (*Conf.* 8.12.29).

51. One may turn to *Conf.* 10.7–25 for Augustine's explicit theory of memory, or to *Conf.* 5 and 6 for a running critique of the Skeptics for their denial that human beings could *comprehendere* any truth with certainty (5.10.19 and 6.4.6). Or one may note the reference to acquiring wisdom in *De doctrina christiana* 1.8.8. But one may also note hundreds of times in his sermons where he spoke of cognition as seizing and holding and grasping an idea or lesson or word. Often in the *Tractatus in Joannis evangelium*, for example, he urged his listeners to take in (*capere*) as much of the lesson as they could understand (1.17; 36.7). They also did right to ask, "How can I apprehend [*apprehendere*] the Word of God" that abides forever? (*Tractatus in Joannis evangelium* 7.1).

52. *Conf.* 8.12.29; *De doctrina christiana* 2.18.28.

53. *De civitate Dei* 1.29; cf. 19.17.

54. *Conf.* 2.5.10.

55. *Conf.* 3.1.1 (cf. 3.2.2 on the spectacle of theater); 7.17.23 (cf. 3.4.8, about books that did not mention Christ and that initially failed to seize him entirely).

56. *Conf.* 10.31.43, 10.31.47; 10.34.53, 10.35.56; 10.36.59–10.37.60.

57. *Conf.* 10.34.52, quoting Psalm 25(24):15.

58. *Conf.* 5.12.22; 6.6.10 (translation altered).

59. One might unknowingly err in relating to such temporal goods, but Augustine argued here that if one's purpose is entirely temporal, and if one seeks to possess things in common rather than privately, one would merely

be subject to the ordinary human temptation of which 1 Corinthians 10:13 refers, and the corresponding sins are easily forgiven.

60. *De trinitate* 12.9.14.

61. *Conf.* 4.4.7; 4.10.15.; cf. 4.6.11 and 4.11.17.

62. *Conf.* 4.12.18, cf. 4.12.19; *De civitate Dei* 2.17; *Tractatus in Joannis evangelium* 5.17, 6.12, 17.16 (commenting on John 5:18, and quoting Philippians 2:6).

63. *De doctrina christiana* 1.22.21; *Conf.* 8.2.5.

64. *Conf.* 5.10.19 and 6.4.6. *Tractatus in Joannis evangelium* 7.1, quoting John 1:14.

65. *De civitate Dei* 19.1; cf. 8.8.

66. O'Donovan, *The Problem of Self-Love,* 46, 52, 58.

67. *De trinitate* 13.4.7.

68. *De doctrina christiana* 1.4.4. We must place the early chapters of *De doctrina* within the apologetic or philosophical genre because Augustine began this work by appealing to *a priori* categories that he believed universal to all human experience. In the very next sentence, in 1.5.5, Augustine began to introduce the claims of revelation, but most of book one of *De doctrina* continues to support those claims by appealing to philosophical universals.

69. *De doctrina christiana* 1.8.8. *Conf.* 6.1.1 (though this passage is not necessarily apologetic, it reports a phase in Augustine's life in which he might have been the object of apologetic appeal). *De civitate Dei* 8.8 (cf. 13.8); 14.8.

70. *De trinitate* 8.3.4.

71. *Conf.* 7.21.27.

72. *Ep.* 157.4; the Vulgate uses the verb *accipere,* but Augustine's epistolary allusion uses the verb *possidere.*

73. *De civitate Dei* 12.1; 19.4 (quoting Habakkuk 2:4, Romans 1:17, Galatians 3:11, or Hebrews 10:38).

74. In the Vulgate, see Psalms 15:5, 72:26, 118:57, 141:6, and also note Jeremiah 10:16, 51:19, and Lamentations 3:24. The Latin words *hereditas, pars,* and *portio* all serve to translate the Hebrew *cheleq.* Although the Vulgate does not use *possessio* in these cases, it can hardly be a coincidence that most of the instances in which Augustine spoke of "possessing God" occur in his *Enarrationes in Psalmos.* See 5.1, 5.14, 17.32, 32/2.17–18, 36/1.4, 55.16, 62.10, 145.11.

75. *Conf.* 1.2.2: "How shall I call upon my God, my God and my Lord, since, in truth, when I call upon him, I call him into myself? What place is there within me where my God can come? How can God come into me, God who made heaven and earth? Oh Lord my God, is there anything in me that can contain you? In truth, can heaven and earth, which you have made and in which you have made me, contain you? Or because without you whatever

is would not be, does it hold that whatever exists contains you? . . ." *Conf.* 1.3.3: "Do heaven and earth therefore contain you, since you fill them? Or do you fill them, and does there yet remain something further, since they do not contain you? . . . But since all things cannot contain you in your entirety, do they then contain a part of you, and do all things simultaneously contain the same part? Or do single things contain single parts, greater things containing greater parts and smaller things smaller parts? Is one part of you greater, therefore, and another smaller? Or are you entire in all places, and does no one thing contain you in your entirety?"

76. *Conf.* 8.4.9: "Lead us, O Lord, and work within us: arouse us, and call us back; enkindle us, and draw us to you [*fac excita et revoca nos, accende et rape*]; grow fragrant and sweet to us. Let us love you, and let us run to you." In 7.1.2, Augustine had noted that many of his previous errors had stemmed from the Manichaean idea that all things might contain (*capere*) the presence of a God who must be material. In 7.18.24, he had confessed himself unable to take in (*capere*) the food of the Mediator Christ Jesus who was truth incarnate, until he first embraced (*amplexo*) the Mediator; embracing or clinging was clearly a different way of having and relating than was grasping or containing.

77. *Conf.* 10.6.8.

78. *Conf.* 13.1.1.

79. *Tractatus in Joannis evangelium* 14.12–13.

80. *De civitate Dei* 21.26; *Tractatus in epistolam Joannis* 2.10. In *Tractatus in Joannis evangelium* 50.4 Augustine was commenting on John 11:57, which reports that Jewish leaders had given orders that anyone who knew where Jesus was should inform upon or arrest (*adprehendere*) Jesus. This allowed the preacher a double entendre: "Let them come to the church, let them hear where Christ is, and let them seize [but also learn of] him!" Here the rhetorical and exegetical exception proves the rule: except where scripture supplied such a usage, Augustine tended to avoid the notion of grasping Christ.

81. *Conf.* 11.29.39, quoting Philippians 3:12: "*ut per eum apprehendam, in quo et apprehensus sum.*" The Vulgate uses *comprehendere*.

82. For examples of Augustine quoting Philippians 3 against the Pelagians, see *Tractatus in epistolam Joannis* 4.6, *De trinitate* 9.1.1, and especially *De peccatorum meritis et remissione* 2.13.20 and *Contra duas epistulas Pelagianorum* 3.5.15. Quotation of Philippians 3:14 uses the literal Greek reading noted in NRSV footnote. Quotation of Philippians 3.12 translates from the Vulgate: "*et comprehensus sum a Christo Jesu.*"

83. *De trinitate* 6.5.7: "*et nobis haerere deo bonum est quia perdet omnem qui fornicatur ab eo.*" *De civitate Dei* 10.3: "*bonum enim nostrum, de cuius fine inter philosophos magna contentio est, nullum est aliud quam illi cohaerere*"; cf. *Conf.* 1.9.15, 7.17.23. *Tractatus in Joannis evangelium* 14.2: "*vis habere gaudium*

sempiternum? inhaere illi qui sempiternus est"; cf. *Conf.* 4.12.18, 6.6.9, 10.17.26; also cf. *De doctrina christiana* 1.4.4 and *De civitate Dei* 10.3 ("*hic autem finis est adhaerere Deo*") and 10.18.

84. Where the word "cling" appears in English translations (or as "cleave" in older translations), Augustine most often employed *inhaereo, adhaereo, cohaereo,* and *haereo* itself. *Amplexo* (embrace) is sometimes a synonym; *habeo* and *teneo* (more general words for having) could also be synonyms but are such broad terms that, according to context, they might stand either for *haereo* verbs or for *prehendeo* verbs. Nuances of meaning in the haereo complex might vary along a continuum of sticking, adhering, attaching, bonding, clinging, hanging onto, attending to, embracing, uniting, coalescing, and cohering; the *Oxford Latin Dictionary* lists most of these meanings for all of the *-haereo* verbs.

85. *De trinitate* 8.3.4, 8.4.6. *De doctrina christiana* 1.4.4; cf. 1.3.3, 1.10.10.

86. *De civitate Dei* 10.3; *Conf.* 7.11.17. *De doctrina christiana* 1.23.23. *Tractatus in Joannis evangelium* 14.2. *De civitate Dei* 10.3. *Tractatus in Joannis evangelium* 14.9. *Conf.* 4.12.18. *Conf.* 7.17.23. *Conf.* 6.6.9; cf. 10.28.39 vis-à-vis 10.29.40. *Conf.* 1.9.15.

87. *De doctrina christiana* 2.41.62. *Tractatus in Joannis evangelium* 122.2. *De civitate Dei* 1.10, 18.18, 10.17; cf. *Serm.* 91.7: "Cling unto Christ, who by descending and ascending has made Himself the Way. Do you wish to ascend? Hold fast to Him that ascends. For by your own self you cannot rise." *Conf.* 7.18.24 makes clear that Augustine himself could not gain enough strength to embrace and enjoy God "until [he] embraced [*amplecterer*] 'the mediator between God and man, the man Christ Jesus, who is over all things, God blessed forever.'" For, he said, "I did not hold fast [*non enim tenebam*] to Jesus my God, a humble man clinging to him who was humble, nor did I know in what thing his lowliness would be my teacher." Cf. also *Conf.* 10.43.68–70, where the love that the Father has shown by sending his only Son to suffer and die as mediator between God and sinners, is Augustine's final answer to the question he had posed in 10.28.39 and 10.29.40—how he might cling to God fully, with a continence able to resist every kind of temptation that continues to afflict him as a Christian.

88. *Serm.* 91.7; translation altered. *Enarrationes in Psalmos* 5.1. See *De trinitate* 7.3.5 for an example of Augustine's citing of Romans 5:5. *Tractatus in Joannis evangelium* 27.1. *Conf.* 11.29.39, quoting Philippians 3:12.

89. *Conf.* 4.3.5; 4.14.23 (cf. *De doctrina christiana* 2.12.17); 13.18.22. *Tractatus in Joannis evangelium* 9.10. *De civitate Dei* 13.21.

90. *Conf.* 2.3.8; 6.12.22.

91. *De doctrina christiana* 1.34.38; *Tractatus in Joannis evangelium* 10.13; cf. *De civitate Dei* 1.10. Cf. *Conf.* 5.12.22, where the verb is *amplexo.*

92. *Conf.* 6.15.25.

93. *Conf.* 4.4.7 (my translation).

94. Some manuscript texts of *Conf.* 4.4.7 read "*tu agglutinas inter haerentes sibi,*" and a number of translations follow this reading. Both the logic of the image and the parallel texts, which the rest of my paragraph treats, allow for such a notion.

95. *Conf.* 4.12.18; 6.10.16.

96. *Conf.* 8.6.15.

97. *De civitate Dei* 12.9; cf. 10.6.

98. *Conf.* 12.11.12.

99. Cf. Deuteronomy 10:14; 1 Kings 8:27; 2 Chronicles 2:6,18; Psalm 115(113):16 and Nehemiah 9:6. In *Conf.* 12.8.8 Augustine identified the heavens created in Genesis 1:1 with this "heaven of the heavens," created "before all days" and thus prior to the material heaven or sky created on the third day according to Genesis 1:6.

100. Nygren, *Agape and Eros,* 464.

101. *Conf.* 12.9.9, 12.11.12, 12.15.21.

102. *Conf.* 12.10.10; cf. 7.10.16. Galatians 2:20. Romans 10:17.

103. *Conf.* 13.2.2: "Your creation subsists out of the fullness of your goodness, to the end that a good that would profit you nothing, and that was not of your substance and thus equal to you, would nevertheless not be nonexistent, since it could be made by you. What claim on you had heaven and earth, which you made in the beginning?" Cf. 9.10.25.

104. *Conf.* 13.2.3; 13.3.4; 13.8.9; 13.9.10.

105. *Conf.* 5.4.7, quoting 2 Corinthians 6:10; translation altered.

106. *De doctrina christiana* 1.1.1. Augustine continued: "For He says, 'He that has, to him shall be given' [Matthew 13:12]. Therefore He will give to those that have, that is, to those benevolently using that which they have received He will increase and heap up what He gives." Also cf. *Ep.* 192.1, where this principle applies particularly to the debt of love (Romans 13:8): ". . . since it cannot be given unless it is possessed, so neither can it be possessed unless it is given; nay at the very time when it is given by a man it increases in that man."

107. *De civitate Dei* 14.13.

108. *De civitate Dei* 14.28. Perverse love of self is not really love of one's true self at all, but love of domination. In a way, one does not love one's true self at all, for perverse self-love, according to Augustine, is really self-hatred; cf. *De doctrina christiana* 1.23.23; *De trinitate* 8.6.9, 14.14.18.

109. *De civitate Dei* 14.13. Thus, however paradoxical it may first seem, "in a surprising way, there is something in humility to exalt the mind and something in exaltation to abase it." Cf. 12.1, 12.3, 14.3–4, 14.28. Also cf. *De trinitate* 12.9.14–12.11.16.

110. *De civitate Dei* 11.1, vis-à-vis 14.28; cf. 14.15, 14.25, 19.6–8 and 22.22.

111. *De doctrina christiana* 1.24.24, 1.23.23; cf. *De trinitate* 8.6.9, 14.14.18; *Enchiridion* 77; *Serm.* 90.6; 87.4. As evidence for the possibility of such self-hatred, Augustine consistently quoted the Latin reading of Psalm 11:5(10:6), which he did not know to be a mistranslation: "*qui diligit iniquitatem odit animam suam.*" For a commentary on Augustine's use of this verse see Canning, *The Unity of Love for God and Neighbour,* 135–41.

112. *De trinitate* 13.13.17. *Serm.* 96.1–2 (probable date is 416 or 417). *De continentia* 13.29.

113. *Conf.* 13.7.8.

114. *De continentia* 1.1, 12.26; *Ep.* 140.37. Cf. the parallel argument concerning patience in *De patientia,* as summarized at 22.25–26.

115. *De continentia* 2.5, cf. 17; 2.4 (quoting Matthew 15:11,17–20); 2.3.

116. *De continentia* 2.5–3.6; 4.11; 5.13, 8.19; 8.19–20, 13.29; 5.12 (citing Romans 6:14); 5.13.

117. *De continentia* 5.13. Psalm 141(140):3–4; cf. *De continentia* 1.2 and passim, where Augustine's Latin differs from the Vulgate and reads: "*Pone, Domine, custodiam ori meo, et ostium continentiae circum labia mea. . . .*" *De continentia* 5.13; 7.17; 13.28 (quoting Philippians 2:13); 13.28; 14.29 (citing Galatians 2:20, Romans 7:17, and Colossians 3:1–4); 12.26 (cf. 1.1); 12.26 (alluding to the just-quoted statement by Paul in Romans 14:23, that "whatever does not proceed from faith is sin"). Note that many of the anti-Pelagian arguments in *De continentia* also appear in the companion treatise *De patientia.*

118. Turning to word studies as a methodology for discerning the underlying grammar of Augustine's thought has risked such a flattened reading, since issues of chronology, development, setting, and genre tend to recede from attention as one focuses instead on word usage. The main corrective is simply to test the learnings that have emerged through this method from another angle, as I do in this section. Questions of historical development have not been entirely absent even from our study of Augustine's grammar of grasping and of clinging, however, and all of the texts that received major attention (see note 46 above) are from the mid-390s on. Even the word study, then, has implied no claim that the underlying structure of Augustine's thought was consistent except after he entered a mature stage of thought, when he reread Paul in the mid-390s, laid out the lineaments of his doctrine of love in *De doctrina christiana,* and reinterpreted his own conversion experience through the writing of *Confessiones.*

119. See note 12 above.

120. Luther remarked and Nygren quoted him to say that Augustine offered nothing about faith until the Pelagians "woke [him] up and made him

into a man." Nygren, *Agape and Eros,* 561, quoting the Wiemar edition of Luther's works, *Tischreden,* vol. 4, p. 56, 23; also see Nygren's conclusion, 739–41.

121. Besides, when we notice Augustine breaking through to "anti-Pelagian" conclusions about the sovereignty of God's grace already in 396, in his letter *De diversis quaestionibus VII ad Simplicianum,* prior even to the writing of *Conf.,* we are forced to mark the emergence of "the later Augustine" rather early in his theological career. See note 123 below.

122. While Nygren was not oblivious to these kinds of themes, John Burnaby's judgment would apply to all of them: Nygren, he noted, found it "unnecessary to do more than refer briefly to the characteristic doctrines of Grace and Predestination, in which the agape motif is most evidently at work." Burnaby, "Amor in St. Augustine," 175; cf. 177ff. on Nygren's corresponding treatment of Augustine on Christ's incarnation.

123. The transition in Augustine's thought is traceable in a series of works from the five years prior to the time Augustine began to write the *Confessiones.* Augustine wrote *De libero arbitrio* in sections from 391 to 395; positing a fully autonomous free will solved some philosophical and psychological puzzles, but toward the end (see 3.3.8–3.4.9) Augustine was discovering a new problem: According to this theory, the will must will itself, but that suggested an endless regression of causality. The Pelagians would later throw this text back at Augustine, but he soon concluded instead (cf. *Conf.* 8) that it was impossible for a fractured will to will itself into a single right will, and that this left no possible cause for the righting of the will except God's grace; Augustine's account of continence would coincide entirely with this argument. The next stage in Augustine's transition to a robust theology of grace is evident in two unfinished works on Romans that Augustine began in 394 or 395—*Expositio quarumdam propositionum ex epistola ad Romanos and Epistulae ad Romanos inchoata expositio.* Proposition 60 of the *Expositio LXXXIV propositionum,* for example, shows Augustine struggling to draw a fine line of distinction between the good works believers do through the Holy Spirit's gift of love, and the work of faith that remains our work, although God foresees it and gives the Holy Spirit accordingly. With the writing of *De diversis quaestionibus VII ad Simplicianum* in 396 Augustine had clearly come to a new understanding of Paul, and apparently of his own conversion experience; though God's choice of some to receive grace was as inscrutable as it must be just (16 and 22), Augustine now had no doubt that our faith, our willing to believe, and our power to act in love must all be based on God's enabling grace (21). As he later commented in the *Retractationes* 2.2, "I have tried hard to maintain the free choice of the human will, but the grace of God prevailed." For fuller expositions of Augustine's transition in the mid-390s and his rereading of

Paul, see Markus, *Conversion and Disenchantment* (8–12, 21–23); Paula Fredriksen Landes, introduction to Augustine, in *Augustine on Romans: Propositions from the Epistle to the Romans and Unfinished Commentary on the Epistle to the Romans,* ed. and trans. Paula Fredriksen Landes, Early Christian Literature Series 6 (Chico, Calif.: Scholars Press, 1982), ix–xii; J. Patout Burns, *The Development of Augustine's Doctrine of Operative Grace* (Paris: Etudes augustiniennes, 1980), 2–51; and Brown, *Augustine of Hippo,* 146–57.

124. *Conf.* 10.29.40 (also see 10.31.35, 10:37.60). Brown, *Augustine of Hippo,* 160, 177, 343; Augustine, *De dono perseverantiae* 20.53.

125. *Conf.* 8.11.27. The historicity of this "vision" is irrelevant to the argument here. I am inclined to assume that it accurately reflects intuitions that Augustine did experience at the time of his conversion, and that Augustine later turned to the narrative of a "vision" in order to articulate those intuitions. But even if someone could prove that Augustine invented the narrative a dozen years after his experiences of 386, the fact that he chose to portray his conversion in this way (among other ways) would be of more rather than less interest to theological ethics.

126. James Wetzel has commented: "Augustine's description of his crisis turns on the figure of continence. She is in personified form external to him, a fair indication that continence is not within him. He is addressed by the very virtue he lacks. . . . Continence tells him, by speaking to him from the outside, that it cannot emerge as a virtue from his inner resources. He has reached an impasse." *Augustine and the Limits of Virtue,* 151.

127. *Conf.* 8.12.30; 8.11.27.

128. Nygren, *Agape and Eros,* 502–3, 530.

129. *De civitate Dei* 14.15.

130. *Serm.* 86.1 (undated). In 86.2 Augustine added that when the rich young man came seeking Jesus' counsel, "Great was the thing he loved, and of little value was that he was unwilling to renounce." He called Jesus master, but had such an "overpowering love of what was valueless" that he "lost possession of what was of great price."

131. *Serm.* 96.1 (dated 416–17).

132. Nygren, *Agape and Eros,* 529–32. Burnaby aptly summarized Nygren's objection this way: "[T]he descent of divine grace in Christ is not 'unmotivated': its ultimate purpose is the ascent of *caritas* to God, for which it supplies the means by touching the heart with that delight in God and his righteousness (*delectatio justitiae*), which is stronger than all the attractions of the temporal world. And this is to contaminate with a 'teleological motivation' the purity, the incomprehensible miracle, of the divine agape. The theocentric antimoralism of Augustine's defense of Grace against Pelagius remains unreconciled with the frank eudaemonism of eros, in which 'our gaze is

turned unwaveringly upon our self and what can satisfy its needs.' Or in Lutheran terms, the *theologia humilitatis* is no more than a means for advancing to a *theologia gloriae*." Burnaby, "Amor in St. Augustine," 177–78).

133. *Serm.* 85.1 (dated in the late 420s); emphasis added. Also see *Serm.* 137.9: "Whoever seeks anything from God besides God, does not seek God chastely. Consider, Brethren; if a wife love her husband because he is rich, she is not chaste. For she loves not her husband, but her husband's gold. Whereas if she love her husband, she loves him both in nakedness and poverty. . . . But if she love her husband indeed, she loves him even more when poor, since she loves with pity too."

134. Burnaby, *Amor Dei*, 89–90; 251–52.

135. Hebrews 12:2. At first it may seem surprising that Augustine rarely cited this text, even though it captures something at the very core of his theology so well. But the Epistle to the Hebrews seems not to have been a text that Augustine lingered over. I count no more than a half dozen references to the letter in the *Confessions,* for example, and there are no extant sermons where Hebrews provides the lesson for exposition. See, however, the broad allusions to Hebrews 12:2 in the prayer that closes Augustine's tenth homily or tractate on the Gospel of John.

136. See *Conf.* 13.34.49, where Augustine was bringing to a close his survey of all that God had created in the six days of Genesis 1, which pointed toward God's will to fashion and bond together all things according to a certain order most fully visible in Christ and the Church: "We have seen that things taken one by one are good, and that together they are very good, in your Word, in your Only-begotten, both heaven and earth, the head and the body of the Church, in your predestination before all times, without morning and evening." God has now begun accomplishing this ordering in time, he continued, for re-creation is the continuing work of the Holy Spirit. Also cf. *Tractatus in epistolam Joannis* 10.3, and see the section "The One Love" in chapter 2.

137. *Tractatus in Joannis evangelium* 17.16, commenting on John 5:18 and quoting Philippians 2:6.

138. Augustine listed the two works together in a letter that is important for the dating of both: *Ep.* 231, to Darias, paragraph 7. The two works begin in strikingly similar ways and share many parallel arguments. Both begin by insisting that the characteristic under study is both a great virtue and a gift of God. Just as *De continentia* takes pains to explain the "higher continence" of the heart, *De patientia* argues that the greatest struggle is not against visible persecutors and outward suffering, but against the devil, who attacks the believer in hidden ways, and whom one must resist patiently as did the patriarch Job. Both argue against the Pelagians that when the respective virtue depends on pride and the strength of human will, it is a false virtue. Only *De*

continentia is explicitly anti-Manichaean, but *De patientia* 21.24 argues against quasi-Manichaean assumptions. Both reiterate at or near their end that continence or patience is a gift of God.

139. *De patientia* 2.2–5.6; cf. 13.16–14.17.

140. See for example *Tractatus in Joannis evangelium* 83.3: "For he that loves not God, how loves he his neighbor as himself, seeing that he loves not even himself. Such a one is both impious and iniquitous; and he that loves iniquity, manifestly loves not, but hates his soul."

141. For a complementary treatment of how Augustine integrated what we now call teleological and deontological principles, see Frederick S. Carney, "The Structure of Augustine's Ethic," in *The Ethics of St. Augustine,* ed. William S. Babcock, JRE Studies in Religion, no. 3 (Atlanta: Scholars Press, 1991), 11–38. Carney argues that for Augustine, neither love alone nor truth alone is the guiding principle, but rather, the two form a "double matrix" in which neither outweighs or subsumes the other; virtue must rest on the foundation of truth if it is to be virtue at all.

142. Nygren, *Agape and Eros,* 544. Nygren later suggested (641) that these conflicting definitions haunt Augustine's legacy: "The possibility of a pure and unselfish love of God became a burning question for Mediaeval theology; and the reason was that it started like Augustine with the assumption that all love is acquisitive love and therefore, in the last resort, self-love. But if in every act of love man seeks his own bonum, how is it with Christian love, of which the Apostle says (1 Cor. 13:5) that it seeketh not its own?"

143. See *Tractatus in Joannis evangelium* 46.5, 51.12–13, 123.5; *Serm.* 96.2; *Serm.* 137.9. *Tractatus in Joannis evangelium* 51.13 clarifies that the call to sacrifice for the sake of Christ's cause applies to all Christians, not just the clergy and bishops. Quotation is from *Tractatus in Joannis evangelium* 123.5.

144. Burnaby, *Amor Dei,* 18.

145. Cf. *Conf.* 2.2 on Augustine's desire to love and to be loved, and then *Conf.* 3.1, which adds that he was in love with love itself. James O'Donnell has pointed out triadic and trinitarian patterns throughout his commentary on the *Conf.;* see his summary at *Augustine: Confessions,* 3:203.

146. *De trinitate* 8.8.12–8.12.14, 9.2.2.

147. Cf. *Ep.* 192.1: "Moreover, how can that [the debt of love, according to Romans 13:8] be denied to friends which is due even to enemies? To enemies, however, this debt is paid with caution, whereas to friends it is repaid with confidence. Nevertheless, it [love] uses every effort to ensure that it receives back what it gives, even in the case of those to whom it renders good for evil."

148. The temporal priority of God's action in Jesus Christ reveals the logical priority of God's action relating to creation from eternity. While Augustine was famously certain of the immutability of the eternal God, he

also suggested in the strongest and most poignant of terms that in Jesus Christ, the fullness of the Trinity does in fact risk and suffer. For in the incarnation of "Jesus my God" human beings see "at their feet . . . the Godhead, weak because of its participation in our 'coats of skin' . . ." (*Conf.* 7.18.24).

149. *Tractatus in Joannis evangelium* 65.1; cf. 83.3.

CHAPTER FOUR   Augustinian Continence as a Response to the Gospel Imperative

1. Cf. *Conf.* 8.6.14.

2. *Conf.* 8.12.29.

3. *Conf.* 8.12.29, cf. Matthew 19:21 and *Vita S. Antoni* 2. According to the *Vita*, Anthony had gone to church pondering New Testament precedents for relinquishing possessions, just as Augustine was already considering a life of continence. In neither case did their subsequent chance encounter with a New Testament text suggest a course of action that was entirely new to them, but rather a kind of divine exclamation point telling them that such a course was in fact to be their own.

4. Romans 13:13–34: "Let us live honorably as in the day, *not in reveling and drunkenness, not in debauchery and licentiousness, not in quarreling and jealousy. Instead, put on the Lord Jesus Christ, and make no provision for the flesh,* to gratify its desires." (Emphasized text indicates the portion that Augustine quoted in *Conf.* 8.12.29).

5. *Conf.* 8.12.30.

6. Such as Acts 4 and 15, Romans 12, 1 Corinthians 6–10, James, 1 John, and the Gospels themselves, when read for clues to the purposes they served in the communities that produced them many decades after the events they recorded and interpreted.

7. Such as the *Didache, The Shepherd of Hermas, The Martyrdom of Justin, The Passion of Perpetua and Felicitas, The Life of Anthony,* the sermons of John Chrysostom, or books 8 through 10 of the *Confessions.*

8. *De doctrina christiana* 2.50.60; cf. *Conf.* 7.9.15.

9. *Conf.* 8.12.30.

10. Augustine may have intended readers to be puzzled. James O'Donnell has suggested that the issue of sexual continence "was not part of what Augustine had bargained for when he set out to search for wisdom, nor was it what most people approaching Christianity in this period were worrying about." Thus, "[t]he struggle to decide whether to lead a completely celibate life is the one feature of the conversion narrative that ought to come as a sur-

prise. If it were only a matter of finding the answers to deep questions, Bk. 7 would be the end of the narrative" (O'Donnell, *Augustine: Confessions*, 1:xxxvii–xxxviii). O'Donnell finds the key to unlocking this puzzle in a lost work of Ambrose, *De sacramento regenerationis sive de philosophia,* which he wrote during the period when Augustine was in Rome, and which Augustine later cited. In arguing that the philosophers lacked the true way, according to O'Donnell, "Ambrose found it polemically necessary and useful to counter the claims of the philosophers to have achieved a higher standard of moral life by chastity; 'continence is the pedestal on which right worship rests', says Ambrose. That was a challenge Augustine accepted: to become not merely Christian, but a Christian who outdoes the philosophers in all their excellences" (1:xxxix).

11. See, for example, Rosemary Radford Ruether, "Misogynism and Virginal Feminism in the Fathers of the Church," in *Religion and Sexism: Images of Woman in the Jewish and Christian Traditions,* ed. Rosemary Radford Ruether (New York: Simon and Schuster, 1974), 156–69. For an even more scathing example, see the chapter on Augustine in Uta Ranke-Heinemann, *Eunuchs for the Kingdom of Heaven: Women, Sexuality, and the Catholic Church,* trans. Peter Heinegg (New York: Doubleday, 1990), 75–98. For a critical but more measured treatment that seeks to assess how Augustine both transcended and reinforced the social, cultural, and ecclesial assumptions he had inherited, see Kim Power, *Veiled Desire: Augustine on Women* (New York: Continuum, 1996). Readers may also wish to refer to Margaret R. Miles, *Desire and Delight: A New Reading of Augustine's Confessions* (New York: Crossroad, 1991), where the opening pages include an eloquent appeal for readings that "somehow manage to see simultaneously the problems and dangers of Augustine's thought—the authoritarianism, the exclusionary strategies—*and* its extraordinary power and beauty" (11–12).

12. When Jerome implied just that, in opposition to Jovinian's defense of Christian marriage as a status equal to consecrated virginity, Augustine took a middle course that, if anything, was closer to Jovinian's position. See Jerome, *Adversus Jovinianum;* Augustine, *De bono conjugali* and *De sancta virginitate.* Cf. Elizabeth A. Clark, "'Adam's Only Companion': Augustine and the Early Christian Debate on Marriage," *Recherches Augustiniennes* 21 (1986): 139–62; and David G. Hunter, "Augustinian Pessimism? A New Look at Augustine's Teaching on Sex, Marriage, and Celibacy," *Augustinian Studies* 25 (1994): 157–65.

13. *Conf.* 6.13.23.

14. Augustine seems initially to have viewed the Christian life as the most promising way to live out the ideal life of the philosopher, which many (including his closest friends, according to *Conf.* 6.12.21 and 6.14.24) argued was incompatible with the cares and burdens of family life. Augustine's initial

retirement to the Cassiciacum estate of one Verecundus (*Conf.* 9.3.5, 9.4.7; cf. Augustine's first Christian writings from this period, especially *Soliloquia* 1.10.17–1.14.24) confirms that this desire to live a life of "unbroken leisure in love of wisdom, as we had long desired" (*Conf.* 6.12.21) was an important factor in his decision for celibacy. The main problem with this explanation is how much evidence (psychological, linguistic, and theological) it leaves out.

15. See pp. 62–64 and note 11 in chapter 3.

16. *Conf.* 2.2.3–4; 5.13.23; 6.13.23, 6.15.25 (cf. Brown, *Augustine of Hippo,* 61–63); 8.2.3; 10.37.60–62.

17. *Conf.* 4.2.2.

18. Direct evidence for this claim comes from the agony that Augustine recorded upon the departure of this woman (*Conf.* 6.15.25), and from the bishop's own admission, by way of the record of a conversation with his friend Alypius (*Conf.* 6.12.22), that the quality of his sexual relation with her differed entirely from Alypius' own furtive sexual experiences, and only lacked "the honored name of matrimony." Cf. also *De bono conjugali* 5, where Augustine noted that a faithful relation of concubinage "perhaps . . . may, not without reason, be called marriage." Indirect evidence comes from Augustine's later ability to recognize the potential equality, tenderness, and *societas* of companionate marriage (cf. *De bono conjugali* 1–3 and *De civitate Dei* 12.28, 14.11); whatever the limitations of this ability according to modern standards, it far outstripped that of other church fathers, as Clark argued in "'Adam's Only Companion,'" 139–62. For a fine assessment of Augustine's relationship with the mother of his son that plumbs its psychological complexities and influence on his thought, see Power's chapter, "Augustine the Lover," in *Veiled Desire,* 94–107.

19. Felix B. A. Asiedu has argued persuasively for the intriguing thesis that when Augustine's long-time partner returned to North Africa with a vow renouncing sexual relations with any other man, she actually provided him with the model of continence that was more pivotal to his conversion than any of the other conversion narratives he recorded in book eight of the *Confessions.* (See Asiedu, "The Example of a Woman: Sexual Renunciation and Augustine's Conversion to Christianity in 386," paper presented at University of Pennsylvania, 1994, available on the Internet World Wide Web at http://ccat.sas.upenn.edu/jod/augustine/felix.) Asiedu's larger argument that continence set the terms of Augustine's conversion coincides with my own. If Asiedu is right about the role that this woman played in setting those terms, however, then the injustice of the way that Augustine "muted" her narrative (to use Asiedu's term) looms all the larger. After all, Augustine's practice in the *Confessions* was apparently to name those who contributed to his pilgrimage to God, and to leave most others unnamed. In fairness, however, one other

possibility is that he was protecting her identity, because she was still alive, perhaps living in a convent in his own archdiocese.

20. *Conf.* 9.9.19.

21. The glimpse is inadvertent because Augustine's main intention was to mock and demythologize the pantheon of Roman paganism. The absurdity of the pagan system degenerated into "the buffoonery of farce" and deprived divinity of its last measure of dignity when the Romans portioned out functions to the gods in "minute penny packets, with instructions that each of those divinities should be supplicated for his special responsibility."

22. All references in this paragraph are from *De civitate Dei* 6.9. I am grateful to John Cavadini for pointing out this overlooked text to me some years ago.

23. *De civitate Dei* 14.26. *De nuptiis et concupiscentia* 1.8.9, quoting 1 Thessalonians 4:3–5; cf. also 12.13, which refers to the lust of the flesh as "so violent a master."

24. This is certainly the picture that Possidius painted in his *Vita Augustini*.

25. Cf. Brown, *The Body and Society,* 388; Brown, *Augustine of Hippo,* 180; Schlabach, "Friendship as Adultery."

26. Margaret Miles has suggested such a thesis in *Desire and Delight.*

27. Cf. note 10 of chapter 3.

28. Stressing the role of continence in Augustine's conception of right Christian love may seem to raise its own set of problems for feminists—first because it involves a dependence on God that might seem to foster subservience toward human powers, and second because the roots of any general theory of Augustinian continence lie in Augustine's problematic male experience of sexuality. At a theoretical level the first problem requires no lengthy reply because it rests on a dubious assumption. Dependence on God does not (as some assume) lead inexorably to subservience toward human patriarchs; prophetic traditions within both Israel and Christianity argue that monotheistic faith that the Lord God alone is king, or that God has now made Jesus Christ the Lord of history, should instead provide a basis for critiquing and resisting every unjust human power. (For a sustained argument to this effect see Kathryn Tanner, *The Politics of God: Christian Theologies and Social Justice* [Minneapolis: Fortress Press, 1992]. Other arguments against any automatic linkage between metaphysical hierarchy and social hierarchy may be found in Jean Porter, *The Recovery of Virtue: The Relevance of Aquinas for Christian Ethics* [Louisville, Ky.: Westminster/John Knox Press, 1990], 58–62; and Michael Shute, "Emergent Probability and the Ecofeminist Critique of Hierarchy," in *Lonergan and Feminism,* ed. Cynthia S. W. Crysdale [Toronto: University of Toronto Press, 1994], 146–74. Also see Peter L. Berger, *The Sacred*

Canopy: Elements of a Sociological Theory of Religion [Garden City, N.Y.: Anchor, 1967], 98–101.) Nonetheless, at another level we will need to deal (in chapter 5) with the gap between Augustine's recognition that God alone can "dominate over others without pride" (*Conf.* 10.36.59) and his attempt to dominate others out of love rather than pride despite that recognition. As to the second worry about the exclusive maleness of Augustinian continence, chapter 3 has shown that while Augustine's own experience of sexual continence informed his general theory of continence, he represented its wider meaning not so much through phallic imagery as through androgynous images of the hand. In any case, Augustinian continence turned out to be not just somber self-restraint but the way to enjoy a "chaste embrace"—to enter into joyfully mutual relationship through right desire, rectified in respect for the other.

29. *De sermone Domini* 1.1.1–1.2.4, 1.2.9, 1.4.11. Cf. *Retractationes* 1.18.2, commenting on *De sermone Domini* 1.4.12. In retracing his earlier writings in his *Retractationes,* Augustine sought to identify, explain, or correct passages which might be taken to conflict with what he had come to understand as orthodox doctrine. His single largest worry was passages that might lend themselves to Pelagian interpretation.

30. "Whoever comes to me and does not hate father and mother, wife and children, brothers and sisters, yes, and even life itself, cannot be my disciple."

31. *De sermone Domini* 1.15.40–41, with citations from Galatians 3:28 or Colossians 3:11, and Matthew 22:30.

32. *De sermone Domini* 1.15.41.

33. *De sermone Domini* 1.19.56–58.

34. *De sermone Domini* 1.21.70. Though Augustine was somewhat attuned to what was "profitable for [the enemy's] salvation" (1.23.80), the emphasis in this text, as Canning noted, "is on the perfection, freedom and security of the individual soul who fulfills the Lord's commandment to love his enemies" (*Unity of Love for God and Neighbour,* 202). Canning also points to parallel texts from Augustine's early writings, namely, *De quantitate animae* 34.78 and *De vera religione* 245–46. Just how interested Augustine was in the question of how people might move toward moral perfection is evident in 1.19.20, where he felt the need to provide a rather fanciful gloss on Matthew 5:41–42. He saw in the text a puzzle: Why did Jesus not tell his disciples to go two *more* miles when compelled to go one, and thus reach the perfection of the number three?

35. *De sermone Domini* 1.20.63. Augustine found evidence that God scourges those God loves in Proverbs 3:12; mention of scourging follows the Septuagent. Augustine also cited the beatings that Jesus promised in Luke 12:47–48.

36. Augustine strained to find a basis for violent sanctions in the New Testament by citing the words of Peter that seemed to strike down Annanias

and Sapphira in Acts 5, and Paul's delivering of a sinner to Satan for the destruction of his flesh, according to 1 Corinthians 5.

37. On Augustine's lack of criteria specifying when an interior "readiness of mind" to respond nonviolently to aggression should actually translate into exterior action, see Lisa Sowle Cahill, "Nonresistance, Defense, Violence, and the Kingdom in Christian Tradition," *Interpretation* 38 (October 1994) 385, cf. 387.

38. *Ep.* 189.6 to Boniface.

39. *De civitate Dei* 19.12–14. Read closely, book nineteen of *De civitate Dei* actually provides no normative statement at all that Christians should seek peace when they wage war, but only a series of descriptive statements that everyone does in fact seek peace. Augustine's theses are that earthly peace is only "some kind of shadow of [true] peace," which in turn supports the larger argument that "pride is a perverted imitation of God" (both statements are in 19.12). For normative statements urging Christian soldiers to seek peace even in war, one must turn to less systematic writings such as *Ep.* 189 to Boniface. The continuing just war tradition has detailed many of the criteria that Augustine first suggested, but it has not detailed the requirement that soldiers and leaders be free of all hatred and desire for revenge—probably because it could not.

40. *Contra Faustum Manichaeum* 1.22.74. *De civitate Dei* 22.4–22.5, 22.11–22.22, 22.25–22.29.

41. *Retractationes* 1.18.5: ". . . the question of the reason for the Master's command that we love our enemies, although in another place He commands hatred of parents and children, must be solved in a different way from the way in which it was solved here, that is, that we should love our enemies to win them to the kingdom of God, and we should hate those among our kindred who stand in the way of the kingdom of God." Cf. Canning, *The Unity of Love for God and Neighbour,* 174–78, which argues that Augustine "systematically and firmly rejects" the argument in *De sermone Domini* 1.15.41, as well as similar statements of this early approach in *De vera religione* 247 and *De genesi contra Manichaeos* 1.19.30.

42. The early-second-century *Shepherd of Hermas* is, in its charming naiveté, one of the best witnesses to vague unease with a changing social situation for Christians who only intermittently faced persecution, but who now faced the temptations of social tolerance and economic prosperity for some but not all of their number.

43. Chrysostom's priestly eloquence rather than his political acumen earned him an abduction into the episcopacy at Constantinople, where his mixture of moral rigorism and uninvited political position was doomed to break down. Chrysostom was ordained a priest in Antioch in 386, the year of Augustine's conversion. In 397 a plot brought him to Constantinople and

to the episcopacy there against his will, so that the imperial court might enjoy his fame and eloquence. His ascetic demands and bluntness soon alienated both the empress and less scrupulous clergy, so that by 403 he was in exile and died. Both Chrysostom's career and prolific output have invited comparisons with Augustine. The recent work of Elaine Pagels ("The Politics of Paradise: Augustine's Exegesis of Genesis 1–3 versus That of John Chrysostom," *Harvard Theological Review* 78 [1985]: 67–99; and *Adam, Eve, and the Serpent* [New York: Random House, 1988]) probably draws too sharp of a contrast, however. Pagels claimed that for Chrysostom, unlike Augustine, "The use of force, the driving energy of imperial society, is utterly alien to church government" because the church corrects only by persuasion ("Politics of Paradise," 73). This may be technically correct, yet it ignores the extent to which Chrysostom's persuasive skills served the cause of a power struggle in Antioch between the church and the city's old elites (cf. Alain Natali, "Eglise et évergetisme à Antioche à la fin du 4e Siècle d'après Jean Chrysostome," *Studia Patristica* 17, no. 3 [1982]: 1176–84).

44. Chrysostomus Baur, *John Chrysostom and His Time,* trans. M. Gonzaga (London: Sands, 1959), 1:231–58; see especially 1:252.

45. On the common thread of antiperfectionism that runs through Augustine's critiques of not only the Donatists and the Pelagians but also the Manichaeans, see James J. O'Donnell, *Augustine,* Twayne's World Authors Series (Boston: Twayne Publishers, 1985), 12.

46. E.g., *De moribus Manichaeorum* 16.52–17.58.

47. *De continentia* 2.5, 5.13; *De patientia* 5.5, 13.16–14.17. Cf. *De spiritu et littera* 30.52; *Tractatus in epistolam Joannis* 7.2; *Enchiridion* 30.

48. *De patientia* 17.20; *De trinitate* 13.10.13.

49. *Serm.* 88.5–6, 12, 17–18.

50. *Serm.* 88.17. A few lines later: "Cry out then by abstaining from going, by repressing in thy heart this worldly [*temporalem*] concupiscence; hold on with a strong and persevering cry unto the ears of the Savior, that Jesus may 'stand still' and heal thee."

51. *Serm.* 88.12, quoting Psalm 112(111):9 and citing Luke 12:33, Luke 6:30, and Luke 19:8.

52. All paraphrases and quotations in this paragraph come from *Serm.* 88.13.

53. Cf. Mark 10:49. *Serm.* 88.18: "But if he persevere and get the better of them by his endurance, and faint not in good works; those very same persons who before hindered him will now respect him. For they rebuke, and hinder, and withstand him so long as they have any hope that he will yield to them. But if they shall be overcome by the perseverance of those who make progress, they turn around and begin to say, 'He is a great man, a holy man, happy is he to whom God has given such grace.' Now do they honour him,

they congratulate and bless and laud him; just as the multitude did which was with the Lord." Perhaps Augustine could have noticed that when the mass of "evil and lukewarm Christians" ceases to marginalize more ardent disciples of Christ by charging them as naifs and fanatics, then praises them as exceptionally graced saints, that praise might in fact prove the more effective strategy to marginalize them and dismiss the challenge of their witness.

54. *Serm.* 88.17–19, with quotation from Matthew 11:28. Augustine's comment on the wide inclusiveness of God's house was this: "His house is not too narrow for thee; the kingdom of God is possessed equally by all, and wholly by each one; it is not diminished by the increasing number of those who possess it, because it is not divided. And that which is possessed by many with one heart, is whole and entire for each one."

55. *Serm.* 88.19; cf. 88.20–25.

56. *Serm.* 88.19. Augustine referred to the Donatists separately, two paragraphs later, in 88.21, where he wrote of those who "forsake unity" altogether and thus "violate charity." "Is Africa the world?" he went on to ask rhetorically, "Is this present time the harvest? Is Donatus the reaper?"

57. *Serm.* 88.19, quoting Ephesians 5:11.

58. *Serm.* 88.14.

59. *Serm.* 88.14. Cf. of course *Conf.* 7.9.13–15 and *De civitate Dei* 10.29 on what Augustine did and did not find in Platonic thought. What is striking about the statement in *Serm.* 88.14 is the forthright way that Augustine expressed the inadequacy of a *Logos*/Word spirituality alone.

60. Cf. *Conf.* 11.1.1; *Tractatus in Joannis evangelium* 51.11; *De patientia* 17.20; *De trinitate* 13.10.13.

61. *Serm.* 88.12.

62. *Serm.* 88.12, quoted on p. 107. For a similar example of Augustine allegorizing a text in a way that makes its ethical implications *more* concrete than a literal reading would require, see *Ep.* 140.2, where Augustine interprets the "breadth" in Ephesians 3:18–19 ("I pray that you may have the power to comprehend, with all the saints, what is the breadth and length and height and depth, and to know the love of Christ that surpasses knowledge, so that you may be filled with all the fullness of God") as neighbor love extending to love of enemy.

63. For an extensive exposition of Augustine's ecclesiology in the theological sense of the term, see Pasquale Borgomeo, *L'Eglise de ce temps dans la prédication de Saint Augustin* (Paris: Etudes augustiniennes, 1972). Borgomeo chose a fruitful line of inquiry by focusing on Augustine's sermons in his research, but his methodology remained that of the intellectual rather than the social historian. A work like Borgomeo's remains to be written that attends more closely to the social issues and forces evident just below the surface of Augustine's sermons.

64. *De civitate Dei* 19.26.

65. *De civitate Dei* 11.1 (cf. 12.1), 14.28.

66. Also prominent in this sermon is 1 John 2:15: "The love of the Father is not in those who love the world."

67. All quotations in this paragraph are from *Serm.* 96.1.

68. *Serm.* 96:1, cf. Matthew 16:25, Mark 8:35, Luke 9:24.

69. *Conf.* 10.29.40, 10.31.35, 10.37.60.

70. *De continentia* 12.26, *De patientia* 3.3–5.6. On the possibility that God might, however, make use of delayed gratification in order to teach us to desire rightly, see *Serm.* 61.6 (dated between 412 and 416) on Matthew 7:7 ("Ask and it will be given you . . .").

71. Even in *De patientia* 5.6, however, Augustine might note that what some people will endure for wickedness should "much admonish us how great things ought to be borne for the sake of a good life, that it may also hereafter be eternal life. . . ."

72. *Serm.* 96.2. Augustine also noted here that when the prodigal son of Luke 15 "returned to himself" after loving himself wrongly, he actually returned not to himself but to his father—and that by self-denial. (Cf. *Conf.* 7.10.16 to recall the deep and markedly Neoplatonic resonances that the phrase "he returned to himself" originally had for Augustine.) One would be hard-pressed to find a more concise statement of how right self-love is necessarily theocentric for Augustine!

73. *Serm.* 96.2–3.

74. Against this tendency in the larger tradition see John Howard Yoder, *The Politics of Jesus* (Grand Rapids: William B. Eerdmans, 1972), 96–98, 132–34.

75. *Serm.* 96.4.

76. All quotations in this paragraph are from *Serm.* 96.4.

77. All quotations in this paragraph are from *Serm.* 96.4.

78. All quotations from *Serm.* 96.5. Cf. *Tractatus in epistolam Joannis* 2.12, 5.9.

79. *Serm.* 96.6, 8–10; block quotation is from 96.9. For another discussion of the various meanings of "the world," see *Tractatus in epistolam Joannis.* In 5.9, Augustine cited a textual basis for his subdivision in the good sense of the world; the Johannine writer, he believed, had spoken of heaven, earth, and created inhabitants in John 1:10, but had also spoken of the redeemed "world" spread throughout this physical world in 1 John 2:2. In 2.2–3, a particularly explicit anti-Donatist section of *Tractatus in epistolam Joannis,* Augustine had equated worldwide extension with the catholicity that was a mark of the true church.

80. *Serm.* 96.9; emphasis added.

81. A less stark description might have admitted the hope Augustine had earlier expressed, that the company of nominal Christians who discouraged new believers from seriously following Christ were already candidates for such transformation as reaches toward the eschaton that is not yet here. And a stark contrast between the following and the persecuting church could eventually enjoy attempts at paradoxical resolution through theological formulae such as Luther's suggestion that the Christian is "*simul justus et peccator,*" while the true church is an "invisible" within the institutionally and sociologically visible church.

82. Even *De civitate Dei* lacks a full ecclesiology to match its nuanced Christian philosophy of history, as H. Richard Niebuhr suggested in *Christ and Culture,* 215–16. Robert Markus also noted that "the development of Augustine's thought on the 'heavenly city' is not quite parallel to the development of his thought on the 'earthly city'" (*Saeculum* 118).

83. Many of the confusions that have led some Christian ethicists to accuse other Christians of being "perfectionists" would be avoidable if we would distinguish between a *realized perfectionism* that claims moral perfection is possible in this life, and an *eschatological perfectionism* that eschews such claims, yet holds that God's promise to complete all things in Jesus Christ has already, in this life, begun to draw the Christian into perfection. Such a typology might aid historical interpretation. In our case, the famous fact that Augustine denounced every sign of the realized perfectionism when he perceived it among Donatists or Pelagians should not obscure the fact that he himself sought to uphold an "eschatological perfectionism." (A complete typology would also have to include what we might call *cosmic perfectionism,* which identifies some metaphysical principle as moving all things inexorably toward cosmic completion. The Platonized Christian thought of Pseudo-Dionysius and of Thomas Aquinas would offer examples. For an argument as to why Augustine's perfectionism fits—in the last analysis and in spite of his debt to Neoplatonism—within the eschatological rather than the cosmic category, see Oliver O'Donovan, *The Problem of Self-Love,* 130–36, especially 135.

CHAPTER FIVE   The Judgment of Augustinian Continence

1. Paul Ramsey argued in fact that Augustine grounded his just war theory in love of neighbor more clearly than much of the later tradition. See *War and the Christian Conscience,* 15–59, and especially 15, 37.

2. Cf. Pope John Paul II, *Tertio mellennio adveniente* [As the third millennium draws near], apostolic letter of 14 November 1994, para. 35:

"Another painful chapter of history to which the sons and daughters of the church must return with a spirit of repentance is that of the acquiescence given, especially in certain centuries, to intolerance and even the use of violence in the service of truth." Also cf. the Second Vatican Council, *Dignitatis humanae* [On the right of the person and communities to social and civil liberty in religious matters], 7 December 1965, para. 12.

3. While I agree with interpreters such as Emilien Lamirande who insist that it is quite inaccurate to call Augustine the father of the Inquisition (Lamirande, *Church, State, and Toleration: An Intriguing Change of Mind in Augustine,* Saint Augustine Lecture 1974 [Villanova, Pa: Villanova University Press, 1975], 70–71), and although I will take pains to note the sanctions that Augustine opposed, that does not absolve Augustine of all responsibility. I believe Charles J. Scalise identified the proper issue and struck the right balance when he wrote: "Augustine did not want to persecute the Donatists. He is personally no forerunner of the 'inquisition' of the medieval period or of our own violent era. He fashioned his coherent exegetical theory more out of a sense of reluctance and resignation than out of vengeance and hatred. Ironically, however, its very character as the 'kindly harshness' of a father's love or of a physician's remedy has rendered Augustine's view an infinitely more effective tool in the hands of later vengeful oppressors. The appearance of biblically warranted 'logic' has deceptively masked the hatred of Christian inquisitors throughout the history of the church." See Scalise, "Exegetical Warrants for Religious Persecution: Augustine vs. the Donatists," *Review and Expositor* 93 (Fall 1996): 502.

4. In clarifying my own hermeneutical and methodological assumptions, the work of Alasdair MacIntyre on the "rationality of traditions" and of Stanley Hauerwas on casuistry in the Christian community have been most helpful. I also recommend a small book on biblical interpretation by a Brazilian liberation theologian, Carlos Mesters. See especially the final three chapters of MacIntyre, *Whose Justice? Which Rationality?* (Notre Dame, Ind.: University of Notre Dame Press, 1988), 349–403; Hauerwas, "Casuistry as a Narrative Art," in *The Peaceable Kingdom,* 116–34; and Mesters, *Defenseless Flower: A New Reading of the Bible,* trans. Francis McDonagh (Maryknoll, N.Y.: Orbis Books, 1989).

5. In fact, Bruce J. Malina ended his study of Jesus' call to deny oneself in Mark 8:34 and parallels with the provocative suggestion that in a modern individualist cultural context, it is difficult if not impossible to implement self-denial as Jesus originally understood it. All first-century Mediterranean people had what social psychologists would now call collectivist selves, constituted through group identities. To deny oneself meant above all to renounce primary identification with family and kin in favor of a new fictive kinship group, the "new Israel" being born within the old. Especially in the United

States, however, the entire culture has already died to any such collectivist self. "We, male and female, are taught to kill our collectivist inclinations by processes of enculturation and socialization. Note how our killing of the collectivist self enables the individualist self to emerge in all its exaggerated glory." Bruce J. Malina, "'Let Him Deny Himself' (Mark 8:34 & par): A Social Psychological Model of Self-Denial," *Biblical Theology Bulletin* 24 (Fall 1994): 118.

6. *Conf.* 10.36.58–10.37.62. Augustine's analysis of the third and most intransigent of the three temptations in 1 John 2:16 is extremely complex. A fuller exposition of this text appears on pp. 134 ff.

7. For an astute argument both on the limits of good intentions and against ethics of control see Sharon D. Welch, *A Feminist Ethic of Risk* (Minneapolis: Fortress Press, 1990), 2–4, 23–43.

8. *Conf.* 10.36.59.

9. Cf. *Ep.* 189.6, *De civitate Dei* 19.7.

10. Yoder, *The Royal Priesthood,* 198, 252.

11. *Ep.* 138.2.13. Of course, as Augustine correctly went on to observe, even Jesus did not follow the precept "turn the other cheek" slavishly and legalistically when he was being interrogated. For other indications of Augustine's tendency to interiorize Jesus' ethic, in years following *De sermone Domini* of 394, see *Contra Faustum Manichaeum* 1.22.74–76 (397–98 or 400) and *Ep.* 47.5 (398).

12. *Ep.* 47.5 includes both Augustine's prohibition against personal self-defense and this quotation.

13. *De sermone Domini* 1.19.59.

14. Cahill, "Nonresistance, Defense . . . ," 385.

15. *Contra Faustum Manichaeum* 1.22.74.

16. Cf. *Enchiridion* 58: "All the events, then, of Christ's crucifixion, of His burial, of His resurrection the third day, of His ascension into heaven, of His sitting down at the right hand of the Father, were so ordered, that the life which the Christian leads here might be modelled upon them, *not merely in a mystical sense, but in reality*" (emphasis added).

17. *De doctrina christiana* 3.5.9 vis-à-vis *De doctrina christiana* 3.10.14.

18. *Conf.* 7.18.24; cf. 7.20.26–7.21.27. See Schlabach, "Augustine's Hermeneutic of Humility," 314–22.

19. *Tractatus in Joannis evangelium* 58.4.

20. In *Conf.* 13.17.20–13.18.22, Augustine interpreted the Genesis 1:9 creation of dry ground from amid the turbid waves of the sea as God's gathering of the embittered into a compassionate society, and interpreted the earth's bearing fruit in Genesis 1:11 as the sprouting of truth and justice, issuing in bread for the hungry, housing for the needy, and clothing of the

naked. In *Serm.* 125, Augustine allegorized the "thirty-eight" years that the paralytic at the pool of Siloa had lain ill (John 5:2) as all the works of the law that fall short of righteousness, for they lack the "two" needed to reach the significant number "forty"—love of God and love of neighbor.

21. *Ep.* 138.20; cf. Brown, *Augustine of Hippo,* 292, 332. On Augustine's relations with the new class of Christian rulers more generally, see Markus, *Saeculum,* 146–51.

22. *Conf.* 4.12.18.

23. *Serm.* 128.5. Cf. *Serm.* 90.6: "Love the Lord, and so learn to love yourselves; that when by loving the Lord you shall have loved yourselves, you may securely love your neighbor as yourselves. For when I find a man that does not love himself, how shall I commit his neighbor whom he should love as himself to him? And who is there, you will say, who does not love himself? Who is there? See, 'He that loves iniquity hates his own soul.' Does he love himself, who loves his body, and hates his soul to his own hurt, to the hurt of both his body and soul? And who loves his own soul? He that loves God with all his heart and with all his mind. To such a one I would at once entrust his neighbor. 'Love your neighbor as yourself.'"

24. Schlabach, "Augustine's Hermeneutic of Humility," 299–330.

25. Note that I am making no judgment here against paternalism on behalf of every penultimate good, as when medical personnel constrain a deranged and suicidal patient who is not capable of exercising "informed consent."

26. For documentation of the relevant laws, see Lamirande, *Church, State, and Toleration,* 9–12. Also cf. Brown, *Augustine of Hippo,* 334.

27. Critical editions identify the location even more exactly as the Basilica Restituta. Only textual rather than archaeological evidence concerning this site is available, along with speculation that the building's name owes to a dispute with, and then a recovery from, either Arian or Donatist Christians. If the latter, the site would bear even greater symbolic freight. Cf. Vincenzo Monachino, *La cura pastorale a Milano, Cartagine e Roma nel sec. IV,* Analecta Gregoriana, vol. 41 (Rome: Apud aedes Universitatis Gregorianae, 1947), 144–45.

28. Ephesians 5:27.

29. *Serm.* 90.4.

30. *Serm.* 90.5–6. Augustine commented specifically on "love that comes from a pure heart, a good conscience, and sincere faith," according to 1 Timothy 1:5.

31. *De correctione Donatistarum* (= *Ep.* 185) 1.3; *Tractatus in epistolam Joannis* 1.13, 2.2–3, 3.7, 6.10, 10.8; *Ep.* 61.1; *Serm.* 90.7; cf. 90.10.

32. *Serm.* 90.6, 8–9.

33. Cf. *Tractatus in epistolam Joannis* 1.12, 6.9–13, and *Ep.* 61.1.

34. *Serm.* 90.9. In arguing for the primacy of love, Augustine cited Gala-tians 5:6, where Paul insists that "in Christ Jesus neither circumcision nor un-circumcision counts for anything; the only thing that counts is faith working through love." On love extending to all humans, including enemies, cf. *Serm.* 133.6–8,10.

35. All quotations are from *Serm.* 90.9.

36. All quotations are from *Serm.* 90.9. Cf. *Conf.* 12.14.17, where Au-gustine had also written of "slaying" one's enemies through love, by convict-ing them of sin so that they will be slain to themselves through repentance and self-denial, in order to live anew.

37. *De correctione Donatistarum* (= *Ep.* 185) 2.11, 6.21–24. Cf. *Ep.* 93.2.5. Augustine's citation of Luke 14:23 in 6.24 is only one in a series of al-legedly biblical precedents for Augustine's position; see especially 5.19–6.24. The irony is that in the hope of preserving "the mark of the Redeemer" upon its sheep (6.23), the church itself was arguably obscuring if not destroying that mark upon itself, insofar as it witnessed to something different from Christ's own cruciform way of redeeming.

38. Cf. *Tractatus in epistolam Joannis* 8.10–11.

39. Although Augustine did not favor torture or capital punishment against the Donatists, lethally "irreversible judgment" was a threat that backed nonlethal sanctions nonetheless, so long as the sword of imperial coercion was involved. While clarifying his record against oft-repeated but unsub-stantiated claims that he justified lethal force for religious purposes, we must insist that involving the civil authority in matters of church discipline moved logically in that direction.

40. Evidence that Augustine only envisioned sanctions such as fines, confiscation of Donatist property, and exile, but not torture and capital pun-ishment, appears in *De correctione Donatistarum* (= *Ep.* 185) 3.14, 7.26; *Ep.* 93.5.19; *Ep.* 133; *Ep.* 134. For documentation of the relevant laws, see Lami-rande, *Church, State, and Toleration,* 9–12. Also see pp. 59–63 of Lamirande for evidence that Augustine's rejection of capital punishment against the Do-natists was a deliberate departure from the recommendations of an earlier Catholic chronicler of the controversy, Optatus of Milevis, upon whom Au-gustine depended in other ways.

41. *Ep.* 93.5.16–17. See *Ep.* 61.1.5 for Vicentius' argument and cf. *De correctione Donatistarum* (= *Ep.* 185) 2.7, 3.13. On Augustine's earlier wor-ries about the pastoral difficulties from an influence of resentful ex-Donatists passing as Catholics, see also *De correctione Donatistarum* (= *Ep.* 185) 7.25.

42. Markus, *Saeculum,* 138. We find evidence for his opposition to co-ercion in a letter of 396, and we might find evidence in *Contra partem Donati* of 398, except that the work is lost and forces us to rely on Augustine's own later summary; see *Ep.* 34.1 and *Retractationes* 2.5.

43. W. H. C. Frend, *The Donatist Church: A Movement of Protest in Roman North Africa* (Oxford: Clarendon Press, 1952), 239–41. On Augustine's private designation of the Donatists as heretics, Frend cited *Ep.* 29.11, a letter to Alypius from 395. Reading through 29.12, however, we find evidence for a policy of nonviolent persuasion even in this private letter: "At Hasna, where our brother Argentius is presbyter, the Circumcelliones [Donatist extremists], entering our church, demolished the altar. The case is now in process of trial; and we earnestly ask your prayers that it may be decided in a peaceful way, and as becomes the Catholic Church, so as to silence the tongues of turbulent heretics."

44. Markus, *Saeculum,* 136. But note Lamirande's contrary view in *Church, State, and Toleration,* 32.

45. In *Church, State, and Toleration* Lamirande came to similar conclusions, though he spoke of Augustine's pastoral concerns in warmer terms, suggesting for example that the image of gathering in lost sheep was "more fundamental" to his thinking than the Lukan exhortation *"compelle intrare."* See 24–26, 33–34, 75.

46. Cf. note 40 above. See for example *Ep.* 133 to Marcellinus in 412 concerning the sentence to be given a group of "Circumcelliones and clergy of the Donatist faction" who had confessed to killing one Catholic presbyter and maiming another. Augustine urged that the punishment *not* be as severe as the crimes committed—so that even in his capacity as a Roman official, Marcellinus the Christian would be more merciful than the law of "an eye for an eye" would have required. As a "Christian judge," Marcellinus should let paternal affection and humanity motivate him rather than a "passion for revenge." Augustine urged him not to let "the sufferings of Catholic servants of God, which ought to be useful in the spiritual upbuilding of the weak, be sullied by the retaliation of injuries on those who did them wrong, but rather, tempering the rigor of justice, let it be your care as sons of the Church to commend both your own faith and your Mother's clemency." For similar appeals for clemency, see *Ep.* 100 and *Ep.* 134.

47. On the violent wing of Donatism, see *Ep.* 43.8.24, *Ep.* 133.1; Brown, *Augustine of Hippo,* 229, 233, 335. For an example of how difficult dialogue was, or seemed to Augustine, see his account of a conversation with the Donatist bishop Fortunius in *Ep.* 44, dated 398.

48. Brown, *Augustine of Hippo,* 235–40. See also Pagels, "The Politics of Paradise."

49. Markus, *Saeculum,* 114–16, 126–27, 133–34, 139, 146–48.

50. See *Ep.* 23.1 to the Donatist bishop Maximinus. Augustine began the letter by insisting on the authenticity of his salutation: "Seeing, therefore, that in this duty of writing to you I am actually by love serving you, I do only what is reasonable by calling you 'my lord,' for the sake of that one true Lord who

gave us this command [to serve one another by love—Gal. 5:13]. Again, as to my having written 'well-beloved,' God knows that I not only love you, but love you as I love myself; for I am well aware that I desire for you the very blessings which I am fain to make my own." Also see *Ep.* 33.1. Frend may have been sensing this personal dimension to the Donatist controversy when he wrote: "One has the impression that the triumph of the Catholics in 411 was a personal triumph of Augustine and his friends, and that this triumph did not outlast the death of their leader" (*The Donatist Church,* 229).

51. *Conf.* 10.36.57–10.37.62.

52. *Conf.* 10.36.59–10.37.62. In concluding this discussion, Augustine wrote: "Behold, O Truth, I see in you that I ought not to be moved by my praises on account of myself, but for my neighbor's good. Whether I am so, I do not know. Concerning this matter I know less about myself than you do." In one way, agapeists such as Nygren and R. Niebuhr have been right to suspect that desire for mutual love is something less than Christian: Augustine's model of self-criticism (however inconclusive) in these chapters urges us to remain ever vigilant and ready to confess when mutual love degenerates into something less than Christian, whether collective egotism or mere reciprocity. Admitting this still does not mean that mutual love is itself sub-Christian, however, or that we are wrong to recognize our need for it.

53. *Tractatus in epistolam Joannis* 7.8. In his introduction to the homilies Burnaby noted that in its context this most famous saying "is the preacher's defense of compulsion in the service of love—the sad monument of an uneasy conscience, seeking to assure itself that the end justifies the means" (John Burnaby, ed. and trans., *Augustine: Later Works,* Library of Christian Classics, vol. 8 [Philadelphia: Westminster Press, 1955], 257). For Augustine's larger defense of paternalism also see 7.11, 9.4–9.6.

54. We do not need to rely on *Conf.* 10.37.60 alone here. Ironically, we may also note *Tractatus in epistolam Joannis* 8.9: "Consider now the works that pride may do: notice how they may resemble or even equal those of charity." Augustine listed standard acts of vainglory: feeding the hungry, clothing the naked, or fasting, all done out of pride. In the previous paragraph (8.8) he had discussed the love of dominance that resulted in human inequality. This time, however, he failed to notice that if pride can disguise itself as charity when one gives alms, it can also disguise itself when one dominates others allegedly for their good.

55. *Tractatus in epistolam Joannis* 1.11–13, 2.2–4, 3.4–9, 6.2–13. 9.2, 10.9–10.

56. *Tractatus in epistolam Joannis* 6.13.

57. *Tractatus in epistolam Joannis* prologue, 1.4, 1.6–7; 3.7 (emphasis added): "*Sed absit ut nos ab ipsis. . . .*" The rest of the paragraph at 3.7 reads: "But the latter is unthinkable: we have the testament of the Lord's inheritance,

we read the Psalm and find it said: 'I will give the nations for thine inheritance, and the ends of the earth for thy possession' [Psalm 2:8; cf. homily 1.8 and 13]. We hold Christ's inheritance: they do not, for they will not have communion with the world, with the universal company of them that are redeemed by the Lord's blood. We stand secure in the unity of the inheritance, and whoever refuses communion therewith has gone out from it."

58. Cf. *Conf.* 2.2.2, 2.4.9 ff., 3.1.1, 4.4.7 ff., 8.4.9 (which is a clue to the whole of book eight). *Tractatus in epistolam Joannis* 1.3, 1.9–13, 5.2 f., 8.14, 10.3.

59. *De correctione Donatistarum* (= *Ep.* 185) 9.35. Cf. *Ep.* 43.3.6.

60. Burnaby, *Augustine: Later Works,* 266 n. 18. As Burnaby had also observed already in *Amor Dei,* "Much . . . of the passion with which Augustine longed for peace came from the weariness of spirit which the Donatist controversy must have caused him." Quoting a passage from Augustine's *Expositions on the Psalms,* Burnaby placed the object of that passion in the peace of the city of mutual love "'whence no friend goes out, where no enemy enters, where there is no tempter, no stirrer of faction, no divider of the people of God,'" but instead there is "'peace in purity among the children of God, all full of love to one another, beholding one another full of God, when God will be all in all . . . [and all have God] for our peace.'" See Burnaby, *Amor Dei,* 55; quotation is from *Enarrationes in Psalmos* 84.10.

61. See O'Donovan, *The Problem of Self-Love,* 130–36, especially 135; and pp. 117–18 above.

62. Here I express my debt to Robert Markus on the question of Augustine's ecclesiology, yet beg to differ on the question of eschatology. Markus argued in *Saeculum* that if anything, Augustine's ecclesiology was *more* Donatist and carried over more North African exclusivity than did that of Tyconius. Tyconius was the former Donatist who supplied Augustine with "a theology of the Church's holiness as eschatological" and thus "the foundation on which Augustine built his theology of the 'two cities'" (117; cf. 120). Tyconius had also helped Augustine distinguish between the heavenly city already at rest and the heavenly city still on pilgrimage amid the earthly city. As Markus noted, this meant that the Church "is subject to the permanent tension between what is here and now and the eschatological reality to be disclosed in and through it. This eschatological tension is what underlay the ambivalence of Augustine's concept of the Church" (120). Yet according to Markus, Augustine also identified the present, sociologically describable "Church" with the "City of God" far more closely than did Tyconius. "Primarily the Church is [sic] what it will be" (120), wrote Markus. And ironically that made Augustine's ecclesiology more Donatist than that of the ex-Donatist Tyconius. Furthermore, Markus is surely right about the eschatological tension in

Augustine's ecclesiology, at least insofar as Tyconian eschatology allowed Augustine to account for the ambiguity and mixture in the church's present historical existence: "Though identical with the City of God, there is room in it, for the time being, for the earthly city, too" (120). But that is not the whole story. When Markus went on to wrestle with the ways that Augustine's policy of religious coercion disturbed the coherence of Augustine's entire theology of history (133 ff.), he recognized the contradictory nature of that policy, but did not revise his account of Augustine's eschatological tension. Divided by schism, North African Christians were not yet what they might be in the eschaton, a community of mutual love. Dogmatic confidence that his church *was* in its primary identity already the City of God both bolstered Augustine's policy and collapsed his eschatology.

63. On the more widespread need that fourth-century church leaders felt to "convince themselves that, essentially, nothing had changed and that their Church was still the Church of the martyrs," see R. A. Markus, *The End of Ancient Christianity* (Cambridge, England: Cambridge University Press, 1990), 90–95.

64. *De continentia* 2.5–3.7, 7.17–19, 13.29; *Serm.* 125.9; *Tractatus in Joannis evangelium* 41.12.

65. *Serm.* 88.17–18. Stanley Hauerwas reflects the character of this Augustinian spirituality in "Tragedy and Joy: The Spirituality of Peaceableness," final chapter of *The Peaceable Kingdom,* 135–51.

66. The first phrase quoted is from *Conf.* 7.14.28. Ironically, even in paragraphs adjacent to Augustine's problematic command to "love and do what you will" in disciplining errant brothers and sisters, he remembered that God had demonstrated loving power not primarily through a rod but on the cross (*Tractatus in epistolam Joannis* 7.9). Likewise, the perfection of charity that made mutual love possible came with the readiness to die for others and forgive, as "our Lord displayed in himself, by dying for all" (*Tractatus in epistolam Joannis* 5.4; cf. 5.12). *Tractatus in epistolam Joannis* 10.3, 65.1, 67.2, 83.3.

67. See pp. 34–36 in chapter 2, and the comments of Peter Brown in note 33 of that section.

68. Cf. *De bono conjugali* 1: "Forasmuch as each man is a part of the human race, and human nature is something social, and has for a great and natural good, the power also of friendship; on this account God willed to create all men out of one, in order that they might be held in their society not only by likeness of kind, but also by bond of kindred."

69. That effort to dominate righteously is at the heart of what John Howard Yoder has identified as the "Constantinian temptation," which in every competing version insists that it is the Christian's duty to make history come out right. Cf. Yoder, *The Royal Priesthood,* 152–57, 198–203.

70. *De continentia* 2.5–3.7, 8.19–20. For positive affirmations that the perfection of neighbor love in love for enemy is possible in this life, see *Serm.* 5.2; *Serm.* 56.14–15; *Serm.* 314; and *Serm.* 317.

1. Anne E. Carr, *Transforming Grace: Christian Tradition and Women's Experience* (San Francisco: Harper and Row, 1988), 174–75; Andolsen, "Agape in Feminist Ethics," 76–77; Mary H. Schertz, "God's Cross and Women's Questions: A Biblical Perspective on the Atonement," *Mennonite Quarterly Review* 68, no. 2 (April 1994): 207; Schertz, "Creating Justice in the Space Around Us: Toward a Biblical Theology of Peace between Men and Women," with a response by Lydia Neufeld Harder, in *Peace Theology and Violence against Women,* ed. Elizabeth G. Yoder, Occasional Papers, no. 16 (Elkhart, Ind.: Institute of Mennonite Studies, 1992), 24. The phrase "project of God" is from Schertz, "Creating Justice."

2. See book one of *De civitate Dei* and the critique by Mary Pellauer, "Augustine on Rape: One Chapter in the Theological Tradition," in *Violence against Women and Children,* ed. Carol J. Adams and Marie M. Fortune (New York: Continuum, 1995), 207–41.

3. *De patientia* 2.2 -7.6.

4. Gill-Austern, "Love Understood as Self-Sacrifice and Self-Denial," 313.

5. Jeanne Stevenson Moessner, "A New Pastoral Paradigm and Practice," in *Women in Travail and Transition: A New Pastoral Care,* ed. Maxine Glaz and Jeanne Stevenson Moessner (Minneapolis: Augsburg Fortress, 1991), 199, 205; Gill-Austern, "Love Understood as Self-Sacrifice and Self-Denial," 304–5, 309–10, 313–18.

6. Gill-Austern, "Love Understood as Self-Sacrifice and Self-Denial," 315–16.

7. In *Agape: An Ethical Analysis,* Outka was prepared both to critique Nygren (50–54) and to make a place for self-love or at least self-regard (285–91). Ramsey stayed closer to Nygren with a consistent argument in his *Basic Christian Ethics* that Christian love is "love for self *inverted*" (100, sic; also note Ramsey's defense of Nygren on 115, note 14). Yet Ramsey had to concede that Christian ethics must provide "some definition of legitimate concern for the self," even if it does so "only as a secondary and derivative part" of its enterprise (159). After all, "as a part of vocational service grounded in Christian love for neighbor, an individual has great responsibility for the development and use of all his natural capacities, or else he takes responsibility for rashly throwing them away." Ramsey may actually have provided a clue

as to why thinkers indebted to Nygren's analysis find they cannot fully accept his claims. As ideals—or in Nygren's preferred anti-Platonic usage, as motifs—agape and eros may each enjoy their distinct conceptual purity. Particularly in a deontological system of ethics, agape may even function for Christians as a kind of categorical imperative (cf. O'Connor, "The 'Uti/Frui' Distinction in Augustine's Ethics," 49). Like Kant's categorical imperative, it obtains and stands prior to any actual application in the "sensible world," and the philosopher derives it without consideration for the causal demands of that world. Yet if we analyze Ramsey's statement we notice that as soon as we insert agape into the world of time ("development") and causative force ("natural capacity"), a world that requires prudence even of idealists (lest they act "rashly"), agape finds it may actually have an interest in eros. To motivate actual human beings to acts of self-denying love, in other words, agape may need to move them *toward* self-denial *from* a foundation in right self-love.

8. Gill-Austern, "Love Understood as Self-Sacrifice and Self-Denial," 316–18. Gill-Austern's interpretation of the Parable of the Good Samaritan drew upon Moessner, "A New Pastoral Paradigm and Practice."

9. Nygren, *Agape and Eros,* 735. Nygren was here summarizing Luther's position as he understood it, but with obvious approval.

10. O'Donovan, *The Problem of Self-Love,* 158–59.

11. 1 Corinthians 15:28.

12. Likewise, Gill-Austern and other Christian feminists have concluded that to avoid destructive conceptions of self-sacrifice and self-denial, and replace them with a properly Christian conception of self-giving love, we should turn to trinitarian theology. See Gill-Austern, "Love Understood as Self-Sacrifice and Self-Denial," 319–20; Andolsen, "Agape in Feminist Ethics," 69, 79–80; Farley, "New Patterns of Relationship," 627–46.

13. 1 Corinthians 11:27–32.

14. Gill-Austern, "Love Understood as Self-Sacrifice and Self-Denial," 313–14.

15. Schertz, "Creating Justice in the Space Around Us," 24. Also cf. Schertz, "God's Cross and Women's Questions," 207–8.

16. Stephen G. Post, *Christian Love and Self-Denial: An Historical and Normative Study of Jonathan Edwards and Samuel Hopkins* (New York: University Press of America, 1987), 94–97, 101, 111. If my own use of the Hebrews 12:2 statement that Jesus endured the cross for the joy set before him has seemed a minor bit of biblical evidence to some readers, Post's discussion of Jesus' longing for communion, even as the cross loomed, confirms that it stands with the Gospel accounts themselves: "To correct those understandings of the cross which emphasize the total denial of self-love, consider first the possibility that Christ came to be loved as well as to love. If he had not hoped for a response to his love, then why did he cry out over Jerusalem before his

crucifixion, using the metaphor of a hen longing to gather her brood under her wings? Is there not real pathos and tragedy here, comprehensive only if Christ *sought* the beloved community he could not find? Later, Christ was troubled by his three major disciples, who were unable to stay awake and pray with him at Gethsemane. Finally, he cried out from the cross, 'Forgive them, for they know not what they do.' These events indicate that Christ did not want his love to be rejected, but rather longed for the reciprocity upon which he could build community. That he had to go the extra mile through crucifixion does not discount the possibility that his love was motivated by a desire to be accepted and loved, i.e., by a certain form of self-love. As King writes, Christian love 'goes the second mile *to restore community* (italics mine).' It forgives 'seventy times seven *to restore community* (italics mine) as well'" (95, *sic*).

17. Schertz, "Creating Justice in the Space Around Us," 24–25. Schertz continued: "To accept and to absorb violence prematurely is neither true to the biblical portrayal of the cross nor an effective resource against violence— since such action leads only to more violence. Such a view of the cross [as a last resort when other creative initiatives for restoring just and right relation- ships fail], it seems to me, may open up new possibilities for genuine service, repentance, prophecy and creative confrontation with the powers of violence on a variety of levels while, at the same time, criticizing the false service of perpetrating violence through acquiescence."

18. Welch, *A Feminist Ethic of Risk*, 23–24. Policies then pursue the holy grail of risk-free invulnerability through nuclear armament that in fact puts all life at risk—and this in the guise of clear-headed rationality. A thorough- going Augustinian should recognize this as the height of that *superbia* by which human beings overstretch their capacities and, but for God's grace, plunge even farther into the abyss. Welch would undoubtedly be surprised to find herself associated with Augustinianism (see 111–13), and yet she also quotes the Augustinian political philosopher Jean Bethke Elshtain approv- ingly precisely as she draws her critique of "the ethic of control" to a close (46–47).

19. Welch, *A Feminist Ethic of Risk*, 20, 22, 74, 78.

20. If I am more reluctant than Augustine to turn to the state, it is in part because living in the century of Gandhi and King, we can see creative possi- bilities opening up that he could not, from the very principle by which he allowed for police action in defense of the innocent but not personal self- defense: Responsibility for protecting third parties lies with the community and its representatives. The more deliberately the community itself takes on that responsibility by depending upon its own communal resources, the less it will need to rely on state violence. The work of Gene Sharp on civilian-based

defense suggests that is true even for secular society, but should enliven the church's imagination to find ways to exercise social responsibility that are less prone than Augustine's to confuse the church's cause with that of the state. Cf. Gene Sharp, *The Politics of Nonviolent Action,* 3 vols., ed. Marina Finkelstein (Boston: Extending Horizons, 1973); Sharp, *Social Power and Political Freedom,* Extending Horizons Books (Boston: P. Sargent Publishers, 1980).

21. On the requirements of a forgiveness that does not mean moving prematurely to reconciliation, see Karen Lebacqz, "Love Your Enemy: Sex, Power, and Christian Ethics," in *Annual of the Society of Christian Ethics, 1990* (Washington, D.C.: Georgetown University Press, 1990), 13–14.

22. I am thinking of an aunt of mine, who divorced a violent and abusive husband many years ago, remarried him, and finally left for good in order to protect her children. Later she entered a much healthier marriage at a time when her church was only beginning to accept divorce and remarriage. Recently the first husband called her to his deathbed to ask forgiveness. The measure of reconciliation they experienced may only have been possible *because* her remarriage and his imminent death together ensured that it could in no way be confused with a false reconciliation that allowed them to renew a dysfunctional cycle of violence, remorse, and forgetfulness.

23. Gill-Austern, "Love Understood as Self-Sacrifice and Self-Denial," 317.

24. This very last point is one of the main lessons from Dorothy Jean Weaver, "On Imitating God and Outwitting Satan: Biblical Perspectives on Forgiveness and the Community of Faith," *Mennonite Quarterly Review* 68, no. 2 (April 1994): 151–69.

25. Post, *Christian Love and Self-Denial,* 111.

26. Moessner, "From Samaritan to Samaritan," 323.

27. Niebuhr, *Human Destiny,* 69.

28. *Conf.* 10.36.58.

29. See Welch's critique of "the erotics of domination" in Welch, *A Feminist Ethic of Risk,* 111–13; in her critique of Augustine's role Welch followed Pagels, "The Politics of Paradise" and *Adam, Eve, and the Serpent.* These arguments should be weighed against those of Tanner, *The Politics of God.* See note 28 in chapter 4.

30. *Serm.* 125.7.

31. Romans 5:5.

32. *De civitate Dei* 1.29.

33. Cf. *Conf.* 11.13.16, 11.30.40, and the discussion in between.

34. I have addressed some of the issues in these paragraphs in my paper, "Deuteronomic or Constantinian: What Is the Most Basic Problem for Christian Social Ethics?" in *The Wisdom of the Cross: Essays in Honor of John Howard*

Yoder, ed. Stanley Hauerwas, Chris K. Huebner, Harry Huebner, and Mark Thiessen Nation (Grand Rapids, Mich.: William B. Eerdmans, 1999), 449–71.

35. James J. O'Donnell, *Late Have I Loved Thee,* videocassette (Santa Fe, N.M.: Della Robbia Productions, 1992).

36. *Conf.* 4.10.15, quoting Psalm 80:3(79:4). See pp. 38–40 and 51–52 in chapter 2.

37. See *Conf.* 7.18.24–7.21–27, 10.42.67–10.43.70. Cf. articles by John Cavadini listed in note 22 of chapter 2.

38. Cf. *Conf.* 7.18.24.

39. Cf. Romans 5 and Ephesians 2.

Works Cited

Collections

CCSL   *Corpus Christianorum, Series Latina.*
CLCLT   *Cetedoc Library of Christian Latin Texts.* Textbase on CD-ROM. Turnhout: Brepols, Universitas Catholica Lovaniensis, Lovanii Novi, 1994.
CSEL   *Corpus Scriptorum Ecclesiasticorum Latinorum.*
NPNF¹   *A Select Library of the Nicene and Post-Nicene Fathers of the Christian Church.* First Series.
PL   *Patrologia Latina.*
WSA   *The Works of Saint Augustine: A Translation for the 21st Century.*

Augustine (Primary Texts)

Augustine's writings are listed below according to their Latin titles, together with the translation(s) consulted. In some situations I have consulted multiple translations; for *De trinitate*, Edmund Hill's translation is quoted in the text unless otherwise indicated. For Augustine's sermons and letters, I have used the *NPNF*¹ translations where available, and turned to the other translations listed as necessary. In all cases in which I have used *NPNF*¹ translations, I have taken the liberty of updating their archaic English without comment.

De bono conjugali. CSEL 41.
    *On the Good of Marriage. NPNF*¹ 3. 397–413.
De civitate Dei. CCSL 47–48.
    The City of God. Translated by Henry Bettenson. Introduction by David Knowles. Harmondsworth, Middlesex: Penguin, 1972.
Confessiones. CCSL 27.
    The Confessions of St. Augustine. Translated by John K. Ryan. New York: Doubleday, 1960.

De continentia. CSEL 41.
  Continence. WSA I/9. 189–216.
  On Continence. NPNF[1] 3. 377–93.
De correctione Donatistarum. = *Ep.* 185.
  The Correction of the Donatists. NPNF[1] 4. 629–51.
De diversis quaestionibus VII ad Simplicianum. CCSL 44.
De doctrina christiana. CCSL 32.
  On Christian Doctrine. Translated with an introduction by D. W. Robert-
    son, Jr. The Library of Liberal Arts. New York: Macmillan, 1958.
De dono perseverantiae. PL 45.
  On the Gift of Perseverance. NPNF[1] 5. 521–52.
Contra duas epistulas Pelagianorum. CSEL 60.
  Against Two Letters of the Pelagians. NPNF[1] 5. 372–434.
Enarrationes in Psalmos. CCSL 38–40.
Enchiridion ad Laurentium de fide et spe et caritate. CCSL 46.
  Enchiridion. NPNF[1] 3. 229–76.
Epistolae ad Romanos inchoata expositio. CSEL 84.
  Unfinished Commentary on the Epistle to the Romans. In *Augustine on Romans.*
    Edited and translated by Paula Fredriksen Landes. Early Christian Lit-
    erature Series 6. Chico, Calif.: Scholars Press, 1982. 51–89.
Epistulae. CSEL 34, 44, 57.
  Letters. NPNF[1] 1. 209–593.
  Letters. Translated by Wilfrid Parsons, S.N.D. Vols. 9–12, 14 of *Writings of
    Saint Augustine.* The Fathers of the Church, vols. 12, 18, 20, 30, 32.
    Washington: Catholic University of America Press, 1951–56.
Expositio quarumdam propositionum ex epistola ad Romanos. CSEL 84.
  Propositions from the Epistles to the Romans. In *Augustine on Romans.* Edited
    and translated by Paula Fredriksen Landes. Early Christian Literature
    Series 6. Chico, Calif.: Scholars Press, 1982. 1–49.
Contra Faustum Manichaeum. CSEL 25.1.
  Reply to Faustus the Manichaean. NPNF[1] 4. 151–345.
De genesi contra Manichaeos. PL 34.
De libero arbitrio. CCSL 29.
  The Problem of Free Choice. Translated and annotated by Mark Pontifex. An-
    cient Christian Writers 22. Westminster, Md.: Newman Press, 1955.
De moribus ecclesiae catholicae. PL 32.
  Of the Morals of the Catholic Church. NPNF[1] 4. 37–63.
De moribus Manichaeorum. PL 32.
  Of the Morals of the Manichaeans. NPNF[1] 4. 65–89.
De natura et origine animae. [Alt. title: *De anima et eius origine.*] *CSEL* 60.
  A Treatise on the Soul and Its Origin. NPNF[1] 5. 309–71.
De nuptiis et concupiscentia. CSEL 42.
  On Marriage and Concupiscence. NPNF[1] 5. 258–308.

De patientia. CSEL 41.
> *On Patience. NPNF¹* 3. 525–36.
De peccatorum meritis et remissione et de baptismo parvulorum ad Marcellinum. CSEL 60.
> *On the Merits and Forgiveness of Sins, and on the Baptism of Infants. NPNF¹* 5. 11–78.
De quantitate animae. CSEL 89.
Retractationes. CCSL 57.
> *The Retractations.* Translated by Mary Inez Bogan. The Fathers of the Church 60. Washington: Catholic University of America Press, 1968.
De sancta virginitate. CSEL 41.
> *Of Holy Virginity. NPNF¹* 3. 417–38.
De sermone Domini in monte. CCSL 35.
> *Our Lord's Sermon on the Mount. NPNF¹* 6. 1–63.
Sermones. PL 38–39.
> *Sermons on Selected Lessons of the New Testament.* [Sermons 51–147]. *NPNF¹* 6. 237–545.
> *Sermons. WSA.* III/1–10.
Soliloquia. CSEL 89.
De spiritu et littera. CSEL 60.
> *On the Spirit and the Letter. NPNF¹* 5. 80–114.
Tractatus in epistolam Joannis ad Parthos. PL 35.
> *Ten Homilies on the First Epistle of St. John.* Translated by John Burnaby. Augustine: Later Works. The Library of Christian Classics 8. Philadelphia: Westminster Press, 1955. 251–348.
Tractatus in Joannis evangelium. CCSL 36.
> *Homilies on the Gospel of John. NPNF¹* 7.
De trinitate. CCSL 50–50A.
> *The Trinity. WSA* I/5.
> *The Trinity.* Translated by Stephen McKenna. The Fathers of the Church 18. Washington: Catholic University of America Press, 1963.
De vera religione. CCSL 32.

Other Primary Sources

Aquinas, Thomas. *Summa Theologiae.* Latin text and English translation. Blackfriars Edition. New York: McGraw-Hill, 1964.
Athanasius. "Life of Antony." In *A Select Library of the Nicene and Post-Nicene Fathers of the Christian Church,* vol. 4. Second series, edited by Philip Schaff and Henry Wace, 188–221. Peabody, Mass.: Hendrickson Publishers, 1994.
Jerome. "Against Jovinianus." In *A Select Library of the Nicene and Post-Nicene Fathers of the Christian Church,* vol. 6. Second series, edited by Philip Schaff

and Henry Wace, 346–416. Peabody, Mass.: Hendrickson Publishers, 1994.

Lightfoot, J. B., and J. R. Harmer, trans. "The Shepherd of Hermas." In *The Apostolic Fathers*, 2d ed., edited and revised by Michael W. Holmes, 189–290. Grand Rapids, Mich.: Baker Book House, 1989.

Luther, Martin. "Heidelberg Disputation." 1518. Translated by Harold J. Grimm in *Career of the Reformer I*. Vol. 31 of *Luther's Works*, edited by Harold J. Grimm, Helmut T. Lehmann, gen. ed., 35–70. Philadelphia: Fortress Press, 1957.

———. "Wartburg Postil." In *Sermons II*. Vol. 52 of *Luther's Works*, edited by Hans J. Hillerbrand, Helmut T. Lehmann, gen. ed., translated by John G. Kunstmann and S. P. Hebart. Philadelphia: Fortress Press, 1974.

Plotinus. *The Enneads*. Edition no. 3 revised by B. S. Page. Translated by Stephen MacKenna, with an introduction by Paul Henry. London: Faber and Faber, 1962.

Possidius. "The Life of St. Augustine." In *The Western Fathers; Being the Lives of SS. Martin of Tours, Ambrose, Augustine of Hippo, Honoratus of Arles, and Germanus Auxerre*, edited and translated by Frederick Russell Hoare, 191–244. New York: Sheed and Ward, 1954.

Augustine and Patristics (Secondary Sources)

Asiedu, Felix B. A. "The Example of a Woman: Sexual Renunciation and Augustine's Conversion to Christianity in 386." Paper presented at University of Pennsylvania, 1994.

Baer, Helmut David. "The Fruit of Charity: Using the Neighbor in *De Doctrina Christiana*." *Journal of Religious Ethics* 24, no. 1 (Spring 1996): 47–64.

Baur, Chrysostomus. *John Chrysostom and His Time*. Translated by M. Gonzaga. London: Sands, 1959.

Bonner, G. I. "*Libido* and *Concupiscentia* in St. Augustine." *Studia Patristica* 6 (1962): 303–14.

Borgomeo, Pasquale. *L'Eglise de ce temps dans la prédication de Saint Augustin*. Paris: Etudes augustiniennes, 1972.

Brown, Peter. *Augustine of Hippo: A Biography*. Berkeley: University of California Press, 1969.

———. *The Body and Society: Men, Women, and Sexual Renunciation in Early Christianity*. Lectures on the History of Religions, vol. 13. New York: Columbia University Press, 1988.

Burnaby, John. *Amor Dei: A Study of the Religion of St. Augustine*. The Hulsean Lectures for 1938. London: Hodder and Stoughton, 1938.

————. "Amor in St. Augustine." In *The Philosophy and Theology of Anders Nygren,* edited by Charles W. Kegley. Carbondale: Southern Illinois University Press, 1970.

————. "Ten Homilies on the First Epistle of St. John." Introduction in *Augustine: Later Works.* The Library of Christian Classics, vol. 8, 251–58. Philadelphia: Westminster Press, 1955.

Burns, J. Patout. *The Development of Augustine's Doctrine of Operative Grace.* Paris: Etudes augustiniennes, 1980.

Canning, Raymond. *The Unity of Love for God and Neighbour in St. Augustine.* Heverlee, Belgium: Augustinian Historical Institute, 1993.

Carney, Frederick S. "The Structure of Augustine's Ethic." In *The Ethics of St. Augustine,* edited by William S. Babcock. JRE Studies in Religion, no. 3, 11–38. Atlanta: Scholars Press, 1991.

Cavadini, John. "Making Truth: A New Commentary on Augustine's *Confessions.*" Review of *Augustine: Confessions,* edited with introduction and commentary by James J. O'Donnell (Oxford: Clarendon Press, 1992). *Religious Studies Review* 21, no. 4 (October 1995): 291–98.

————. "The Structure and Intention of Augustine's *De trinitate.*" *Augustinian Studies* 23 (1992): 103–23.

————. "The Sweetness of the Word: Salvation and Rhetoric in Augustine's *De doctrina christiana.*" In *De Doctrina Christiana: A Classic of Western Culture,* ed. Duane W. H. Arnold and Pamela Bright. Christianity and Judaism in Antiquity, vol. 9. Notre Dame, Ind.: University of Notre Dame Press, 1995.

————. "Time and Ascent in *Confessions* XI." In *Augustine: Presbyter Factus Sum.* Papers originally presented at a conference at Marquette University, November 1990, ed. Joseph T. Lienhard, Earl C. Muller, and Roland J. Teske. New York: P. Lang, 1993.

————. "Voice and Vision in the *Confessions:* The Place of Bk. XIII." Unpublished paper. Notre Dame, Ind., 1995.

Cipriani, Nello. "Lo schema dei tri vitia (voluptas, superbia, curiositas) nel De vera religione: Antropologia soggiacente e fonti." *Augustinianum* 38 (1998): 157–95.

Clark, Elizabeth A. "'Adam's Only Companion': Augustine and the Early Christian Debate on Marriage." *Recherches Augustiniennes* 21 (1986): 139–62.

Courcelle, Pierre Paul. *Recherches sur les Confessions de Saint Augustin.* Paris: E. de Boccard, 1950.

Dideberg, Dany. "Caritas: Prolegomenes à une étude de la théologie augustinienne de la charité." In *Signum pietatis: Festgabe für Cornelius Petrus Mayer zum 60. Geburtstag,* edited by Adolar Zumkeller. Cassiciacum, vol. 40, 369–81. Wurzburg: Augustinus-Verlag, 1989.

Frend, W. H. C. *The Donatist Church: A Movement of Protest in Roman North Africa.* Oxford: Clarendon Press, 1952.

Holte, Ragnar. *Béatitude et sagesse; Saint Augustin et le problème de la fin de l'homme dans la philosophie ancienne.* Paris; Worcester, Mass.: Etudes augustiniennnes; Augustinian Studies, Assumption College, 1962.

Hultgren, Gunnar. *Le commandement d'amour chez Augustin; Interprétation philosophique et théologique d'après les écrits de la période 386–400.* Paris: Vrin, 1939.

Hunter, David G. "Augustinian Pessimism? A New Look at Augustine's Teaching on Sex, Marriage and Celibacy." *Augustinian Studies* 25 (1994): 153–77.

————. "The Date and Purpose of Augustine's *De Continentia.*" *Augustinian Studies* 26, no. 2 (1995): 7–24.

Lamirande, Emilien. *Church, State, and Toleration: An Intriguing Change of Mind in Augustine.* Saint Augustine Lecture 1974. Villanova, Pa: Villanova University Press, 1975.

Landes, Paula Fredriksen. "Introduction." In *Augustine on Romans: Propositions from the Epistle to the Romans and Unfinished Commentary on the Epistle to the Romans,* edited and translated by Paula Fredriksen Landes. Early Christian Literature Series 6. Chico, Calif.: Scholars Press, 1982.

Langan, John. "The Elements of St. Augustine's Just War Theory." *Journal of Religious Ethics* 12 (1984): 19–38.

Lawless, George. "*Auaritia, Luxuria, Ambitio, Lib. Arb.* 1.11.22: A Greco-Roman Literary Topos and Augustine's Asceticism." *Studia Ephemeridis Augustinianum* 62 (1998): 317–31.

Markus, Robert A. *Conversion and Disenchantment in Augustine's Spiritual Career.* Saint Augustine Lecture 1984. Villanova, Pa.: Villanova University Press, 1989.

————. *The End of Ancient Christianity.* Cambridge, England: Cambridge University Press, 1990.

————. *Saeculum: History and Society in the Theology of St. Augustine.* 2d ed. 1970. Cambridge, England: Cambridge University Press, 1988.

Miles, Margaret R. *Desire and Delight: A New Reading of Augustine's Confessions.* New York: Crossroad, 1991.

Monachino, Vincenzo. *La cura pastorale a Milano, Cartagine e Roma nel sec. IV.* Analecta Gregoriana, vol. 41. Rome: Apud aedes Universitatis Gregorianae, 1947.

Natali, Alain. "Eglise et évergetisme à Antioche à la fin du 4e Siècle d'après Jean Chrysostome." *Studia Patristica* 17, no. 3 (1982): 1176–84.

Norris, Frederick W. "Black Marks on the Communities' Manuscripts." 1994 NAPS Presidential Address. *Journal of Early Christian Studies* 2, no. 3 (Winter 1994): 443–66.

O'Connor, William Riordan. "The 'Uti/Frui' Distinction in Augustine's Ethics."
    Augustinian Studies 14 (1983): 45–62.

O'Donnell, James J. *Augustine.* Twayne's World Authors Series. Boston: Twayne
    Publishers, 1985.

———. *Augustine: Confessions.* Latin text with English commentary. 3 vols. Ox-
    ford and New York: Oxford University Press, 1992.

———. "The Authority of Augustine." *Augustinian Studies* 22 (1991): 7–35.

———. *Late Have I Loved Thee.* Videocassette. Santa Fe, N.M.: Della Robbia
    Productions, 1992.

O'Donovan, Oliver. *The Problem of Self-Love in St. Augustine.* New Haven: Yale
    University Press, 1980.

———. "*Usus* and *Fruitio* in Augustine, *De Doctrina Christiana I.*" *Journal of
    Theological Studies* 33 [new series], no. 2 (October 1982): 361–97.

Pagels, Elaine H. *Adam, Eve, and the Serpent.* New York: Random House, 1988.

———. "The Politics of Paradise: Augustine's Exegesis of Genesis 1–3 versus
    That of John Chrysostom." *Harvard Theological Review* 78 (1985): 67–99.

Pellauer, Mary. "Augustine on Rape: One Chapter in the Theological Tradition."
    In *Violence against Women and Children,* edited by Carol J. Adams and
    Marie M. Fortune, 207–41. New York: Continuum, 1995.

Plaskow, Judith. *Sex, Sin, and Grace: Women's Experience and the Theologies of
    Reinhold Niebuhr and Paul Tillich.* Washington, D.C.: University Press of
    America, 1980.

Power, Kim. *Veiled Desire: Augustine on Women.* New York: Continuum, 1996.

Rackett, Michael R. "Anti-Pelagian Polemic in Augustine's *De Continentia.*" *Au-
    gustinian Studies* 26, no. 2 (1995): 25–50.

Ruether, Rosemary Radford. "Misogynism and Virginal Feminism in the Fathers
    of the Church." In *Religion and Sexism: Images of Woman in the Jewish and
    Christian Traditions,* edited by Rosemary Radford Ruether, 150–83. New
    York: Simon and Schuster, 1974.

Scalise, Charles J. "Exegetical Warrants for Religious Persecution: Augustine vs.
    the Donatists." *Review and Expositor* 93 (Fall 1996): 497–506.

Schlabach, Gerald W. "Augustine's Hermeneutic of Humility: An Alternative
    to Moral Imperialism and Moral Relativism." *Journal of Religious Ethics* 22,
    no. 2 (Fall 1994): 299–330.

———. "Friendship as Adultery: Social Reality and Sexual Metaphor in
    Augustine's Doctrine of Original Sin." *Augustinian Studies* 23 (1992): 125–47.

———. "'Love Is the Hand of the Soul': The Grammar of Continence in Au-
    gustine's Doctrine of Christian Love." *Journal of Early Christian Studies* 6,
    no. 1 (Spring 1998): 59–92.

Wetzel, James. *Augustine and the Limits of Virtue.* Cambridge, England: Cam-
    bridge University Press, 1992.

General

Adams, Carol J., and Marie M. Fortune, eds. *Violence against Women and Children.* New York: Continuum, 1995.

Andolsen, Barbara Hilkert. "Agape in Feminist Ethics." *Journal of Religious Ethics* 9, no. 1 (Spring 1981): 69–83.

Barr, James. "Words for Love in Biblical Greek." In *The Glory of Christ in the New Testament.* Oxford: Clarendon Press, 1987.

Bender, Harold S. "The Anabaptist Vision." *Church History* 13 (March 1944): 3–24.

Benhabib, Seyla. "The Generalized and the Concrete Other: The Kohlberg-Gilligan Controversy and Feminist Theory." *Praxis International* 5 (January 1986): 402–24.

Berger, Peter L. *The Sacred Canopy: Elements of a Sociological Theory of Religion.* 1967. Garden City, N.Y.: Anchor, 1969.

Berry, Wanda W. "Images of Sin and Salvation in Feminist Theology." *Anglican Theological Review* 60, no. 1 (January 1978): 25–54.

Brown, Joanne Carlson, and Rebecca Parker. "For God So Loved the World?" In *Christianity, Patriarchy, and Abuse: A Feminist Critique,* ed. Joanne Carlson Brown and Carole R. Bohn. New York: Pilgrim Press, 1989.

Cahill, Lisa Sowle. "Nonresistance, Defense, Violence, and the Kingdom in Christian Tradition." *Interpretation: A Journal of Bible and Theology* 38 (October 1984): 380–97.

Carr, Anne E. *Transforming Grace: Christian Tradition and Women's Experience.* San Francisco: Harper and Row, 1988.

Daly, Mary. *Beyond God the Father: Toward a Philosophy of Women's Liberation.* Boston: Beacon Press, 1973.

———. *Pure Lust: Elemental Feminist Philosophy.* Boston: Beacon Press, 1984.

d'Arcy, M. C. *The Mind and Heart of Love: Lion and Unicorn: A Study in Eros and Agape.* 1947. Cleveland: Meridian, 1967.

Dunfee, Susan Nelson. *Beyond Servanthood: Christianity and the Liberation of Women.* Lanham, Md.: University Press of America, 1989.

———. "The Sin of Hiding: A Feminist Critique of Reinhold Niebuhr's Account of the Sin of Pride." *Soundings* 65 (Fall 1982): 316–27.

Esquivel, Julia. "Christian Women and the Struggle for Justice in Central America." In *Speaking of Faith: Global Perspectives on Women, Religion, and Social Change,* edited by Diana L. Eck and Devaki Jain, 4–14. Philadelphia: New Society Publishers, 1987.

Farley, Margaret A. "New Patterns of Relationship: Beginnings of a Moral Revolution." *Theological Studies* 36, no. 4 (1975): 627–46.

Flanagan, Owen, and Kathryn Jackson. "Justice, Care, and Gender: The Kohlberg-Gilligan Debate Revisited." *Ethics* 97 (April 1987): 622–37.

Fletcher, Joseph. *Situation Ethics: The New Morality.* Philadelphia: Westminster Press, 1966.

Fox, Matthew. *Original Blessing.* Santa Fe, N.M.: Bear, 1983.

Frantz, Nadine Pence. "Women: Bearing the Cross of Discipleship." *Women's Concerns Report of the Mennonite Central Committee on Women's Concerns,* March–April 1990, 1–2.

Gill-Austern, Brita L. "Love Understood as Self-Sacrifice and Self-Denial: What Does It Do to Women?" In *Through the Eyes of Women: Insights for Pastoral Care,* edited by Jeanne Stevenson Moessner, 304–21. Minneapolis: Fortress Press, 1996.

Gilligan, Carol. *In a Different Voice: Psychological Theory and Women's Development.* Cambridge, Mass.: Harvard University Press, 1982.

Glaz, Maxine, and Jeanne Stevenson Moessner, eds. *Women in Travail and Transition: A New Pastoral Care.* Minneapolis: Augsburg Fortress, 1991.

Hall, Thor. *Anders Nygren.* Makers of the Modern Theological Mind. Waco, Tex.: Word Books, 1978.

Hauerwas, Stanley. *The Peaceable Kingdom: A Primer in Christian Ethics.* Notre Dame, Ind.: University of Notre Dame Press, 1983.

Hershberger, Guy Franklin. *The Way of the Cross in Human Relations.* Scottdale, Pa.: Herald Press, 1958.

Hunter, James Davison. *Culture Wars: The Struggle to Define America.* New York: Basic Books, 1991.

John Paul II, Pope. *Tertio Mellennio Adveniente [As the Third Millennium Draws Near].* Apostolic letter, 1994.

Kant, Immanuel. *Groundwork of the Metaphysic of Morals.* Translated and analyzed by H. J. Paton. 1948. The Academy Library. New York: Harper and Row, 1964.

Lebacqz, Karen. "Love Your Enemy: Sex, Power, and Christian Ethics." In *Annual of the Society of Christian Ethics, 1990,* 3–23. Washington, D.C.: Georgetown University Press, 1990.

Lindbeck, George A. *The Nature of Doctrine: Religion and Theology in a Postliberal Age.* Philadelphia: Westminster Press, 1984.

MacIntyre, Alasdair. *After Virtue: A Study in Moral Theory.* 2d ed. Notre Dame, Ind.: University of Notre Dame Press, 1984.

———. *Whose Justice? Which Rationality?* Notre Dame, Ind.: University of Notre Dame Press, 1988.

Malina, Bruce J. "'Let Him Deny Himself' (Mark 8:34 & par): A Social Psychological Model of Self-Denial." *Biblical Theology Bulletin* 24 (Fall 1994): 106–19.

McCann, Dennis. *Christian Realism and Liberation Theology: Practical Theologies in Creative Conflict.* Maryknoll, N.Y.: Orbis Books, 1981.

Mesters, Carlos. *Defenseless Flower: A New Reading of the Bible.* Translated by Francis McDonagh. 1983. Maryknoll, N.Y.: Orbis Books, 1989.

Moessner, Jeanne Stevenson. "From Samaritan to Samaritan: Journey Mercies." In *Through the Eyes of Women: Insights for Pastoral Care,* edited by Jeanne Stevenson Moessner, 322–33. Minneapolis: Fortress Press, 1996.

———. "A New Pastoral Paradigm and Practice." In *Women in Travail and Transition: A New Pastoral Care,* edited by Maxine Glaz and Jeanne Stevenson Moessner, 198–225. Minneapolis: Augsburg Fortress, 1991.

———, ed. *Through the Eyes of Women: Insights for Pastoral Care.* Minneapolis: Fortress Press, 1996.

Niebuhr, H. Richard. *Christ and Culture.* Harper Torchbooks/Cloister Library. New York: Harper and Row, 1956.

Niebuhr, Reinhold. *Human Destiny.* Vol. 2 of *The Nature and Destiny of Man.* 1943. The Scribner Lyceum Editions Library. New York: Scribner's, 1964.

———. *Human Nature.* Vol. 1 of *The Nature and Destiny of Man.* 1941. The Scribner Lyceum Editions Library. New York: Scribner's, 1964.

———. "Intellectual Autobiography." In *Reinhold Niebuhr: His Religious, Social, and Political Thought,* edited by Charles W. Kegley and Robert W. Bretall. The Library of Living Theology, vol. 11, 1–23. New York: Macmillan, 1956.

———. *An Interpretation of Christian Ethics.* New York and London: Harper and Brothers, 1935.

———. *Love and Justice.* Edited by D. B. Robertson. Cleveland: World Publishing, Meridian, 1967.

———. *Moral Man and Immoral Society.* Reprint ed. The Scribner Lyceum Editions Library. New York: Scribner's, 1960.

———. "Reply to Interpretation and Criticism." In *Reinhold Niebuhr: His Religious, Social, and Political Thought,* edited by Charles W. Kegley and Robert W. Bretall. The Library of Living Theology, vol. 11, 429–51. New York: Macmillan, 1956.

———. "Why the Christian Church Is Not Pacifist." In *Christianity and Power Politics,* 1–32. New York: Charles Scribner's Sons, 1940.

Nygren, Anders. *Agape and Eros: The Christian Idea of Love.* Translated by Philip S. Watson. New York: Harper and Row, 1969.

———. "Intellectual Autobiography." Translated by Peter W. Russell. In *The Philosophy and Theology of Anders Nygren,* edited by Charles W. Kegley, 1–29. Carbondale: Southern Illinois University Press, 1970.

Outka, Gene. *Agape: An Ethical Analysis.* New Haven and London: Yale University Press, 1972.

Porter, Jean. *The Recovery of Virtue: The Relevance of Aquinas for Christian Ethics.* Louisville, Ky.: Westminster/John Knox Press, 1990.

Post, Stephen G. *Christian Love and Self-Denial: An Historical and Normative Study of Jonathan Edwards and Samuel Hopkins.* New York: University Press of America, 1987.

———. *A Theory of Agape: On the Meaning of Christian Love.* Lewisburg, Pa.: Bucknell University Press, 1990.

Ramsey, Paul. *Basic Christian Ethics.* New York: Scribner's, 1950.

———. *War and the Christian Conscience; How Shall Modern War Be Conducted Justly?* Published for the Lilly Endowment Research Program in Christianity and Politics. Durham, N.C.: Duke University Press, 1961.

Ranke-Heinemann, Uta. *Eunuchs for the Kingdom of Heaven: Women, Sexuality, and the Catholic Church.* Translated by Peter Heinegg. New York: Doubleday, 1990.

Rooney, Phyllis. "A Different Different Voice: On the Feminist Challenge in Moral Theory." *The Philosophical Forum* 22, no. 4 (Summer 1991): 335–61.

Roth, John D., ed. *Refocusing a Vision: Shaping Anabaptist Character in the 21st Century.* Goshen, Ind.: Mennonite Historical Society, 1995.

Ruether, Rosemary Radford. *Sexism and God-Talk: Toward a Feminist Theology.* Boston: Beacon Press, 1983.

Saiving, Valerie. "The Human Situation: A Feminine View." In *Womanspirit Rising: A Feminist Reader in Religion,* edited by Carol P. Christ and Judith Plaskow. A Harper Forum Book, 25–42. San Francisco: Harper and Row, 1979.

Schertz, Mary H. "Creating Justice in the Space Around Us: Toward a Biblical Theology of Peace between Men and Women." With a response by Lydia Neufeld Harder. In *Peace Theology and Violence against Women,* edited by Elizabeth G. Yoder, 5–28. Occasional Papers 16. Elkhart, Ind.: Institute of Mennonite Studies, 1992.

———. "God's Cross and Women's Questions: A Biblical Perspective on the Atonement." *Mennonite Quarterly Review* 68, no. 2 (April 1994): 194–208.

Schlabach, Gerald W. "Beyond Two- Versus One-Kingdom Theology: Abrahamic Community as a Mennonite Paradigm for Engagement in Society." *Conrad Grebel Review* 11, no. 3 (Fall 1993): 187–210.

———. "The Blessing of Abraham's Children: A Theology of Service." *Mission Focus* 19, no. 4 (December 1991): 52–55.

———. "Deuteronomic or Constantinian: What Is the Most Basic Problem for Christian Social Ethics?" In *The Wisdom of the Cross: Essays in Honor of John Howard Yoder,* edited by Stanley Hauerwas, Chris K. Huebner, Harry Huebner, and Mark Thiessen Nation, 449–71. Grand Rapids, Mich.: William B. Eerdmans, 1999.

————. "More Than One Task: North American Nonviolence and Latin American Liberation Struggle." Epilogue in *Relentless Persistence: Nonviolent Action in Latin America,* edited by Philip McManus and Gerald Schlabach, with a foreword by Leonardo Boff, 252–65. Philadelphia: New Society Publishers, 1991.

————. *To Bless All Peoples: Serving with Abraham and Jesus.* Peace and Justice Series, no. 12. Scottdale, Pa.: Herald Press, 1991.

Sharp, Gene. *The Politics of Nonviolent Action.* 3 vols. Edited by Marina Finkelstein. Boston: Extending Horizons, 1973.

————. *Social Power and Political Freedom.* Extending Horizons Books. Boston: P. Sargent Publishers, 1980.

Shute, Michael. "Emergent Probability and the Ecofeminist Critique of Hierarchy." In *Lonergan and Feminism,* edited by Cynthia S. W. Crysdale. Toronto: University of Toronto Press, 1994.

Sittler, Joseph. *The Structure of Christian Ethics.* With a foreword by Franklin Sherman. Baton Rouge: Louisiana State University Press, 1958.

Tanner, Kathryn. *The Politics of God: Christian Theologies and Social Justice.* Minneapolis: Fortress Press, 1992.

Tillich, Paul. *Love, Power and Justice: Ontological Analyses and Ethical Applications.* Given as Firth lectures in Nottingham, England, and as Sprunt lectures in Richmond, Virginia. London: Oxford University Press, 1954.

Troeltsch, Ernst. *The Social Teaching of the Christian Churches.* Translated by Olive Wyon, with an introduction by Richard Niebuhr. New York: Macmillan, 1931. Reprint, Chicago: University of Chicago Press, 1981.

Vacek, Edward Collins. *Love, Human and Divine: The Heart of Christian Ethics.* Moral Traditions and Moral Arguments Series. Washington, D.C.: Georgetown University Press, 1994.

Vatican Council, Second. *Dignitatis Humanae [On the Right of the Person and Communities to Social and Civil Liberty in Religious Matters],* 1965.

Warnach, Victor. *Agape: Die Liebe als Grundmotiv der neutestamentlichen Theologie.* Düsseldorf: Patmos-Verlag, 1951.

————. "Agape in the New Testament." In *The Philosophy and Theology of Anders Nygren,* edited by Charles W. Kegley, 143–55. Carbondale: Southern Illinois University Press, 1970.

Warren, Karen J. "The Power and the Promise of Ecological Feminism." *Environmental Studies* 12 (1990): 125–46.

Weaver, Dorothy Jean. "On Imitating God and Outwitting Satan: Biblical Perspectives on Forgiveness and the Community of Faith." *Mennonite Quarterly Review* 68, no. 2 (April 1994): 151–69.

Welch, Sharon D. *A Feminist Ethic of Risk.* Minneapolis: Fortress Press, 1990.

White, Lynn, Jr. "The Historical Roots of Our Ecological Crisis." *Science* 155 (March 1967): 1203–7.

Yoder, Elizabeth G., ed. *Peace Theology and Violence against Women*. Occasional Papers 16. Elkhart, Ind.: Institute of Mennonite Studies, 1992.

Yoder, John Howard. *The Christian Witness to the State*. Institute of Mennonite Studies Series no. 3. Newton, Kan.: Faith and Life Press, 1964.

————. *The Politics of Jesus*. Grand Rapids, Mich.: William B. Eerdmans, 1972.

————. *The Politics of Jesus*. 2d ed. Grand Rapids, Mich.: William B. Eerdmans, 1994.

————. *Reinhold Niebuhr and Christian Pacifism*. A Concern Reprint. Scottdale, Pa.: Concern, n.d. Also printed in the *Mennonite Quarterly Review* 29 (April 1955).

————. *The Royal Priesthood: Essays Ecclesiological and Ecumenical*. Edited with an introduction by Michael G. Cartwright. Grand Rapids, Mich.: William B. Eerdmans, 1994.

Index

content of, 31, 50–51
  specification, 51–53, 57, 152–53,
    170–71
continent. *See* continence, as operative
    mode of *caritas*
cosmic, 179n33
of creatures, 27, 36–40, 60, 101, 135,
    167
  "in God," 27, 38, 40–41, 43–44,
    47, 50–51, 53, 57–58, 127, 138,
    147, 151–52, 164, 166, 168, 171
  by refraction through love of God,
    53
cruciform, xx, 129
doctrine of, xxi, 27, 31, 48, 56, 59,
    112, 123–24, 126, 128, 143, 170
of domination, 36, 45, 62, 80, 139
of enemy, xv, xix–xx, 10, 22, 36–37,
    40–42, 52–58, 102, 107, 111,
    113, 119, 128–33, 144, 152,
    168, 221n62
  "in God," 168
  "for the sake of [*propter*] God," 41
  test of neighbor love, 41
as eschatological, 49, 149
ethic of, 14, 22–23, 25
as evangelical, 42, 49, 70–71, 157
false loves, 31, 44
  "in God," 60
the four loves, 2, 27, 29–47, 52, 147
fragmentation of, 3, 63, 144–45
of friends, 34, 36–41, 53, 70–71, 77,
    99, 104, 134, 138, 147, 150,
    164
Gestalt vision of, 38, 43, 47, 53, 56,
    59, 147–48, 152–53, 163
as gift of God, 8, 32, 134, 166
as global (catholic), 129
of glory, 112
for God, 6, 8, 11, 29–33, 96–97, 112,
    125, 129, 156, 167
  all loves referred to, 30
  as elusive, 31, 48, 50, 147, 154
  and love of neighbor, 31
  priority of, 27, 30, 37
  response to God's love, 50

transforms all other loves, 86–87,
    147
  See also clinging, to God
of God, 86
  ambiguity of the genitive, 31
  both transcendent and incarnate, 48
  and love of neighbor, 27–29
  See also love, God's; love, for God
God is (1 John 4:16), 48
God's, 17, 66, 153
  analogy of the carpenter, 42
  as disinterested, 14–15
  gratitude for, 59
  in Jesus Christ, 157
  participation in, 48–49
  as saving initiative, 17, 33, 42, 50,
    74, 167
  for sinners, 5, 176n10
as God's gift, 50, 66, 75, 77–78, 151
as God's saving initiative, 90, 151
as "hand of the soul," 65–67, 78–79,
    164, 171
as hermeneutical key, 29–30, 51
as incarnate, 53
law of, 14, 33
love commands, 28–30, 33, 86, 154
  nineteenth-century interpretation,
    176n10
of love itself, 89
mortal, 30–31, 147
mutual, 3, 11, 14–17, 34, 45, 90, 111,
    134, 137, 150, 162–63, 168
  in the body of Christ, 50–51, 90,
    129, 134–35, 141, 154, 165–66
  community of, xvi, xxi
  criteria, 156
  desire for, 89–90
  in eternity, 16–17
  God's, 88
  as God's ultimate will for all
    creatures, 45, 50, 59, 88, 90,
    135, 146–48, 151–53, 156,
    167–68; *See also* ecology of all
    creatures "in God"
  in history, 15–17
  as the Holy Spirit, 48, 150, 165, 171

Nygren, Anders (*cont.*)
  critique of, 9, 11–12, 147, 177n21
    O'Donovan's, 151
  influence of, xix, 4, 9

obedience, 89–90
objectivism, historical, xxii–xxiii
O'Connor, William Riordan, 177n22,
    233n7
O'Donnell, James J., 63, 169, 187n8,
    188n22, 189n28, 191n39,
    199n12, 201n25, 214n10,
    220n45
O'Donovan, Oliver, 10–12, 38, 48–49,
    60, 72, 139, 146–47, 151,
    174n14, 187n9, 191n46,
    193n69, 195n97, 223n83
omnipotence, 163
the One, 60
oppression, xv
ordinary time, 24, 112, 144–45, 168
orthodoxy, Christian, 21, 163
Ostia vision, 32, 66
otherworldliness, 100–104
Outka, Gene, 149, 175n6

pacifism, xvii, 120, 131
  Christian, xv, xxiv, 131, 156
  Mennonite, 156, 182n54
  Reinhold Niebuhr's critique of, 13
paganism, 98, 133
Pagels, Elaine H., 220n43, 228n48,
    235n29
Parable, parables, 157
  Good Samaritan, 150, 161
  Laborers in the Vineyard, 6
  Lost Sheep, 176n11
  Prodigal Son, 176n11
  Sower, 176n11
  Wedding Banquet, 128–29, 131
  Wheat and Chaff, 108–9
  Wheat and Tares, 108–10, 126, 129
paradox, Niebuhrian, 13–17, 161,
    198n6
Parker, Rebecca, 183n57

participation in the life of God, 48–49,
    80, 87–88, 90, 138, 149, 152,
    165, 167
Passion of Perpetua and Felicitas, 214
pastoral concession, 149
pastoral ministry, 1, 3, 25, 146, 148–49,
    151, 154–55, 185n77
paternalism, xxiii, 56, 126–27, 131,
    136–37, 140, 165
On Patience, 64, 87, 148, 209n114
patience, 87, 111, 124, 126, 137,
    140–41, 152, 160, 171
  as gift of God, 82
patriarchy, 203n45
Patricius, 97–98
Paul, 5–6, 13, 57, 73, 75, 78, 80, 84, 88,
    94, 96, 100, 102, 171
Paul and Jesus in agreement, 5
peace, 103–4, 139
  of Babylon, 112
  earthly, 54
  peace witness, peacemaking, xiv–xv,
    xxii
  Stoic, 101
Pelagianism, 101, 105, 188n15, 194n75
  Augustine's critique of, xxi, 61, 63–64,
    75, 81–84, 100, 105, 188n18
Pelagius, 84
Pellauer, Mary, 232n2
perfection, human, possibility of, 14
perfectionism, xxi, 101, 103, 105, 110,
    117, 129, 142, 166
  realized vs. eschatological vs. cosmic,
    223n83
persecution
  by Christians, xviii, 56, 102, 110, 119,
    128–39, 165
  of Christians, 115, 120, 126, 140
  of "good Christians" by "evil
    Christians," 106–8, 110, 115
perseverance, 108
persuasion, 131, 133, 157
philia, 4, 11, 89
  Nygren's neglect of, 89
phronesis. See judgment